Blendtec
Lifestyles Recipe Book

Over 20 years ago Blendtec began making home grain mills. Success with the grain mill led to the development of a home bread mixer. Later, a blender was incorporated into the design of the bread mixer and the combination was a huge hit.

Over 10 years ago, as the smoothie revolution was heating up, retail food outlets turned to Blendtec to adapt blender technology for commercial use. Blendtec developed the first blender to use a microprocessor to govern the motor; no buttons, switches or knobs. Later advancements included a sound enclosure and the first blender with programmability, auto-start and stop, and safety interlock features. Soon the new technology was taking the market by storm.

The commercial blender market has seen many changes in recent years. Smoothies and frozen coffees are just the latest products to create their own market segment. Blendtec has joined with major retail restaurant chains as well as local operations in providing the public with the best blended taste available. Today, Blendtec blenders are found worldwide.

The commercial success of Blendtec products have led to the introduction of professional quality machines for home use. Today, Blendtec blenders are used in the home to make a variety of recipes; from frozen drinks to hot soups. Blendtec blenders enhance your ability to prepare many different foods with ease and precision. This recipe book contains some of Blendtec's favorite recipes for you to enjoy.

DISCLAIMER: All nutritional or health related information contained within this book is for reference purposes only and should not be taken as medical advice. For specific questions about your individual health or diet, please consult a physician.

How to Use the Blender

Every Blendtec blender is programmed with Smart-Touch™ tec-nology. Experienced chefs have teamed up with engineers to create specific cycles for the recipes in this book and much more. To operate these unique cycles, simply press the desired button, and the blender will speed up, slow down, and stop according to the recipe's demands. Also included are manual controls to increase or decrease the speed of the blender, and a high speed pulse. To operate the speed function, hold down the **Speed Up** or **Speed Down** button until you reach the desired speed and release. The blender will then run for 50 seconds. The Pulse button creates a high speed blend that will run until you take your finger off the button. To stop the blender at any time, press any lower row button.

Blending 101

Before we give you some delicious and easy recipes, let's talk about the "art of blending." Blending is about managing temperatures, proportions, and textures.

If you have too much "cold", the ingredients freeze up in the blending jar – forming an air pocket around the blade. When this occurs, take out two oz. (by volume) of ice and add one ounce of liquid. If the blend is too runny, decrease the liquid by one ounce and add two oz. of ice. (You don't have to be exact, experience is the best teacher. Proper adjustments of frozen and liquid ingredients should not affect the taste.)

When blending hot liquids remove the centerpiece of the lid. Failure to remove the 'steam cap' may cause the lid to pop off during processing. To prevent ingredients from coming out through the hole, cover it with a paper towel. Do not trap steam inside blender jar. Caution: Steam is hot and may cause burns.

The texture of the blended mixture is directly affected by the blade speed and length of the blending time.
Over blending or blending at high speeds may cause ingredients to become over-processed. Insufficient blending time and motor speed will create a lumpy texture. The pulse key gives you flexibility to control the texture. If lumpiness is desired (i.e., salsas, soups), pulse intermittently until desired texture is achieved.

You are now ready to experiment and create your own fantastic recipes – but hopefully you will pass it along. We are always interested in a great new recipe to share with Blendtec owners.

Table of Contents

Healthy living is directly related to lifestyle choice. Your Blendtec blender is designed to bring you delicious, healthy, and valuable nutrition within seconds. In this section, you will learn very simple ways in which you can make healthy and delicious choices. With your Blendtec blender, and a little education, you can turn any of your favorite recipes into a quick and healthy alternative!

All foods, regardless of their source, break down into 3 basic macronutrients: Carbohydrates, Proteins, or Fats. It is the combination and the amount of all three macronutrients that create a balanced or an unbalanced diet. All meals cause certain hormones to be released into the blood: Insulin (fat storage) or Glucagon (fat burning). The type of hormone released depends upon the type, amount, and combination of foods eaten or not eaten.

Carbohydrates

The main sources of carbohydrates are all forms of sugar, breads, vegetables, and fruits. Carbohydrates are all foods that, when broken down, turn into sugar or glucose in your bloodstream. Some carbohydrates absorb quickly causing a rapid rise of sugar or glucose in your bloodstream (High glycemic). Some absorb slowly and steadily keeping your blood sugar stable (Low glycemic). Carbohydrates are the brain's main and only proper energy source. Carbohydrates can be burned by your muscles for engery; however, carbohydrates are not the most efficient muscle energy source.

The best carbohydrate sources are those low in starch, low in sugar, and high in fiber such as:

Fruits: Apples, apricots, berries, cantaloupe, cherries, grapefruits, grapes, honeydew, kiwi, oranges, peaches, pears, pineapple, plums and watermelon
Grains: Black beans, chickpeas, kidney beans, lima beans, lentils, navy beans, pinto beans and white beans
Starches: Sweet potato, whole grain pastas and yams
Vegetables: Artichokes, asparagus, broccoli, cabbage, cauliflower, celery, cucmber, green beans, eggplant, leaf lettuce, onions, radishes, tomatoes and zucchini

Proteins

Protein is the main building block of your body and is the only one of the 3 macronutrients that cannot be stored within the body for later use. Because protein cannot be stored, it then becomes absolutely essential that we regularly consume adequate amounts of quality lean protein containing all 10 essential amino acids at each meal. Adequate amounts of "good," lean protein is vital to good health. In fact, a healthy immune system is centered on the work of antibodies: protein substances used in fighting infection and disease; and therefore crucial to a strong immune system. Protein will also promote stable blood sugar levels, hormone production and balance, body fluid balance, and provide optimal cellular growth, repair, and metabolism.

Protein is essential in the release of glucagon, the fat burning hormone. If you do not consume adequate amounts of lean protein from proper sources, especially within the first 2 meals, your body will begin to store fat instead of burning it.

> **Protein:** eggs, egg whites, fish, lean meats, low-fat cottage cheese, low-fat mozzarella, low-fat tofu and tempeh, skinless fowl and protein powders (rice, soy, whey).

Fat

Yes, it is true, not all fats are good; especially fats that are hydrogenated and/or processed like those in fried foods, margarines, and vegetable shortenings. However, it is important to remember that not all fats are bad, some are even essential. The problem is most Americans have been eating the wrong kind! The right kinds of fats will actually signal your brain to tell you when you are full. Fats also aid in blood sugar stabilization, the absorption of vitamins A, D, E and K, providing raw materials for optimal hormone production, strengthening cell walls, protecting mucous membranes, and providing fuel for long-term energy production.

The best sources for "good" fats that are unprocessed and found naturally within foods.

> **Fats:** Avocados, cold water fish, crab, raw nuts, nut butters, seeds, safflower- based mayonnaise and oils, olive oil, sesame oil and sunflower oils

There is a difference between the dietary fat that you eat in your food and the body fat you carry around inside of you. Just because a certain food contains dietary fat does not necessarily mean that it will turn into body fat when you eat it. All foods, especially high glycemic carbohydrates if eaten in too great abundance can cause weight and/or body fat gain.

Stored body fat is the body's preferred source of energy:

1 gram of carbohydrate = 4 calories of energy
1 gram protein = 4 calories of energy
1 gram fat = 9 calories of energy

Because fat contains over twice the amount of calories in each gram, people who burn fat instead of carbohydrates or proteins will have twice the energy!

Carbohydrates and the Glucose Glycemic Index

All food and/or Macronutrients (Carbohydrates, Proteins, and Fats) break down into their own "sub-culture" once ingested into the body. Carbohydrates break down into a "sub-culture" that is measured by a Glucose Glycemic Index.

A Glycemic Index is a scale upon which all carbohydrates are measured, and shows the specific speed at which any carbohydrate breaks down into a sugar or glucose within the bloodstream.

All carbohydrates will fall within the following Glycemic Range: Very High(VH), High(H), Moderate(M), Low(L), Very Low(VL). Foods with a high glycemic index are considered to be fast-acting because they release glucose into the bloodstream quickly causing a rapid rise or 'spike' in the blood sugar, and then a rise in insulin production. This blood sugar 'spike' may remain within the normal limits; however, any sudden spike in blood sugar will require the body to produce insulin- the fat storage hormone. Please be aware, most fat-free or diet foods, such as rice cakes and popcorn, have a very high glycemic rating and should be avoided, or used very sparingly, if you have diabetes, hypoglycemia, heart disease, high blood cholesterol levels, or difficulty in maintaining an adequate body weight. Most breads, starches, overcooked, and processed foods tend to be high glycemic.

Foods with a low glycemic index are considered slow-acting and release glucose into the bloodstream slowly, resulting in a more stable blood sugar or glucose level and then the release of glucagon- the fat burning hormone. In fact, most fruits and vegetables, especially when eaten in their raw form, are moderate and/or low glycemic foods.

Arranging foods according to their glycemic indexes will give you a full working knowledge and allow you to know which foods to eat plentifully, moderately, and as sparingly as possible. Use the following glycemic index to offset one high-index food with several low-index foods, thus giving you a fair amount of healthy freedom in your choice of foods. All carbohydrates with a low to moderate glycemic index rate are your best choices, as long as you are not allergic to or have a physician's recommended restriction of these foods.

Glycemic Index Rating Chart

Cereals
    All Bran (H) 74
    Cornflakes (VH) 21
    Muesli (H) 96
    Oat Bran (H)..85
    Oatmeal, instant (H) 89
    Oatmeal, slow cooked (M) 49
    Puffed Rice (VH) 132
    Puffed Wheat (VH) 110
    Shredded Wheat 97
Cookies
    Fat Free Cookies (VH) ....110+
    Oatmeal (H) 78
    Shortbread (H) 88
    Water Biscuits (H) 100
Dairy
    Custard (M) 59
    Ice Cream, full fat (M) 69
    Ice Cream, fat free (H) .... 90+
    Milk, skim (M) 46
    Milk, whole (M) 44
    Yogurt, plain and full fat (M) 52
    Yogurt, wth fruit and sugar (H) .... 90+
    Yogurt, frozen and fat free (H) .... 90+
Fruits
    Apple (M) 49
    Apple Juice, unfiltered (M) 55
    Apple Sauce (M) 52
    Apricot (H) 73
    Banana (H) 82

Cherries (L) 23
Dates (H) 95
Grapefruit (L) 26
Grapes (M) 45
Mango (H) 78
Orange (M) 59
Orange Juice (H) 71
Papaya (H) 75
Peach (L) 25
Pear (L) 34
Plum (L) 25
Prunes (M) 52
Raisins (H) 93

Grains
Barley, pearl (L) 36
Barley, rolled (M) 65
Bread, white (H) 100
Bread, wheat (H) 100
French Baguette (VH) 131
Puffed Crisp (VH) 112
Buchwheat (H) 78
Bulgur (M) 65
Millet (H) 81
Macaroni, boiled 5 min. (M) 66
Rice, brown or white (H) 81
Instant, boiled 1 min. (M) 65
Instant, boiled 6 min. (VH) 121
Polished, boiled 5 min. (M) 54
Parbiled, boiled 5 min. (M) 54
Parboiled, boiled 15 min. (H) 70
Rye Bread, pumpernickel (M) 68
Rye Crisp Crackers (M) 45
Rye Kernels (M) 47
Rye Wholemeal (H) 89

Spaghetti
Brown, boiled 15 min. (M) 61
White, boiled 15 min. (M) 67
White, boiled 5 min. (M) 45
Pasta, protein enriched (L) 38
Wholemeal (H) 100
White Flour (H) 100

Wheat Kernels
Pressure Cooked (M) 63
Quick Cooking (H) 75

Nuts
Almonds (VL) 15
Peanuts (VL) 15
Walnuts (VL) 15

Snack Foods

Corn Chips (H) 99
Popcorn (VH) 133
Potato Chips (H) 77
Rice Cakes (VH) 132
Apple flavored (VH) ....132+
Cinnamon flavored (VH) ....132+

Sugars
Fructose (L) 23
Glucose (H) 100
Honey (VH) 126
Lactose (M) 57
Maltose (VH) 153
Sucrose, table sugar (H) 83

Vegetables and Legumes
Artichoke, cooked (L) 25
Asparagus (VL) 22
Baked Beans (H) 70
Beets (M) 68
Black Eye Peas (M) ....
Broccoli, raw (VL) 23
Brussel Sprouts, raw (VL) 23
Carrots (H) 92
Cauliflower, raw (VL) 21
Chickpeas, dried (M) 47
Chickpeas, canned (M) 60
Corn, sweet (H) 76
Garbonzo beans (M) 64
Kidney Beans, canned (H) 43
Lentils, green and dried (L) 36
Lentils, green and canned (H) 74
Lentils, red and dried (L) 38
Lima Beans (M) 46
Parsnips (H) 96
Peas, green and dried (M) 50
Peas, frozen (M) 65
Pinto Beans, canned (M) 64
Pinto Beans, dried (M) 60

Potato
Instant, mashed (VH) 120
Mashed (VH) 117
New, white and boiled (H) 80
New, red and boiled (M) 69
Russet, baked (VH) 116
Soy Beans, baked (VH) 22
Soy Beans, dried (VL) 20
Sweet Potato (M) 69
White Beans, dried (M) 54
Yam (M) 69

Health Conditions

All health conditions are benefited by proper nutrition and a balanced diet. There are many specific health benefits of proper nutrition and balanced diet as they relate to any specific health condition: heart disesase, cancer, AIDS, autoimmune disorders, arthritis, kidney disorders, gastrointestinal disorders, metabolic disorder, bacterial infections, viral infections, etc.

Your Blendtec blender can assist you regardless of the specific health condition you currently face. The reason for this is that the majority, if not all, health conditions can be tremendously benefited by all of the vital nutrients, vitamins, and minerals of fresh fruits, fresh vegetables, freshly ground whole grains, lean proteins, and naturally obtained dietary fats that are all contained in a high fiber, low starch, low sugar, low salt, and a low-fat diet that also includes an adequate daily fluid intake.

Diabetes

Diabetes Mellitus is a chronic disease affecting the metabolism of dietary carbohydrates and results from an inability of the pancreas to produce insulin, and/or make sufficient or effective amounts of insulin, when required by the body. Diabetes is a disease that is dramatically affected by the foods consumed in our daily diets; particularly those foods that are low in fiber, high in starch, and high in sugar; and, should be avoided or consumed very sparingly by most diabetics. However, once you understand the concept and function of insulin, as it relates to carbohydrates in the diet, you will find that the dietary recommendations of a diabetic patient are extremely helpful in maintaining optimal helath; especially when confronted with those diseases involving proper weight management, the heart or coronary system, and the circulatory system.

High levels of blood glucose (sugar) can severely damage the body and its internal organs. Therefore, even in the healthiest person, the main function of insulin is to protect the body and internal organs from damage by reducing blood glucose levels. Insulin is produced when there is an abnormally high level of blood glucose within the bloodstream or a rapid rise in blood glucose within the bloodstream. Only in these two cases is the body forced to produce the hormonal safety mechanism known as insulin. In both cases, insulin lowers or removes this excess glucose from the blood by storing it as body fat within the body. Therefore, insulin is a fat storage hormone. It is this reason that most people with a high glycemic carbohydrate diet have difficulty maintaining adequate body weight as well as healthy blood cholesterol levels.

In place of insulin, properly balanced diets cause the body to produce a hormone called glucagon. Unlike insulin, when glucagon is released, body fat and blood cholesterol are burned rather than stored. Glucagon promotes optimal blood glucose levels, blood cholesterol levels, body fat burning, and energy production. Therefore, glucagon is a fat burning and energy releasing hormone. Insulin and gluacgon are inversely related to one another. When insulin is "needed" or produced by the body, glucagon is not produced. Likewise, when glucagon is produced, insulin is not produced. Therefore, by promoting the release of glucagons, with a properly balanced diet, the diabetic's "need" of insulin dramatically decreases.

In optimal circumstances, properly balanced diets should not require the body to produce insulin. This is the very reason why properly balanced diets are so critical to diabetics and all other persons trying to maintain adequate body weight and cholesterol levels. Many Type II Diabetics are usually able to control their diabetes with a properly balanced diet. Balanced diets allow Type II Diabetics to need very little, if any, insulin with proper compliance to their prescribed treatment. However, Type I or Juvenile Onset Diabetics are insulin dependent and do require insulin; and thereore, balanced diets are even more critical. With a properly balanced diet, the Type I or Juvenile Onset Diabetic's insulin requirements will generally stabilize and even decrease in some cases.

Your Blendtec blender can greatly assist Type I or Type II Diabetics in complying with their prescribed dietary instructions. Your Blendtec blender assists by enabling you to frequently and more fully utilize fresh fruits and vegetables, which are generally low to medium glycemic carbohydrates, and are the very best carbohydrate sources for diabetic patients to consume.

Hypoglycemia and Sugar Cravings

Hypoglycemia is a condition in which the pancreas secretes too much insulin into the blood stream causing abnormally low blood glucose levels. Hypoglycemia is generally caused by a poor dietary intake of high glycemic carbohydrates. Upon digestion, these high glycemic carbohydrates initially cause a rapid rise in blood glucose levels. This initial "spike" may remain within the normal range of the recommended blood glucose levels; however, it triggers a "rebound" low blood sugar effect, as the pancreas secretes more than adequate amounts of insulin to compensate for the initial "spike" in blood glucose levels. Hypoglycemia can also be caused by prolonged fasting.

The brain can only metabolize glucose. However, even in a very healthy person, when your last meal contains too many high glycemic carbohydrates, or your body experiences a prolonged fast, a rebound hypoglycemic state can occur. Properly balanced meals or snacks should be eaten at least every 4 to 6 hours in frequency, excluding sleeping hours, to provide adequate amounts of glucose for brain metabolism. When prolonged fasting occurs, adequate amounts of glucose are not available for proper brain metabolism. The brain, seeking glucose for proper metabolism, is then forced to send a signal to the pancreas to secrete insulin, causing a "hypoglycemic state." This "hypoglycemic state" is the brain's attempt to force you to eat carbohydrates by causing you to experience incredibly strong sugar cravings, even when you're full. More than likely, it is a direct result from your last meal containing too many high glycemic carbohydrates or your body has experienced prolonged fast.

If your brain is forced to continue without a proper glucose source, from low to medium glycemic carbohydrates; eventually, it will begin sending a signal to your body, forcing it to breakdown and metabolize your own muscle tissue as an alternate glucose source. Only by eating a properly balanced diet containing adequate amounts of low to medium glycemic carbohydrates, lean protein, and dietary fat from the proper sources can you avoid falling into this unwanted cycle.

Your Blendtec blender can assist you by enabling you to more fully utilize the low to medium glycemic carbohydrates of most fresh fruits and vegetables and inhibit unwanted "spikes" in blood sugar.

Diverticulitis

Certain foods irritate certain health conditions. An excellent example of this is Diverticulitis. Diverticulitis is a health condition in which small "pouch-like" areas and or/scars are formed in the large intestine from a prolonged irritation to the lining of the bowel, most likely resulting from constipation from a low-fiber diet with inadequate daily fluid intake. Once these diverticula are formed with in the large bowel, there is no treatment to remove them other than the extreme measure of a large bowel resection. Certain foods wil irritate diverticulitis, such a seeds, grains, and nuts. Because these foods are difficult to chew into a very fine form, and once swallowed reman in little bits and pieces within the digestive tract, they then tend to become "trapped" within the diverticula of the large bowel as they pass through on their way to elimination.

Your Blendtec blender can greatly assist you with this difficulty. Your Blendtec blender is able to blend seeds, grains, and nuts so that they do not cause irritation; check with your physician. If you are able to remove the risk of inflammation to the diverticula by using your Blendtec blender to grind the foods into a "safe" form and consistency while retaining the fiber, you may find, with regular initial monitoring, that your physician may allow your to use your Blendtec blender to consume certain foods.

⌂Blendtec®home Product Line

Connoisseur

Total Blender

Mix 'n Blend

Kitchen Mill

For more information on these products, additional recipes, or help with creating a better lifestyle for yourself visit blendtechome.com

Temperature Conversions	
Fahrenheit	Celsius
250°	= 120°
300°	= 150°
350°	= 180°
400°	= 200°
450°	= 230°

Dry Measuring Equivalents		
1 Tablespoon	=3 teaspoons	=15 mL
1/8 cup	=2 Tablespoons	=30 mL
1/4 cup	=4 Tablespoons	=50 mL
1/3 cup	=5 1/3 Tablespoons	=75 mL
1/2 cup	=8 Tablespoons	=125 mL
2/3 cup	=10 2/3 Tablespoons	=150 mL
3/4 cup	=12 Tablespoons	=175 mL
1 cup	=16 Tablespoons	=250 mL

Liquid Measuring Equivalents			
1 cup	=8 ounces	=1/2 pint	
2 cups	= 6 ounces	=1 pint	=1/2 quart
4 cups	=32 ounces	=2 pints	=1 quart
8 cups	=64 ounces	=4 pints	=2 quarts

Ingredient Substitutions

Allspice, 1 teaspoon	1/2 teaspoon ground cinnamon plus 1/2 teaspoon ground cloves
Apple Pie Spice, 1 teaspoon	1/2 teaspoon ground cinnamon plus 1/4 teaspoon ground nutmeg plus
	1/8 teaspoon ground caramon
Baking Powder, 1 teaspoon	1/4 teaspoon baking soda plus 1/2 teaspoon cream of tartar
Balsamic Vinegar, 1 Tablespoon	1 Tablespoon cooking sherry or cider vinegar
Broth - Chicken, Beef, or Vegetable, 1 cup	1 teaspoon chicken, beef, or vegetable bouillon dissolved in 1 cup boiling water
Brown Sugar, 1 cup	1 cup granulated sugar plus 2 Tablespoons molases
Butter/ Margarine, 1 cup	1 cup hard shortening or 7/8 cup vegetable oil
Buttermilk, 1 cup	1 tablespoon vinegar or lemon plus enough milk to make 1 cup.
	Let stand for 5 minutes before using.
Corn Syrup, 1 cup (for thickening)	1 cup granulate sugar plus 1/4 cup water
Cornstarch, 1 Tablespoon	2 Tablespoons flour
Dry Mustard, 1 teaspoon	1 Tablespoon prepared mustard
Garlic, 1 clove	1/8 teaspoon garlic powder or minced dried garlic
Half & Half, 1 cup	7/8 cup milk plus 3 Tablespoons butter
Honey, 1 cup	1 1/2 cups sugar plus 1/4 cup liquid
Leeks, 1/2 cup	1/2 cup sliced shallots or green onions
Molasses, 1 cup	1/2 cup honey
Onion, 1 small	1 teaspoon onion powder
Powdered Sugar, 1 cup	1 cup sugar plus 1 Tablespoon cornstarch processed in food processor
Pumpkin Pie Spice, 1 teaspoon	1/2 teaspoon ground cinnamon plus 1/4 teaspoon ground ginger plus
	1/8 teaspoon ground allspice plus 1/8 teaspoon ground nutmeg
Skim Milk, 1 cup	1/3 cup nonfat dry milk plus 3/4 cup water
Sour Cream, 1 cup	1 cup plain yogurt
Sweetened Condensed Milk, 1 cup	1 cup nonfat dry milk plus 1/2 cup warm water; mix and add 3/4 cup sugar
Tomato Juice, 1 cup	1/2 cup tomato sauce plus 1/2 cup water
Tomato Sauce, 2 cups	3/4 cup tomato paste plus 1 cup water
Whole Milk, 1 cup	1/2 cup evaporated milk plus 1/2 cup water

APPETIZERS

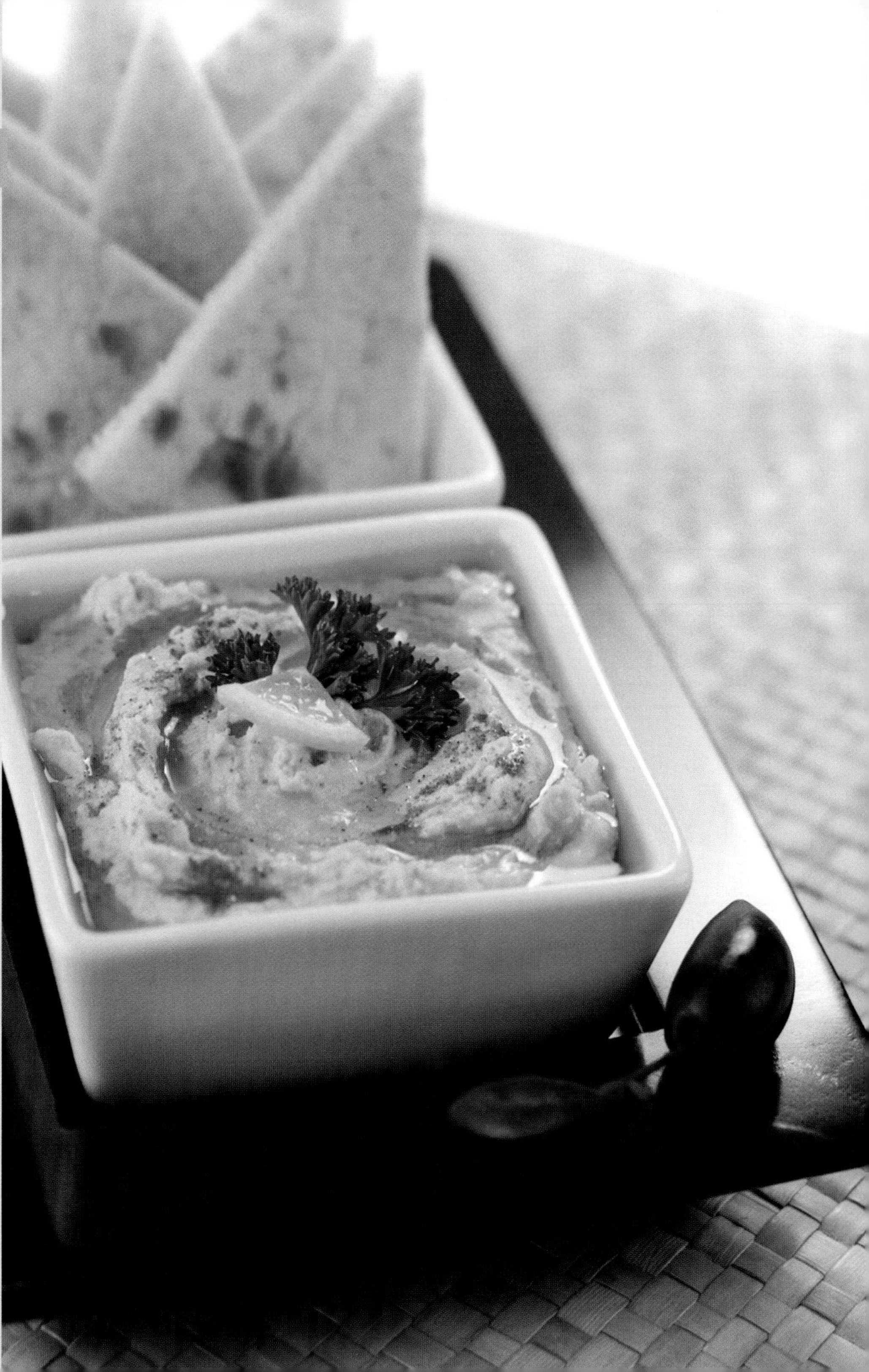

Appetizers Table of Contents

DIPS

To blend a Dip, simply press the **Dips** button.

You can turn any dip recipe into a dressing by substituting milk for cream cheese and adding mayonnaise.

Remember when you are creating your own dip recipe in your Blendtec blender to shred your food products first, place your liquid or liquid-like products in your container next, and add your dry products last.

Most instant or dry soup mixes can quickly be turned into a dip by adding low-fat sour cream and/or plain dairy or nondairy yogurt.

Your Blendtec blender will process most food products to the desired consistency within seconds. If you use foods that have been previously refrigerated, your final product will remain in a "chilled" state, ready to serve.

To thicken Guacamole, add additional ripe avocados.

Cucumber Dill Dip

1 cup low-fat mayonnaise

¾ package (6 oz.) cream cheese

1 medium cucumber (equivalent to 2 cups) - chopped

2 tsp fresh dill*

2 green onions - cut in half

1 Tbsp lemon juice

⅓ tsp Tabasco sauce

Directions: Place ingredients into blender jar and secure the lid. Press the **Dips** button.

*May substitute ½ tsp dried dill

Nutritional Information

Yield: 3 cups
Serving Size: 2 Tablespoons

Amount per serving

Calories: 27.18	Potassium: 34.96 mg
50.20% from Fat	Magnesium: 2.45 mg
12.40% from Protein	Zinc: .08 mg
37.50% from Carb	Copper: .01 mg
Protein: .86 g	Manganese: .01 mg
Total Fat: 1.55 g	Vitamin A: 68.65 IU
Saturated Fat: .85 g	Vitamin E: 12.83 mg
Monosaturated Fat: .55 g	Thiamin: 0.00 mg
Polyunsaturated: .06 g	Riboflavin: .02 mg
Cholesterol: 4.93 mg	Niacin: .02 mg
Carbohydrates: 2.61 g	Pantothenic Acid: .02 mg
Fiber: .27 g	Vitamin B6: .01 mg
Calcium: 11.93 mg	Folate: 2.30 ug
Phosphorous: 13.67 mg	Vitamin B12: .04 ug
Iron: .21 mg	Vitamin C: .68 mg
Sodium: 105.89 mg	Selenium: .35 ug
Sugar: 1.28 mg	

Spinach Vegetable Dip

½ package (5 oz.) frozen spinach, thawed and drained

2 green onions - discard root and cut in half

¾ cup sour cream

½ cup mayonnaise

½ can (4 oz.) water chestnuts - drained

½ package onion dry soup mix

Directions: Place ingredients into blender jar and secure the lid. Press the **Dips** button.

Nutritional Information

Yield: 2 ½ cups
Serving Size: 2 Tablespoons

Amount per serving

Calories: 32.26	Potassium: 71.80 mg
53.80% from Fat	Magnesium: 8.26 mg
7.93% from Protein	Zinc: .09 mg
38.20% from Carb	Copper: .03 mg
Protein: .67 g	Manganese: .07 mg
Total Fat: 2.03 g	Vitamin A: 916.94 IU
Saturated Fat: 1.17 g	Vitamin E: 15.01 mg
Monosaturated Fat: .64 g	Thiamin: .02 mg
Polyunsaturated: .09 g	Riboflavin: .04 mg
Cholesterol: 4.37 mg	Niacin: .10 mg
Carbohydrates: 3.24 g	Pantothenic Acid: .06 mg
Fiber: .58 g	Vitamin B6: .03 mg
Calcium: 22.67 mg	Folate: 10.83 ug
Phosphorous: 15.00 mg	Vitamin B12: .03 ug
Iron: .17 mg	Vitamin C: .60 mg
Sodium: 78.02 mg	Selenium: .64 ug
Sugar: 1.00 mg	

Fruit 'n Cream Dip

¼ cup orange juice

¼ cup lemon juice

¼ cup crushed pineapple

¼ cup heavy cream

½ package (4 oz.) cream cheese

¼ cup sugar

¼ tsp salt

1 orange slice ¼" thick - include peel

Directions: Place ingredients into blender jar and secure the lid. Press the **Dips** button.

Nutritional Information

Yield: 2 cups
Serving Size: 2 Tablespoons

Amount per serving

Calories: 41.69	Potassium: 29.70 mg
40.90% from Fat	Magnesium: 1.65 mg
7.90% from Protein	Zinc: .06 mg
51.20% from Carb	Copper: .01 mg
Protein: .85 g	Manganese: .03 mg
Total Fat: 1.95 g	Vitamin A: 96.31 IU
Saturated Fat: 1.22 g	Vitamin E: 20.39 mg
Monosaturated Fat: .55 g	Thiamin: .01 mg
Polyunsaturated: .07 g	Riboflavin: .03 mg
Cholesterol: 6.53 mg	Niacin: .10 mg
Carbohydrates: 5.49 g	Pantothenic Acid: .02 mg
Fiber: .06 g	Vitamin B6: .02 mg
Calcium: 13.06 mg	Folate: 2.91 ug
Phosphorous: 13.68 mg	Vitamin B12: .05 ug
Iron: .14 mg	Vitamin C: 5.80 mg
Sodium: 58.69 mg	Selenium: .32 ug
Sugar: 4.18 mg	

Tropical Fruit Dip

½ cup low-fat milk

½ cup sour cream

1 small (5 oz.) package instant banana pudding

1 Tbsp shredded coconut

1 Tbsp frozen orange juice concentrate

1 (8 oz.) can crushed pineapple with juice

Directions: Place ingredients into blender jar and secure the lid. Press the **Dips** button.

Nutritional Information

Yield: 2 cups
Serving Size: 2 Tablespoons

Amount per serving

Calories: 45.85	Potassium: 49.94 mg
32.80% from Fat,	Magnesium: 5.04 mg
5.00% from Protein	Zinc: .08 mg
62.20% from Carb	Copper: .02 mg
Protein: .59 g	Manganese: .17 mg
Total Fat: 1.72 g	Vitamin A: 71.78 IU
Saturated Fat: 1.07 g	Vitamin E: 16.95 mg
Monosaturated Fat: .47 g	Thiamin: .02 mg
Polyunsaturated: .08 g	Riboflavin: .03 mg
Cholesterol: 3.47 mg	Niacin: .06 mg
Carbohydrates: 7.35 g	Pantothenic Acid: .07 mg
Fiber: .13 g	Vitamin B6: .02 mg
Calcium: 20.98 mg	Folate: 3.62 ug
Phosphorous: 57.99 mg	Vitamin B12: .05 ug
Iron: .08 mg	Vitamin C: 2.76 mg
Sodium: 88.39 mg	Selenium: .48 ug
Sugar: 1.61 mg	

Caramel Cream Dip

1 (8 oz.) package cream cheese - softened and cut into
    three pieces
½ cup packed brown sugar
¼ cup sugar
1 tsp vanilla

Directions: Place ingredients into blender jar and secure the lid. Press
the **Speed Up** button and hold down until the blender reaches Speed 8.
Allow the blender to run for 30 seconds then press any lower row button
to stop. After cycle is finished, use a rubber spatula to scrape ingredients toward the blade. Run blender at speed 8 again for 20 seconds and
press any lower row button to stop.

Nutritional Information

Serving Size: 2 Tablespoons

Amount per serving

Calories: 71.63	Potassium: 47.92 mg
31.20% from Fat	Magnesium: 3.16 mg
8.36% from Protein	Zinc: .12 mg
60.40% from Carb	Copper: .02 mg
Protein: 1.50 g	Manganese: .02 mg
Total Fat: 2.49 g	Vitamin A: 96.25 IU
Saturated Fat: 1.57 g	Vitamin E: 25.66 mg
Monosaturated Fat: .70 g	Thiamin: 0.00 mg
Polyunsaturated: .09 g	Riboflavin: .04 mg
Cholesterol: 7.94 mg	Niacin: .03 mg
Carbohydrates: 10.87 g	Pantothenic Acid: .01 mg
Fiber: 0.00 g	Vitamin B6: .01 mg
Calcium: 21.78 mg	Folate: 2.62 ug
Phosphorous: 22.22 mg	Vitamin B12: .09 ug
Iron: .37 mg	Vitamin C: 0.00 mg
Sodium: 44.66 mg	Selenium: .67 ug
Sugar: 9.82 mg	

Cheesy Dip

1 small tomato
¼ cup mayonnaise
2 Tbsp milk
Dash black pepper
½ cup cheddar cheese - shredded

Directions: Place ingredients into blender jar and secure the lid. Press
the **Dips** button.

Nutritional Information

Yield: 1 ½ cup
Serving Size: 2 Tablespoons

Amount per serving

Calories: 28.87	Potassium: 26.96 mg
61.70% from Fat	Magnesium: 2.70 mg
20.90% from Protein	Zinc: .19 mg
17.40% from Carb	Copper: .01 mg
Protein: 1.52 g	Manganese: .01 mg
Total Fat: 2.00 g	Vitamin A: 112.42 IU
Saturated Fat: 1.21 g	Vitamin E: 15.67 mg
Monosaturated Fat: .63 g	Thiamin: 0.00 mg
Polyunsaturated: .06 g	Riboflavin: .03 mg
Cholesterol: 6.36 mg	Niacin: .04 mg
Carbohydrates: 1.27 g	Pantothenic Acid: .04 mg
Fiber: .18 g	Vitamin B6: .01 mg
Calcium: 43.87 mg	Folate: 2.06 ug
Phosphorous: 32.48 mg	Vitamin B12: .06 ug
Iron: .06 mg	Vitamin C: .89 mg
Sodium: 77.82 mg	Selenium: .84 ug
Sugar: .74 mg	

Ranch Dip

1 cup buttermilk

2 (1 oz.) packages ranch dressing mix

1 (8 oz.) package cream cheese, softened and cut into 3
   pieces

1 cup mayonnaise

Directions: Place ingredients into blender jar and secure the lid. Press the **Dips** button.

Italian Veggie Dip

1 (8 oz.) package cream cheese – cut in half

⅓ cup milk

1 (1 oz.) package Italian dressing mix

¼ tsp soy sauce

Directions: Place cream cheese at bottom of jar, touching the blade. Place other ingredients in jar in order as listed and secure the lid. Press the **Dips** button.

Note: After cycle is completed, it may be necessary to use a rubber spatula to pull ingredients towards the blade. Secure the lid and press the Pulse button 3 to 4 times.

Nutritional Information

Yield: 3 ½ cups
Serving Size: 1 Tablespoon

Amount per serving

Calories: 40.29	Potassium: 14.71 mg
86.00% from Fat	Magnesium: 2.70 mg
6.10% from Protein	Zinc: .81 mg
7.92% from Carb	Copper: .05 mg
Protein: .62 g	Manganese: 0.00 mg
Total Fat: 3.87 g	Vitamin A: 39.64 IU
Saturated Fat: .94 g	Vitamin E: 10.94 mg
Monosaturated Fat: 1.10 g	Thiamin: 0.00 mg
Polyunsaturated: 1.48 g	Riboflavin: .02 mg
Cholesterol: 4.76 mg	Niacin: .01 mg
Carbohydrates: .80 g	Pantothenic Acid: .01 mg
Fiber: 0.00 g	Vitamin B6: 0.00 mg
Calcium: 10.32 mg	Folate: .95ug
Phosphorous: 10.91 mg	Vitamin B12: .03 ug
Iron: .09 mg	Vitamin C: .04 mg
Sodium: 82.56 mg	Selenium: .31 ug
Sugar: .22 mg	

Nutritional Information

Serving Size: 2 Tablespoons

Amount per serving

Calories: 38.53	Potassium: 32.09 mg
61.10% from Fat	Magnesium: 1.88 mg
18.00% from Protein	Zinc: .13 mg
20.90% from Carb	Copper: 0.00 mg
Protein: 1.68 g	Manganese: 0.00 mg
Total Fat: 2.54 g	Vitamin A: 106.66 IU
Saturated Fat: 1.60 g	Vitamin E: 28.62 mg
Monosaturated Fat: .72 g	Thiamin: 0.00 mg
Polyunsaturated: .09g	Riboflavin: .05 mg
Cholesterol: 8.14 mg	Niacin: .03 mg
Carbohydrates: 1.96 g	Pantothenic Acid: .02 mg
Fiber: 0.00 g	Vitamin B6: .01 mg
Calcium: 22.42 mg	Folate: 2.82 ug
Phosphorous: 25.89 mg	Vitamin B12: .10 ug
Iron: .24 mg	Vitamin C: .05 mg
Sodium: 276.16 mg	Selenium: .69 ug
Sugar: .03 mg	

Guacamole

3 avocados - peeled and pitted

½ cup red bell pepper - quartered

1 Roma tomato - quartered

½ small lemon - peeled

¼ yellow onion - peeled

¾ tsp salt

Directions: Place ingredients into blender jar and secure the lid. Press the pulse button and release after one second. You may need to stop ibetween pulsing and use spatula to scrape ingredients toward blade. Press 8 times or until desired consistency is reached.

Shrimp Dip

½ medium yellow onion

Directions: Place onion into blender jar and secure the lid. Press the Pulse button until onion is chopped.

Add:

¾ cup sour cream

½ package (4 oz.) cream cheese - softened

⅛ tsp garlic salt

1 4 oz. can of tiny cocktail shrimp

Directions: Place cream cheese and shrimp down toward blade with spoon or spatula. Add remaining ingredients, secure the lid, and press the **Dips** button.

Nutritional Information

Yield: 3 cups
Serving Size: 2 Tablespoons

Amount per serving

Calories: 38.36	Potassium: 127.06 mg
72.10% from Fat	Magnesium: 7.21 mg
4.84% from Protein	Zinc: .16 mg
23.10% from Carb	Copper: .04 mg
Protein: .51 g	Manganese: .04 mg
Total Fat: 3.35 g	Vitamin A: 155.13 IU
Saturated Fat: .46 g	Vitamin E: 0.00 mg
Monosaturated Fat: 2.12 g	Thiamin: .03 mg
Polyunsaturated: .45 g	Riboflavin: .03 mg
Cholesterol: 0.00 mg	Niacin: .46mg
Carbohydrates: 2.42 g	Pantothenic Acid: .33 mg
Fiber: 1.62 g	Vitamin B6: .08 mg
Calcium: 3.98 mg	Folate: 14.81 ug
Phosphorous: 13.77 mg	Vitamin B12: 0.00 ug
Iron: .16 mg	Vitamin C: 8.92 mg
Sodium: 75.69 mg	Selenium: .10 ug
Sugar: .36 mg	

Nutritional Information

Yield: 2 cups
Serving Size: 2 Tablespoons

Amount per serving

Calories: 49.62	Potassium: 47.98 mg
66.20% from Fat,	Magnesium: 5.05 mg
22.30% from Protein	Zinc: .18 mg
11.50% from Carb	Copper: .03 mg
Protein: 2.77 g	Manganese: .01 mg
Total Fat: 3.65 g	Vitamin A: 122.32 IU
Saturated Fat: 2.22 g	Vitamin E: 32.86 mg
Monosaturated Fat: 1.03 g	Thiamin: .01 mg
Polyunsaturated: .18 g	Riboflavin: .04 mg
Cholesterol: 20.97 mg	Niacin: .22 mg
Carbohydrates: 1.43 g	Pantothenic Acid: .06 mg
Fiber: .06 g	Vitamin B6: .02 mg
Calcium: 35.48 mg	Folate: 3.33 ug
Phosphorous: 37.15 mg	Vitamin B12: .15 ug
Iron: .33 mg	Vitamin C: .51 mg
Sodium: 38.79 mg	Selenium: 3.35 ug
Sugar: .20 mg	

French Fry Sauce

¼ cup milk

6 oz. cream cheese - softened and cut into 3 pieces

⅓ cup ketchup

2 Tbsp Catalina dressing

½ tsp salt

Directions: Place ingredients into blender jar and secure the lid. Press the **Dips** button.

Nutritional Information

Yield: 2 cups
Serving Size: 2 Tablespoons

Amount per serving

Calories: 35.67	Potassium: 45.24 mg
54.90% from Fat	Magnesium: 2.50 mg
15.00% from Protein	Zinc: .11 mg
30.10% from Carb	Copper: .02 mg
Protein: 1.36 g	Manganese: .01 mg
Total Fat: 32.21 g	Vitamin A: 137.63 IU
Saturated Fat: 1.23 g	Vitamin E: 21.46 mg
Monosaturated Fat: .66 g	Thiamin: 0.00 mg
Polyunsaturated: .18 g	Riboflavin: .06 mg
Cholesterol: 6.11 mg	Niacin: .10 mg
Carbohydrates: 2.72 g	Pantothenic Acid: .02 mg
Fiber: .09 g	Vitamin B6: .02 mg
Calcium: 17.98 mg	Folate: 2.90 ug
Phosphorous: 21.32 mg	Vitamin B12: .08 ug
Iron: .22 mg	Vitamin C: .79 mg
Sodium: 179.12 mg	Selenium: .56 ug
Sugar: 1.37 mg	

JAMS

For sweetest tasting jams, use fresh fruit.

Apricot Jam

2 cups apricots - pitted
¼ cup light corn syrup
½ Tbsp orange peel

Directions: Place ingredients in jar in order as listed and secure the lid. Press the Pulse button for 10 seconds, or until ingredients are blended.

½ cup sugar
3 Tbsp liquid Pectin

Directions: Combine above ingredients in separate container and mix. Add to jar and secure the lid. Press the **Soups** button. Seal and refrigerate or freeze.

Strawberry Jam

2 cups strawberries*
¼ cup light corn syrup
2 Tbsp lemon peel

Directions: Place ingredients in jar in order as listed and secure the lid. Press the Pulse button for 10 seconds, or until ingredients are blended.

½ cup sugar
3 Tbsp liquid Pectin

Directions: Combine above ingredients in separate container and mix. Add to jar and secure the lid. Press the **Soups** button. Seal and refrigerate or freeze.

*Substitute any other berry to create a different flavored jam

Nutritional Information

Yield: 2 cups
Serving Size: 1 Tablespoon

Amount per serving

Calories: 39.50	Potassium: 95.06 mg
0.93% from Fat,	Magnesium: 2.70 mg
2.60% from Protein	Zinc: .03 mg
96.50% from Carb	Copper: .03 mg
Protein: .28 g	Manganese: .02 mg
Total Fat: .04 g	Vitamin A: 293.77 IU
Saturated Fat: 0.00 g	Vitamin E: 0.00 mg
Monosaturated Fat: .01 g	Thiamin: 0.00 mg
Polyunsaturated: .01 g	Riboflavin: .01 mg
Cholesterol: 0.00 mg	Niacin: .21 mg
Carbohydrates: 10.34 g	Pantothenic Acid: .04 mg
Fiber: .62 g	Vitamin B6: .01 mg
Calcium: 4.94 mg	Folate: .88 ug
Phosphorous: 5.87 mg	Vitamin B12: 0.00 ug
Iron: .22 mg	Vitamin C: .39 mg
Sodium: 3.92 mg	Selenium: .22 ug
Sugar: 9.53 mg	

Nutritional Information

Yield: 2 cups
Serving Size: 1 Tablespoon

Amount per serving

Calories: 24.58	Potassium: 20.76 mg
0.62% from Fat,	Magnesium: 1.58 mg
0.93% from Protein	Zinc: .02 mg
98.50% from Carb	Copper: .01 mg
Protein: .06 g	Manganese: .04 mg
Total Fat: .02 g	Vitamin A: 6.26 IU
Saturated Fat: 0.00 g	Vitamin E: 0.00 mg
Monosaturated Fat: 0.00 g	Thiamin: 0.00 mg
Polyunsaturated: .01 g	Riboflavin: .01 mg
Cholesterol: 0.00 mg	Niacin: .06 mg
Carbohydrates: 6.47 g	Pantothenic Acid: .02 mg
Fiber: .30 g	Vitamin B6: 0.00 mg
Calcium: 2.44 mg	Folate: 2.36 ug
Phosphorous: 1.86 mg	Vitamin B12: 0.00 ug
Iron: .11 mg	Vitamin C: 5.81 mg
Sodium: 3.38 mg	Selenium: .13 ug
Sugar: 5.82 mg	

Orange Citrus Marmalade

1 ¾ cup oranges - peeled
¼ cup ruby red grapefruit - peeled
¼ cup light corn syrup
½ Tbsp orange peel

Directions: Place ingredients in jar in order as listed and secure the lid. Press the Pulse button for 10 seconds, or until ingredients are blended.

Add:

½ cup sugar
3 Tbsp liquid Pectin

Directions: Combine above ingredients in separate container and mix. Add to jar and secure the lid. Press the **Soups** button. Seal and refrigerate or freeze.

Nutritional Information

Yield: 2 cups
Serving Size: 1 Tablespoon

Amount per serving

Calories: 24.99	Potassium: 20.68 mg
0.55% from Fat,	Magnesium: 1.20 mg
1.58% from Protein	Zinc: .01 mg
97.90% from Carb	Copper: .01 mg
Protein: .11 g	Manganese: 0.00 mg
Total Fat: .02 g	Vitamin A: .39.20 IU
Saturated Fat: 0.00 g	Vitamin E: 0.00 mg
Monosaturated Fat: 0.00 g	Thiamin: .01 mg
Polyunsaturated: 0.00 g	Riboflavin: .01 mg
Cholesterol: 0.00 mg	Niacin: .03 mg
Carbohydrates: 6.52 g	Pantothenic Acid: .03 mg
Fiber: .27 g	Vitamin B6: .01 mg
Calcium: 4.41 mg	Folate: 3.16 ug
Phosphorous: 1.59 mg	Vitamin B12: 0.00 ug
Iron: .01 mg	Vitamin C: 5.98 mg
Sodium: 3.10 mg	Selenium: .09 ug
Sugar: 6.23 mg	

Plum Jam

2 cups plums – peeled and pitted
¼ cup light corn syrup
½ tsp cinnamon
½ Tbsp lemon peel

Directions: Place ingredients in jar in order as listed and secure the lid. Press the Pulse button for 10 seconds, or until ingredients are blended.

Add:

½ cup sugar
3 Tbsp liquid Pectin

Directions: Combine above ingredients in separate container and mix. Add to jar and secure the lid. Press the **Soups** button. Seal and refrigerate or freeze.

Nutritional Information

Yield: 2 cups
Serving Size: 1 Tablespoon

Amount per serving

Calories: 24.58	Potassium: 16.68 mg
1.13% from Fat,	Magnesium: .81 mg
1.14% from Protein,	Zinc: .01 mg
97.70% from Carb	Copper: .01 mg
Protein: .107 g	Manganese: .01 mg
Total Fat: .03 g	Vitamin A: .35.72 IU
Saturated Fat: 0.00 g	Vitamin E: 0.00 mg
Monosaturated Fat: .01 g	Thiamin: 0.00 mg
Polyunsaturated: 0.00 g	Riboflavin: 0.00 mg
Cholesterol: 0.00 mg	Niacin: .04 mg
Carbohydrates: 6.41 g	Pantothenic Acid: .01 mg
Fiber: .17 g	Vitamin B6: 0.00 mg
Calcium: 1.29 mg	Folate: 3.54 ug
Phosphorous: 1.73 mg	Vitamin B12: 0.00 ug
Iron: .03 mg	Vitamin C: 1.11 mg
Sodium: 3.12 mg	Selenium: .04 ug
Sugar: 6.22 mg	

Apple Cinnamon Jam

2 cups apples – peeled, cored, and steamed

¼ cup molasses

1 tsp cinnamon

½ Tbsp lemon peel

1 Tbsp lemon juice

Directions: Place ingredients in jar in order as listed and secure the lid. Press the Pulse button for 10 seconds, or until ingredients are blended.

Add:

½ cup sugar

3 Tbsp liquid Pectin

Directions: Combine above ingredients in separate container and mix. Add to jar and secure the lid. Press the **Soups** button. Seal and refrigerate or freeze.

Nutritional Information

Yield: 2 cups
Serving Size: 1 Tablespoon

Amount per serving

Calories: 23.48	Potassium: 45.91 mg
0.52% from Fat,	Magnesium: 6.73 mg
0.40% from Protein	Zinc: .01 mg
99.10% from Carb	Copper: .02 mg
Protein: .102 g	Manganese: .05 mg
Total Fat: .01 g	Vitamin A: .2.95 IU
Saturated Fat: 0.00 g	Vitamin E: 0.00 mg
Monosaturated Fat: 0.00 g	Thiamin: 0.00 mg
Polyunsaturated: 0.00 g	Riboflavin: 0.00 mg
Cholesterol: 0.00 mg	Niacin: .03 mg
Carbohydrates: 6.11 g	Pantothenic Acid: .03 mg
Fiber: .14 g	Vitamin B6: .02 mg
Calcium: 6.80 mg	Folate: .09 ug
Phosphorous: 1.66 mg	Vitamin B12: 0.00 ug
Iron: .16 mg	Vitamin C: 5.64 mg
Sodium: 1.00 mg	
Sugar: 5.32 mg	Selenium: .49 ug

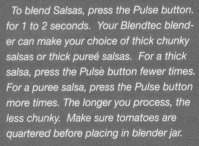

To blend Salsas, press the Pulse button. for 1 to 2 seconds. Your Blendtec blender can make your choice of thick chunky salsas or thick pureé salsas. For a thick salsa, press the Pulse button fewer times. For a puree salsa, press the Pulse button more times. The longer you process, the less chunky. Make sure tomatoes are quartered before placing in blender jar.

Chubb's Chunky Salsa

3 Roma tomatoes – quartered

1 generous portion of cilantro

½ onion – quartered

1 jalapeno

½ Tbsp taco seasoning

Directions: Add ingredients in the order listed above. Secure the lid and press the Pulse button. Depress one second at a time, and let motor come to a complete stop before resuming. Pulse motor until you have achieved the desired consistency.

Nutritional Information

Yield: 1 cup
Serving Size: 2 Tablespoons

Amount per serving

Calories: 16.63	Potassium: 107.22 mg
5.10% from Fat,	Magnesium: 5.23 mg
13.90% from Protein	Zinc: .08 mg
81.00% from Carb	Copper: .03 mg
Protein: .56 g	Manganese: .06 mg
Total Fat: .09 g	Vitamin A: 58.185 IU
Saturated Fat: .02 g	Vitamin E: .02 mg
Monosaturated Fat: .02 g	Thiamin: .02 mg
Polyunsaturated: .06 g	Riboflavin: .01 mg
Cholesterol: 0.00 mg	Niacin: .26 mg
Carbohydrates: 3.28 g	Pantothenic Acid: .05 mg
Fiber: .75 g	Vitamin B6: .05 mg
Calcium: 6.91 mg	Folate: 8.88 ug
Phosphorous: 11.82 mg	Vitamin B12: 0.00 ug
Iron: .16 mg	Vitamin C: 6.34 mg
Sodium: 140.43 mg	Selenium: .05 ug
Sugar: 1.31 mg	

Strawberry Peach Salsa

1 cup peaches

¼ cup strawberries - may leave stems attached

½ medium green bell pepper - quartered

½ medium onion - cut in half

3 Tbsp parsley

1 tsp red wine vinegar

2 Tbsp olive oil

1 Tbsp sugar

½ tsp salt

1 tsp dry mustard

1 tsp thyme

¼ tsp cinnamon

1 tsp rosemary

Directions: Place ingredients in jar in order as listed and secure the lid. Press the Pulse button 5 to 10 times.

Nutritional Information

Yield: 2 cups
Serving Size: 2 Tablespoons

Amount per serving

Calories: 27.16	Potassium: 50.08 mg
55.20% from Fat	Magnesium: 3.05 mg
3.72% from Protein	Zinc: .06 mg
41.00% from Carb	Copper: .02 mg
Protein: .27 g	Manganese: .06 mg
Total Fat: 1.77 g	Vitamin A: 82.07 IU
Saturated Fat: .24 g	Vitamin E: 0.00 mg
Monosaturated Fat: 1.26 g	Thiamin: .01 mg
Polyunsaturated: .19 g	Riboflavin: .01 mg
Cholesterol: 0.00 mg	Niacin: .15 mg
Carbohydrates: 2.95 g	Pantothenic Acid: .03 mg
Fiber: .49 g	Vitamin B6: .02 mg
Calcium: 8.10 mg	Folate: 2.91 ug
Phosphorous: 5.59 mg	Vitamin B12: 0.00 ug
Iron: .43 mg	Vitamin C: 6.46 mg
Sodium: 75.21 mg	Selenium: .13 ug
Sugar: 2.15 mg	

Pineapple Salsa

1 cup fresh pineapple
2 Tbsp orange marmalade
1 Tbsp cilantro
2 tsp jalapeno pepper - remove seeds
2 tsp diced pimento
1 ½ tsp lime juice
¼ tsp salt

Directions: Place ingredients in jar in order as listed and secure the lid. Press the Pulse button 5 to 10 times.

Nutritional Information

Yield: 1 cup
Serving Size: 2 Tablespoons

Amount per serving

Calories: 22.70	Potassium: 45.08 mg
1.26% from Fat	Magnesium: 5.86 mg
2.68% from Protein,	Zinc: .04 mg
96.10% from Carb	Copper: .04 mg
Protein: .17 g	Manganese: .35 mg
Total Fat: .04g	Vitamin A: 51.16 IU
Saturated Fat: 0.00 g	Vitamin E: .01 mg
Monosaturated Fat: 0.00 g	Thiamin: .03 mg
Polyunsaturated: .01 g	Riboflavin: .01 mg
Cholesterol: 0.00 mg	Niacin: .11 mg
Carbohydrates: 6.01 g	Pantothenic Acid: .03 mg
Fiber: .32 g	Vitamin B6: .03 mg
Calcium: 7.20 mg	Folate: 2.71 ug
Phosphorous: 1.88 mg	Vitamin B12: 0.00 ug
Iron: .16 mg	Vitamin C: 3.47 mg
Sodium: 80.08 mg	Selenium: .16 ug
Sugar: 5.33 mg	

Salsa Verde

1 (11 oz.) can tomatillo - drained
½ cup white onion
2 garlic cloves - minced
2 green chilies - minced, keep seeds
¼ cup cilantro
2 Tbsp sugar
½ tsp salt

Directions: Place ingredients in jar in order as listed and secure the lid. Press the Pulse button 5 to 10 times.

Nutritional Information

Yield: 2 cups
Serving Size: 2 Tablespoons

Amount per serving

Calories: 15.96	Potassium: 69.31 mg
11.00% from Fat	Magnesium: 5.13 mg
7.07% from Protein	Zinc: .06 mg
82.00% from Carb	Copper: .02 mg
Protein: .31 g	Manganese: .05 mg
Total Fat: .21g	Vitamin A: 81.06 IU
Saturated Fat: .03 g	Vitamin E: .01 mg
Monosaturated Fat: .03 g	Thiamin: .01 mg
Polyunsaturated: .09 g	Riboflavin: .01 mg
Cholesterol: 0.00 mg	Niacin: .40 mg
Carbohydrates: 3.56 g	Pantothenic Acid: .05 mg
Fiber: .47 g	Vitamin B6: .03 mg
Calcium: 4.72 mg	Folate: 3.11 ug
Phosphorous: 10.68 mg	Vitamin B12: 0.00 ug
Iron: .16 mg	Vitamin C: 3.25 mg
Sodium: 89.60 mg	Selenium: .23 ug
Sugar: 2.56 mg	

Tropical Salsa

1 large grapefruit - peeled

2 medium oranges - peeled

½ medium mango - peeled, pitted

½ small red onion - peeled

½ yellow bell pepper

½ large chili pepper

1 Tbsp cilantro

¼ tsp salt

½ tsp olive oil

Directions: Place ingredients in jar in order as listed and secure the lid. Press the Pulse button 5 to 10 times.

Apple Salsa

2 Granny Smith apples - peeled,cored, and quartered

1 (4 oz.) can chopped green chilies

¼ cup lemon juice

3 Tbsp cilantro

1 clove garlic - minced

1 tsp dried oregano

½ tsp salt

Directions: Place ingredients in jar in order as listed and secure the lid. Press the Pulse button 10 to15 times.

Nutritional Information

Yield: 3 ¼ cups
Serving Size: 2 Tablespoons

Amount per serving

Calories: 16.22	Potassium: 61.78 mg
6.89% from Fat	Magnesium: 3.59mg
6.67% from Protein	Zinc: .03 mg
86.40% from Carb	Copper: .02 mg
Protein: .30 g	Manganese: .01 mg
Total Fat: .14 g	Vitamin A: 192.39 IU
Saturated Fat: .02 g	Vitamin E: 0.00 mg
Monosaturated Fat: .07 g	Thiamin: .02 mg
Polyunsaturated: .02 g	Riboflavin: .01 mg
Cholesterol: 0.00 mg	Niacin: .14 mg
Carbohydrates: 3.88 g	Pantothenic Acid: .09 mg
Fiber: .62 g	Vitamin B6: .03 mg
Calcium: 8.75 mg	Folate: 7.56 ug
Phosphorous: 5.00 mg	Vitamin B12: 0.00 ug
Iron: .06 mg	Vitamin C: 19.81mg
Sodium: 27.54 mg	Selenium: .16 ug
Sugar: 2.90 mg	

Nutritional Information

Yield: 2 cups
Serving Size: 2 Tablespoons

Amount per serving

Calories: 10.84	Potassium: 32.01 mg
3.64% from Fat	Magnesium: 1.53 mg
4.62% from Protein	Zinc: .02 mg
91.70% from Carb	Copper: .01 mg
Protein: .14 g	Manganese: .02 mg
Total Fat: .05 g	Vitamin A: 53.09 IU
Saturated Fat: .01 g	Vitamin E: .01 mg
Monosaturated Fat: 0.00 g	Thiamin: .01 mg
Polyunsaturated: .02 g	Riboflavin: .01 mg
Cholesterol: 0.00 mg	Niacin: .08 mg
Carbohydrates: 2.85 g	Pantothenic Acid: .03 mg
Fiber: .39 g	Vitamin B6: .02 mg
Calcium: 5.49 mg	Folate: 4.84 ug
Phosphorous: 3.59 mg	Vitamin B12: 0.00 ug
Iron: .15 mg	Vitamin C: 5.12 mg
Sodium: 102.20 mg	Selenium: .07 ug
Sugar: 1.71 mg	

Chunky Tomato Parsley Salsa

½ medium onion

Directions: Press the Pulse button 3 to 5 times until onions are chopped.

Add:

¼ cup fresh parsley

5 Roma tomatoes - quartered

¼ jalapeno

¼ tsp salt

Directions: Place ingredients in jar in order as listed and secure the lid. Press the Pulse button 10 to 15 times.

Nutritional Information

Yield: 2 ½ cups
Serving Size: 2 Tablespoons

Amount per serving

Calories: 5.38	Potassium: 58.60 mg
7.51% from Fat,	Magnesium: 3.01 mg
16.20% from Protein	Zinc: .05 mg
76.20% from Carb	Copper: .01 mg
Protein: .25 g	Manganese: .05 mg
Total Fat: .05 g	Vitamin A: 181.87 IU
Saturated Fat: .01 g	Vitamin E: .0.00 mg
Monosaturated Fat: .02 g	Thiamin: .01 mg
Polyunsaturated: .03 g	Riboflavin: .01 mg
Cholesterol: 0.00 mg	Niacin: .13 mg
Carbohydrates: 1.18 g	Pantothenic Acid: .02 mg
Fiber: .35 g	Vitamin B6: .02 mg
Calcium: 6.42 mg	Folate: 3.92 ug
Phosphorous: 6.22 mg	Vitamin B12: 0.00 ug
Iron: .31 mg	Vitamin C: 2.93 mg
Sodium: 32.25 mg	Selenium: .09 ug
Sugar: 1.64 mg	

Lime Sublime Salsa

¾ medium onion

Directions: Press Pulse button 3 to 5 times, or until onions are chopped.

Add:

¼ cup fresh cilantro

½ whole lime - peeled

2 cups canned stewed tomatoes

¼ fresh jalapeno pepper*

¾ tsp salt

Directions: Place ingredients in jar in order as listed and secure the lid. Press the Pulse button 5 to 10 times.

*May add more pepper if hotter taste is desired.

Nutritional Information

Yield: 2 ½ cups
Serving Size: 2 Tablespoons

Amount per serving

Calories: 12.58	Potassium: 128.09 mg
4.28% from Fat,	Magnesium: 6.96 mg
14.20% from Protein	Zinc: .11 mg
81.50% from Carb	Copper: .08 mg
Protein: .52 g	Manganese: .08 mg
Total Fat: .07 g	Vitamin A: 155.02 IU
Saturated Fat: .01 g	Vitamin E: .0.00 mg
Monosaturated Fat: .02 g	Thiamin: .01 mg
Polyunsaturated: .03 g	Riboflavin: .02 mg
Cholesterol: 0.00 mg	Niacin: .39 mg
Carbohydrates: 2.99 g	Pantothenic Acid: .12 mg
Fiber: .63 g	Vitamin B6: .04 mg
Calcium: 9.57 mg	Folate: 4.29 ug
Phosphorous: 12.27 mg	Vitamin B12: 0.00 ug
Iron: .71 mg	Vitamin C: 3.76 mg
Sodium: 190.07 mg	Selenium: 1.23 ug
Sugar: 1.45 mg	

South of the Border Salsa

3 jalapeno peppers - remove stems
1 (4oz.) can green chilies - do not drain
1 ½ Tbsp white vinegar
⅓ cup canned tomato paste
½ tsp dried parsley
½ tsp salt
2 cups stewed tomatoes

Directions: Place ingredients in jar in order as listed and secure the lid. Press the Pulse button 5 to 10 times.

Easy Salsa

1 (20 oz.) can whole tomatoes - do not drain
½ medium onion
½ tsp minced garlic - fresh or dried
1 Tbsp lime juice
1 tsp salt
½ tsp cumin
4 oz. can green chilies – do not drain
2 Tbsp chopped cilantro
1 drop hot sauce

Directions: Place ingredients in jar in order as listed and secure the lid. Press the Pulse button 5 to10 times.

Nutritional Information

Yield: 2 ½ cups
Serving Size: 2 Tablespoons

Amount per serving

Calories: 14.80 (4.96% from Fat,	Magnesium: 8.30 mg
15.20% from Protein, 79.90% from	Zinc: .13 mg
Carb)	Copper: .09 mg
Protein: .66 g	Manganese: .06 mg
Total Fat: .10 g	Vitamin A: 211.33 IU
Saturated Fat: .01 g	Vitamin E: .0.00 mg
Monosaturated Fat: .01 g	Thiamin: .01 mg
Polyunsaturated: .04 g	Riboflavin: .03 mg
Cholesterol: 0.00 mg	Niacin: .55 mg
Carbohydrates: 3.47 g	Pantothenic Acid: .12 mg
Fiber: .80 g	Vitamin B6: .05 mg
Calcium: 8.49 mg	Folate: 6.88 ug
Phosphorous: 14.74 mg	Vitamin B12: 0.00 ug
Iron: .68 mg	Vitamin C: 6.06 mg
Sodium: 215.77 mg	Selenium: 1.38 ug
Sugar: 1.85 mg	
Potassium: 164.40 mg	

Nutritional Information

Yield: 4 cups
Serving Size: 2 Tablespoons

Amount per serving

Calories: 8.33	Potassium: 71.09 mg
5.68% from Fat	Magnesium: 3.27 mg
10.60% from Protein	Zinc: .05 mg
83.70% from Carb	Copper: .03 mg
Protein: .25 g	Manganese: .05 mg
Total Fat: .06 g	Vitamin A: 58.06 IU
Saturated Fat: .01 g	Vitamin E: .0.00 mg
Monosaturated Fat: .01 g	Thiamin: .02 mg
Polyunsaturated: .02 g	Riboflavin: .01 mg
Cholesterol: 0.00 mg	Niacin: .20 mg
Carbohydrates: 1.99 g	Pantothenic Acid: .06 mg
Fiber: .45 g	Vitamin B6: .04 mg
Calcium: 8.75 mg	Folate: 4.91 ug
Phosphorous: 6.98 mg	Vitamin B12: 0.00 ug
Iron: .19 mg	Vitamin C: 5.12 mg
Sodium: 141.96 mg	Selenium: .15 ug
Sugar: 1.401 mg	

Western Salsa

6 ripe tomatoes - quartered

¼ cup fresh cilantro

½ medium onion - cut in half

1 tsp fresh lemon juice

1 serrano chili pepper

1 tsp cider vinegar

1 tsp salt

Directions: Place ingredients in jar in order as listed and secure the lid. Press the Pulse button 10 to 15 times. If blade is spinning freely, remove jar and shake 1 to 2 times. Then place jar back on blender and continue pulsing.

Mango Salsa

½ small red onion

2 medium red tomatoes

1 medium avocado - quartered

1 medium mango - peeled, cored and quartered

2 Tbsp dried coriander

1 Tbsp lemon juice

1 chili

1 clove of garlic minced

Directions: Place ingredients in jar in order as listed and secure the lid. Press the Pulse button 15 to 20 times or until blended to desired consistency.

Nutritional Information

Yield: 2 ½ cups
Serving Size: 2 Tablespoons

Amount per serving

Calories: 5.64	Potassium: 61.81 mg
7.10% from Fat	Magnesium: 3.05 mg
14.90% from Protein	Zinc: .04 mg
78.00% from Carb	Copper: .02 mg
Protein: .24 g	Manganese: .03 mg
Total Fat: .05 g	Vitamin A: 224.39 IU
Saturated Fat: .01 g	Vitamin E: .01 mg
Monosaturated Fat: .01 g	Thiamin: .01 mg
Polyunsaturated: .03 g	Riboflavin: .01 mg
Cholesterol: 0.00 mg	Niacin: .15 mg
Carbohydrates: 1.27 g	Pantothenic Acid: .03 mg
Fiber: .34 g	Vitamin B6: .02 mg
Calcium: 3.43 mg	Folate: 4.39 ug
Phosphorous: 6.66 mg	Vitamin B12: 0.00 ug
Iron: .08 mg	Vitamin C: 3.49 mg
Sodium: 119.44 mg	Selenium: .02 ug
Sugar: .75 mg	

Nutritional Information

Yield: 3 ¾ cups
Serving Size: 2 Tablespoons

Amount per serving

Calories: 21.74	Potassium: 100.52 mg
37.80% from Fat	Magnesium: 5.71 mg
6.15% from Protein	Zinc: .09 mg
56.10% from Carb	Copper: .04 mg
Protein: .37 g	Manganese: .06 mg
Total Fat: 1.01 g	Vitamin A: 105.59 IU
Saturated Fat: .14 g	Vitamin E: 0.00 mg
Monosaturated Fat: .62 g	Thiamin: .02 mg
Polyunsaturated: .14 g	Riboflavin: .02 mg
Cholesterol: 0.00 mg	Niacin: .31 mg
Carbohydrates: 3.38 g	Pantothenic Acid: .15 mg
Fiber: .87 g	Vitamin B6: .06 mg
Calcium: 9.01 mg	Folate: 7.91 ug
Phosphorous: 9.98 mg	Vitamin B12: 0.00 ug
Iron: .20 mg	Vitamin C: 6.73 mg
Sodium: 43.93 mg	Selenium: .23 ug
Sugar: 1.92 mg	

Corn Salsa

¼ medium green bell pepper - cut in half

1 green onion - cut in half

2 Tbsp white wine vinegar

4 oz. green chilies

1 jalapeno chile pepper – seeded and cut in half

1 Tbsp vegetable oil

¼ tsp salt

16 oz. can corn

Directions: Place ingredients in jar in order as listed and secure the lid. Press the Pulse button 5 to10 times until blended to desired consistency.

Nutritional Information

Yield: 2 cups
Serving Size: 2 Tablespoons

Amount per serving

Calories: 36.92	Potassium: 91.98 mg
23.80% from Fat,	Magnesium: 7.33 mg
10.00% from Protein	Zinc: .14 mg
66.20% from Carb	Copper: .02 mg
Protein: 1.05 g	Manganese: .05 mg
Total Fat: 1.11 g	Vitamin A: 142.74 IU
Saturated Fat: .15 g	Vitamin E: 0.00 mg
Monosaturated Fat: .27 g	Thiamin: .03 mg
Polyunsaturated: .62 g	Riboflavin: .03 mg
Cholesterol: 0.00 mg	Niacin: .58 mg
Carbohydrates: 6.95 g	Pantothenic Acid: .09 mg
Fiber: 1.02 g	Vitamin B6: .07 mg
Calcium: 8.94 mg	Folate: 18.88 ug
Phosphorous: 23.41 mg	Vitamin B12: 0.00 ug
Iron: .34 mg	Vitamin C: 7.66mg
Sodium: 71.23 mg	Selenium: .26 ug
Sugar: 1.26 mg	

Thick & Chunky Cilantro Salsa

½ medium onion

⅓ cup cilantro

¼ fresh jalapeno pepper

Directions: Place ingredients in jar in order as listed and secure the lid. Press the lower row Pulse button 3 to 5 times or until ingredients are chopped.

Add:

1 tsp lemon juice

1 tsp vinegar

5 Roma tomatoes - quartered

3 drops Tabasco sauce

¾ tsp salt

Directions: Press the Pulse button 5 times or until salsa is blended to desired consistency.

Nutritional Information

Yield: 2 cups
Serving Size: 2 Tablespoons

Amount per serving

Calories: 12.62	Potassium: 113.60 mg
4.60% from Fat,	Magnesium: 5.22 mg
10.50% from Protein	Zinc: .07 mg
84.80% from Carb	Copper: .05 mg
Protein: .38 g	Manganese: .08 mg
Total Fat: .07 g	Vitamin A: 128.43 IU
Saturated Fat: .01 g	Vitamin E: .02 mg
Monosaturated Fat: .01 g	Thiamin: .03 mg
Polyunsaturated: .603 g	Riboflavin: .01 mg
Cholesterol: 0.00 mg	Niacin: .29 mg
Carbohydrates: 3.06 g	Pantothenic Acid: .10 mg
Fiber: .66 g	Vitamin B6: .06 mg
Calcium: 12.29 mg	Folate: 5.59 ug
Phosphorous: 10.99 mg	Vitamin B12: 0.00 ug
Iron: .22 mg	Vitamin C: 6.86 mg
Sodium: 200.92 mg	Selenium: .23 ug
Sugar: 1.71 mg	

SPREADS

To blend spreads, you will use the Speed buttons (**Speed Up** and **Speed Down**). Pay special attention to the directions so that you will blend each recipe accurately. Before blending to create spreads, make sure jar is completely dry. When blending nut butters, use 2 to 3 cups of nuts at a time.

Fresh Peanut Butter

3 cups roasted peanuts*
Optional, 3 tsps peanut or vegetable oil

Directions: Place ingredients into blender jar and secure the lid. Press the **Speed Up** button until blender reaches speed 1. Allow blender to run the full cycle (it may appear as though it is not running). Remove the lid and with a rubber spatula, scrape peanuts towards the center of the jar. Press the **Speed Up** button and hold down until blender reaches speed 5. Allow the blender to run the full cycle. During this cycle, butter should begin to form around the blade. After the cycle is finished, remove the lid and with a rubber spatula, scrape peanuts toward the center of the jar. Press the **Speed Up** button again until blender reaches speed 5 and continue this process until peanut butter has reached desired consistency.

*May substitute cashews

Honey Nut Butter

½ cup honey
1 ½ cups butter - softened
½ cup roasted peanuts*
⅛ tsp nutmeg
⅛ tsp cinnamon

Directions: Place ingredients in jar in order as listed. Pack butter around blade with a spatula or spoon. Press the **Speed Up** button until blender reaches speed 9. Allow the blender to run until the ingredients begin to mix – this will be approximately 35 seconds. When the display reads 35 seconds, press the **Speed Down** button until the speed reaches speed 3. Allow the blender to run a complete cycle. Chill and serve.

*May substiute cashews

Nutritional Information

Yields: 2 cups.
Serving Size: 2 Tablespoons

Amount per serving

Calories: 37.56	Potassium: 21.26 mg
58.80% from Fat	Magnesium: 12.05 mg
16.00% from Protein	Zinc: .22 mg
25.20% from Carb	Copper: .06 mg
Protein: 1.59 g	Manganese: .12 mg
Total Fat: 2.60 g	Vitamin A: 0.00 IU
Saturated Fat: .36 g	Vitamin E: 0.00 mg
Monosaturated Fat: 1.29 g	Thiamin: .03 mg
Polyunsaturated: .82 g	Riboflavin: .01 mg
Cholesterol: 0.00 mg	Niacin: .62 mg
Carbohydrates: 2.51 g	Pantothenic Acid: .10 mg
Fiber: 1.04g	Vitamin B6: .02 mg
Calcium: 6.50 mg	Folate: 8.86 ug
Phosphorous: 23.39 mg	Vitamin B12: 0.00 ug
Iron: .12 mg	Vitamin C: 0.00 mg
Sodium: 88.71 mg	Selenium: .52 ug
Sugar: .29 mg	

Nutritional Information

Yields: 2 cups
Serving Size: 2 Tablespoons

Amount per serving

Calories: 191.19	Potassium: 14.31 mg
80.50% from Fat	Magnesium: 2.69 mg
0.97% from Protein	Zinc: .08 mg
18.60% from Carb	Copper: .01 mg
Protein: .48 g	Manganese: .03 mg
Total Fat: 217.70 g	Vitamin A: 531.89 IU
Saturated Fat: 11.00 g	Vitamin E: 142.80 mg
Monosaturated Fat: 4.69 g	Thiamin: .01 mg
Polyunsaturated: .78 g	Riboflavin: .01 mg
Cholesterol: 46.75 mg	Niacin: .13 mg
Carbohydrates: 9.18 g	Pantothenic Acid: .05 mg
Fiber: .21 g	Vitamin B6: .01 mg
Calcium: 7.08 mg	Folate: 2.35 ug
Phosphorous: 9.48 mg	Vitamin B12: .04 ug
Iron: .08 mg	Vitamin C: .06 mg
Sodium: 138.80 mg	Selenium: .38 ug
Sugar: 8.77 mg	

Honey Butter

½ cup vegetable oil
½ cup honey
1 ½ cups butter - softened
⅛ tsp nutmeg
⅛ tsp cinnamon

Directions: Place ingredients into blender jar in order as listed and secure the lid. Press the **Speed Up** button until the blender reaches speed 3. After 15 seconds, quickly increase the Speed to speed 9. Press any lower row button to stop when the time reaches 35 seconds. Chill and serve.

Nutritional Information

Yield: 2 cups
Serving Size: 1 Tablespoon

Amount per serving

Calories: 122.58	Potassium: 5.38 mg
85.80% from Fat	Magnesium: .34 mg
0.34% from Protein	Zinc: .02 mg
13.90% from Carb	Copper: 0.00 mg
Protein: .11 g	Manganese: .01 mg
Total Fat: 12.04 g	Vitamin A: 265.94 IU
Saturated Fat: 5.90 g	Vitamin E: 71.40 mg
Monosaturated Fat: 3.06g	Thiamin: 0.00 mg
Polyunsaturated: 2.32 g	Riboflavin: .01 mg
Cholesterol: 22.88 mg	Niacin: .01 mg
Carbohydrates: 4.38 g	Pantothenic Acid: .02 mg
Fiber: .02 g	Vitamin B6: 0.00 mg
Calcium: 3.00 mg	Folate: .43 ug
Phosphorous: 2.79 mg	Vitamin B12: .02 ug
Iron: .03 mg	Vitamin C: .03 mg
Sodium: 61.51 mg	Selenium: .15 ug
Sugar: 4.36 mg	

Maple Nut Butter

½ cup maple syrup
1 ½ cups butter - softened
½ cup roasted peanuts*
⅛ tsp nutmeg
⅛ tsp cinnamon

Directions: Place ingredients in jar in order as listed. Pack butter around blade with a spatula or spoon. Press the **Speed Up** button until blender reaches speed 9. Allow the cycle to run until the ingredients begin to mix – this will take approximately 35 seconds. When the display reads 35 seconds, press the **Speed Down** button until the speed reaches speed 3. Allow the blender to finish the cycle. Chill and serve.

*May substitute cashews

Nutritional Information

Yield: 2 cups
Serving Size: 2 Tablespoons

Amount per serving

Calories: 185.29	Potassium: 29.36 mg
83.90% from Fat,	Magnesium: 3.89 mg
0.94% from Protein	Zinc: .48 mg
15.20% from Carb	Copper: .02 mg
Protein: .45 g	Manganese: .36 mg
Total Fat: 17.72 g	Vitamin A: 531.89 IU
Saturated Fat: 11.00 g	Vitamin E: 142.80 mg
Monosaturated Fat: 4.70 g	Thiamin: .01 mg
Polyunsaturated: .79 g	Riboflavin: .01 mg
Cholesterol: 45.75 mg	Niacin: .12 mg
Carbohydrates: 7.21 g	Pantothenic Acid: .04 mg
Fiber: .19 g	Vitamin B6: 0.00 mg
Calcium: 13.19 mg	Folate: 2.13 ug
Phosphorous: 9.26 mg	Vitamin B12: .04 ug
Iron: .15 mg	Vitamin C: .01 mg
Sodium: 138.28 mg	Selenium: .36 ug
Sugar: 6.06 mg	

Maple Butter

½ cup olive oil

½ cup maple syrup

1 ½ cups butter - softened

⅛ tsp nutmeg

⅛ tsp cinnamon

Directions: Place ingredients into blender jar and secure the lid. Press the **Speed Up** button until the blender reaches speed 3. After 15 seconds, press the **Speed Up** button and increase the speed to speed 9. Press any lower row button to stop when the time reaches 35 seconds. Chill and serve.

Strawberry Butter

½ cup strawberry jam

1 cup butter - softened

3 Tbsp vegetable oil

Directions: Place ingredients into blender jar in order as listed and secure the lid. Press the **Speed Up** button until blender reaches speed 9. Allow the blender to run a complete cycle.

Nutritional Information

Yield: 2 cups
Serving Size: 1 Tablespoon

Amount per serving

Calories: 119.63	Potassium: 12.91 mg
88.60% from Fat	Magnesium: .94mg
0.30% from Protein	Zinc: .22 mg
11.10% from Carb	Copper: 0.00 mg
Protein: .09 g	Manganese: .17 mg
Total Fat: 12.05 g	Vitamin A: 265.94 IU
Saturated Fat: 5.90 g	Vitamin E: 71.40 mg
Monosaturated Fat: 3.06 g	Thiamin: 0.00 mg
Polyunsaturated: 2.33 g	Riboflavin: 0.00 mg
Cholesterol: 22.88 mg	Niacin: .01 mg
Carbohydrates: 3.40 g	Pantothenic Acid: .01 mg
Fiber: .01 g	Vitamin B6: 0.00 mg
Calcium: 6.05 mg	Folate: .33 ug
Phosphorous: 2.68 mg	Vitamin B12: .02 ug
Iron: .07 mg	Vitamin C: 0.00 mg
Sodium: 61.75 mg	Selenium: .14 ug
Sugar: 3.01 mg	

Nutritional Information

Yield: 2 cups
Serving Size: 1 Tablespoon

Amount per serving

Calories: 76.05	Potassium: 5.55 mg
81.80% from Fat	Magnesium: .34 mg
0.41% from Protein	Zinc: .01 mg
17.80% from Carb	Copper: 0.00 mg
Protein: .08 g	Manganese: 0.00 mg
Total Fat: 7.03 g	Vitamin A: 177.27IU
Saturated Fat: 3.81 g	Vitamin E: 17.60 mg
Monosaturated Fat: 1.80 g	Thiamin: 0.00 mg
Polyunsaturated: .97 g	Riboflavin: .01 mg
Cholesterol: 15.25 mg	Niacin: 0.00 mg
Carbohydrates: 3.45 g	Pantothenic Acid: .01 mg
Fiber: .05 g	Vitamin B6: 0.00 mg
Calcium: 2.70 mg	Folate: .76 ug
Phosphorous: 2.65 mg	Vitamin B12: .01 ug
Iron: .03 mg	Vitamin C: .44 mg
Sodium: 42.46 mg	Selenium: .17 ug
Sugar: 2.43 mg	

Hummus

1 Tbsp olive oil

15 oz. canned chickpeas (Garbanzo beans) - drained

½ cup sesame seeds

¼ cup lemon juice

1 clove garlic - peeled

⅛ tsp salt

Directions: Place ingredients into blender jar in order as listed and secure the lid. Press the **Speed Up** button until the blender reaches 1. Allow blender to run a full cycle (it may appear as though the ingredients are not being blended). When the cycle has finished, remove the lid and with a spatula scrape ingredients towards center of the jar. Secure the lid and press the **Speed Up** button until the blender reaches speed 5. During this cycle, the spread will begin to form around the blade. After cycle is finished, remove the lid with a rubber spatula and scrape the ingredients toward the center of the jar. Secure the lid and press the **Speed Up** button until blender reaches speed 5. Repeat this process 4 to 5 times or until spread has reached desired consistency.

Nutritional Information

Yield: 2 cups
Serving Size: 2 Tablespoons

Amount per serving

Calories: 145.46	Potassium: 271.67 mg
34.80% from Fat,	Magnesium: 56.07 mg
16.80% from Protein	Zinc: 1.42 mg
48.40% from Carb	Copper: 40 mg
Protein: 6.36 g	Manganese: .77 mg
Total Fat: 5.85g	Vitamin A: 19.17 IU
Saturated Fat: .76 g	Vitamin E: 0.00 mg
Monosaturated Fat: 2.27 g	Thiamin: 0.11 mg
Polyunsaturated: 2.29 g	Riboflavin: .07 mg
Cholesterol: 0.00 mg	Niacin: .74 mg
Carbohydrates: 18.33 g	Pantothenic Acid: .43 mg
Fiber: 5.64 g	Vitamin B6: .20 mg
Calcium: 98.61 mg	Folate: 155.49 ug
Phosphorous: 142.99 mg	Vitamin B12: 0.00 ug
Iron: 2.71 mg	Vitamin C: 2.87 mg
Sodium: 25.67 mg	Selenium: 2.62 ug
Sugar: 2.94 mg	

Mayonnaise

1 large egg at room temperature

1 Tbsp fresh lemon juice

1 tsp Dijon style mustard

⅛ tsp salt

⅛ tsp pepper

1 cup olive oil

Directions: Place ingredients (except olive oil) into blender jar in order as listed and secure the lid. Press the Pulse button and hold for 10 seconds. Remove the steam cap in center of lid. Press **Speed Up** button again, until blender reaches speed 6. Allow the blender to run for 10 seconds and then begin adding the olive oil. Add oil gradually through steam cap until mixture has thickened. Replace the steam cap and allow the blender to finish the cycle. Refrigerate for 30 minutes.

Nutritional Information

Yields: 1 cup
Serving Size: 1 Tablespoon

Amount per serving

Calories: 122.62	Potassium: 3.19 mg
99.20% from Fat	Magnesium: .17 mg
0.50% from Protein	Zinc: .02mg
0.35% from Carb	Copper: 0.00 mg
Protein: .16 g	Manganese: 0.00 mg
Total Fat: 13.76	Vitamin A: 6.93 IU
Saturated Fat: 1.77 g	Vitamin E: 1.78 mg
Monosaturated Fat: 3.34 g	Thiamin: 0.00 mg
Polyunsaturated: 8.01 g	Riboflavin: .01 mg
Cholesterol: 4.51 mg	Niacin: .01 mg
Carbohydrates: .11 g	Pantothenic Acid: .02 mg
Fiber: .01 g	Vitamin B6: 0.00 mg
Calcium: .82 mg	Folate: .60 ug
Phosphorous: 1.90 mg	Vitamin B12: .01 ug
Iron: .02 mg	Vitamin C: .50 mg
Sodium: 19.75 mg	Selenium: .33 ug
Sugar: .04 mg	

Butter

2 cups heavy whipping cream
¼ tsp salt

Directions: Place whipping cream into blender jar and secure the lid. Press the **Speed Up** button until the blender reaches speed 9. Allow cycle to run for approximately 10 to 15 seconds and press any lower row button to stop. Remove the lid and with a spatula pull the ingredients toward the center. Secure the lid and hold down the Pulse button for 5 seconds. Repeat this procedure 5 to 7 times until liquid starts to appear. After butter is formed, stir with a spatula to group together and then strain. Add salt and refrigerate.

Nutritional Information

Yields: 2 cups
Serving Size: 2 Tablespoons

Amount per serving

Calories: 51.31	Potassium: 11.21 mg
94.50% from Fat	Magnesium: 1.05 mg
2.33% from Protein	Zinc: .03 mg
3.17% from Carb	Copper: 0.00 mg
Protein: .31 g	Manganese: 0.00 mg
Total Fat: 5.53 g	Vitamin A: 219.58 IU
Saturated Fat: 3.44 g	Vitamin E: 60.50 mg
Monosaturated Fat: 1.60 g	Thiamin: 0.00 mg
Polyunsaturated: .21 g	Riboflavin: .02 mg
Cholesterol: 20.46 mg	Niacin: .01 mg
Carbohydrates: .42 g	Pantothenic Acid: .04 mg
Fiber: 0.00 g	Vitamin B6: 0.00 mg
Calcium: 9.73 mg	Folate: .60 ug
Phosphorous: 9.26 mg	Vitamin B12: .03 ug
Iron: 0.00 mg	Vitamin C: .09 mg
Sodium: 42.52 mg	Selenium: .07 ug
Sugar: .02 mg	

Spicy Cheese Ball

1 (8 oz.) package nonfat cream cheese - softened
1 Tbsp lemon juice
2 Tbsp Worcestershire sauce
1 cup cheddar cheese - shredded
⅛ tsp salt
⅛ tsp Tabasco sauce
¼ tsp onion powder
2 green chilies
½ jalapeño pepper – keep seeds*

Directions: Place ingredients in jar in order as listed with spatula. Pack ingredients near the blade and secure the lid. Press the **Speed Up** button until blender reaches speed 9. When the display reads 25 seconds or when all ingredients are blended press any lower row button to stop. Refrigerate for 2 hours or until firm.

1 cup pecans chopped

Directions: Form cheese spread into a ball and roll in the chopped nuts.

for a less spicy dip, remove seeds and rind

Nutritional Information

Yield: 2 cups
Serving Size: 2 Tablespoons

Amount per serving

Calories: 68.15	Potassium: 50.26 mg
69.30% from Fat	Magnesium: 3.67 mg
21.30% from Protein	Zinc: .37 mg
9.49% from Carb	Copper: .01 mg
Protein: 3.61 g	Manganese: 0.00 mg
Total Fat: 5.23 g	Vitamin A: 186.10 IU
Saturated Fat: 3.31 g	Vitamin E: 46.94 mg
Monosaturated Fat: 1.48 g	Thiamin: .01 mg
Polyunsaturated: .17 g	Riboflavin: .07 mg
Cholesterol: 16.60 mg	Niacin: .04 mg
Carbohydrates: 1.61 g	Pantothenic Acid: .04 mg
Fiber: .02 g	Vitamin B6: .02 mg
Calcium: 75.94 mg	Folate: 4.60 ug
Phosphorous: 65.36 mg	Vitamin B12: .15 ug
Iron: .42 mg	Vitamin C: 4.13 mg
Sodium: 118.14 mg	Selenium: 1.72 ug
Sugar: .40 mg	

Deviled Ham Spread

¼ cup milk

1 (8 oz.) package nonfat cream cheese - softened

1 (4.5 oz.) can deviled ham

½ cup pecans

Directions: Place ingredients in jar in order as listed. Pack ingredients around blade of blender jar and secure the lid. Press the **Dips** button.

Nutritional Information

Yield: 2 cups
Serving Size: 2 Tablespoons

Amount per serving

Calories: 71.11	Potassium: 72.23 mg
70.50% from Fat,	Magnesium: 7.44 mg
20.10% from Protein	Zinc: .46 mg
9.43% from Carb	Copper: .05 mg
Protein: 3.62 g	Manganese: .16 mg
Total Fat: 5.64 g	Vitamin A: 105.93 IU
Saturated Fat: 2.01 g	Vitamin E: 27.99 mg
Monosaturated Fat: 2.43 g	Thiamin: .10 mg
Polyunsaturated: .90 g	Riboflavin: .07 mg
Cholesterol: 11.28 mg	Niacin: .46 mg
Carbohydrates: 1.70 g	Pantothenic Acid: .09 mg
Fiber: .33 g	Vitamin B6: .05 mg
Calcium: 23.77 mg	Folate: 3.89 ug
Phosphorous: 51.77 mg	Vitamin B12: .17 ug
Iron: .41 mg	Vitamin C: .08 mg
Sodium: 129.14 mg	Selenium: 2.98 ug
Sugar: .36 mg	

Mexican Spread

2 cups low-fat sour cream

1 (8 oz.) package nonfat cream cheese

1 package (1¼ oz.) taco seasoning

Directions: Place ingredients into blender jar and secure the lid. Press the **Dips** button.

Nutritional Information

Yield: 4 cups
Serving Size: 2 Tablespoons

Amount per serving

Calories: 25.44	Potassium: 16.27 mg
76.40% from Fat	Magnesium: 1.07 mg
10.20% from Protein	Zinc: .85 mg
13.30% from Carb	Copper: 0.00 mg
Protein: .64 g	Manganese: 0.00 mg
Total Fat: 2.13 g	Vitamin A: 133.88 IU
Saturated Fat: 1.33 g	Vitamin E: 18.92 mg
Monosaturated Fat: .61g	Thiamin: .10 mg
Polyunsaturated: .08 g	Riboflavin: .07 mg
Cholesterol: 5.15 mg	Niacin: .46 mg
Carbohydrates: .84g	Pantothenic Acid: .09 mg
Fiber: 12.09 g	Vitamin B6: .05 mg
Calcium: 12.31 mg	Folate: 3.89 ug
Phosphorous: 11.28 mg	Vitamin B12: .17 ug
Iron: .06 mg	Vitamin C: .08 mg
Sodium: 54.61 mg	Selenium: 2.98 ug
Sugar: .02 mg	

Spinach Spread

1 cup sour cream

1 cup mayonnaise

1 package vegetable soup mix

1 tsp onion powder

1 ¼ cups spinach

Directions: Place spinach into blender jar and pack down around the blade with spatula or spoon. Place remaining ingredients into blender jar and secure the lid. Press the **Dips** button.

Cheese Spread

3 Tbsp Milk

1 cup mayonnaise

6-8 slices bacon - crisped and crumbled

¼ cup slivered almonds

1 ½ cup cheddar cheese - shredded

Directions: Place ingredients into blender jar in order as listed and secure the lid. Press the **Dips** button. After blending, it may be necessary to press the Pulse button 3 to 4 times.

Nutritional Information

Yield: 2 cups
Serving Size: 1 Tablespoon

Amount per serving

Calories: 75.30 (83.00% from Fat, 5.45% from Protein, 11.50% from Carb)	Magnesium: 10.54 mg
	Zinc: .11 mg
	Copper: .02 mg
Protein: 1.05 g	Manganese: .10 mg
Total Fat: 7.01 g	Vitamin A: 996.71 IU
Saturated Fat: 1.85 g	Vitamin E: 18.01 mg
Monosaturated Fat: 1.85 g	Thiamin: .01 mg
Polyunsaturated: 3.01 g	Riboflavin: .03 mg
Cholesterol: 5.96 mg	Niacin: .11 mg
Carbohydrates: 2.22 g	Pantothenic Acid: .09 mg
Fiber: .66 g	Vitamin B6: .06 mg
Calcium: 23.14 mg	Folate: 11.63 ug
Phosphorous: 17.48 mg	Vitamin B12: .09 ug
Iron: .31 mg	Vitamin C: .44 mg
Sodium: 200.29 mg	Selenium: .68 ug
Sugar: .11 mg	
Potassium: 47.01 mg	

Nutritional Information

Yield: 2 cups
Serving Size: 2 Tablespoons

Amount per serving

Calories: 176.45	Potassium: 47.48 mg
88.00% from Fat	Magnesium: 9.11 mg
10.50% from Protein	Zinc: .54 mg
1.50% from Carb	Copper: .03 mg
Protein: 4.67 g	Manganese: .04 mg
Total Fat: 17.46 g	Vitamin A: 631.48 IU
Saturated Fat: 5.20 g	Vitamin E: 141.13 mg
Monosaturated Fat: 7.39 g	Thiamin: .02 mg
Polyunsaturated: 3.97 g	Riboflavin: .07 mg
Cholesterol: 16.32 mg	Niacin: .41 mg
Carbohydrates: .67 g	Pantothenic Acid: .11 mg
Fiber: .18 g	Vitamin B6: .02 mg
Calcium: 98.70 mg	Folate: 2.91 ug
Phosphorous: 90.66 mg	Vitamin B12: .16 ug
Iron: .19 mg	Vitamin C: .04 mg
Sodium: 279.81 mg	Selenium: 3.65 ug
Sugar: .18 mg	

Olive Spread

1 Tbsp olive oil

2 (6 oz.) can pitted olives - drained

¼ tsp garlic powder

Directions: Place ingredients into blender jar and secure the lid. Press the **Speed Up** button until blender reaches speed 8. Allow the blender to run for approximately 30 seconds, or until desired consistency is reached, then press any lower row button to stop.

Nutritional Information

Yield: 2 cups
Serving Size: 2 Tablespoons

Amount per serving

Calories: 39.51	Potassium: 2.20 mg
85.20% from Fat	Magnesium: .88 mg
1.78% from Protein	Zinc: .05 mg
13.00% from Carb	Copper: .05 mg
Protein: .19 g	Manganese: 0.00 mg
Total Fat: 3.96 g	Vitamin A: 85.69 IU
Saturated Fat: .53 g	Vitamin E: 0.00 mg
Monosaturated Fat: 2.92 g	Thiamin: 0.00 mg
Polyunsaturated: .36 g	Riboflavin: .01 mg
Cholesterol: 0.00 mg	Niacin: 0.00 mg
Carbohydrates: 1.36 g	Pantothenic Acid: 0.00 mg
Fiber: .68 g	Vitamin B6: 0.00 mg
Calcium: 18.76 mg	Folate: 0.00 ug
Phosphorous: .82 mg	Vitamin B12: 0.00 ug
Iron: .71 mg	Vitamin C: .20 mg
Sodium: 185.47 mg	Selenium: .21 ug
Sugar: .01 mg	

Beverages Table of Contents

Whole Juices   104

Alcohol Substitution Chart

Alcoholic Ingredient	Substitution
Amaretto	1/4 to 1/2 teaspoons Almond extract for 2 Tablespoons Amaretto
Anisette	Anise Italian Syrup or Funnel
Beer or Ale	Chicken Broth, Beef Broth, Mushroom Broth, White Grape Juice, Ginger Ale
Bourbon	1 1/2 to 2 teaspoons vanilla extract for 2 Tablespoons Bourbon
Brandy	1 1/2 to 2 teaspoons vanilla extract for 2 Tablespoons Brandy (For a particular flavor of brandy, use the corresponding extract)
Calvados	Apple juice concentrate or apple juice
Chambord	Rasperry juice, syrup, or extract
Champagne	Ginger ale, sparkling cider, sparkling cranberry juice, sparkling white grape juice
Claret	Diluted currant or grape juice, cherry cider syrup
Cointreau	Orange juice, frozen orange juice concentrate
Cognac	Peach, pear, or apricot juice
Creme de menthe	Spearmint extract mixed with water or grape juice
Coffee Liqueur	1/2 to 1 teaspoon chocolate extract plus, one teaspoon instant coffee, and 2 tablespoons water for 2 tablespoons Liqueur
Curacao	Orange juice concentrate
Framboise	Raspberry juice or syrup
Frangelico	Hazelnut or almond extract
Galliano	Licorice extract
Grand Marnier	2 Tablespoons orange juice concentrate, or 2 Tablespoons orange juice and 1/2 teaspoon orange extract for 2 Tablespoons Grand Marnier
Grenadine	Pomegranite syrup or juice
Hard Cider	Apple juice or apple cider

Alcoholic Ingredient	Substitution
Kahlua	1/2 to 1 teaspoon chocolate extract or 1/2 to 1 teaspoon instant coffee and 2 Tablespoons water for 2 Tablespoons Kahlua
Kirsch	Cherry cider or black cherry, raspberry, boysenberry, currant, or grape juice or syrup
Mirin	White grape juice and lemon juice or zest
Muscat	White grape juice and powdered sugar
Pepperment Schnapps	Mint or peppermint exrtact, mint Italian soda, or mint leaves
Port Wine	Sweet Sherry, Orange Juice, or Apple Juice
Red Burgundy	Red wine vinegar or grape juice
Red Wine	Non-alcoholic wine, beef or chicken broth, diluted red wine vinegar, tomato juice, grape juice, cranberry juice, water
Rum	White grape juice, pineapple juice, apple juice
Sake	Rice vinegar
Schnapps	1 teaspoon corresponding flavor extract for 2 Tablespoons Schnapps
Scotch	1/2 to 2 Tablespoons vanilla extract for 2 Tablespoons Scotch
Sherry	Apple juice, orange juice, or pineapple juice
Tequila	Cactus juice or nectar
Triple Sec	Orange juice concentrate, orange juice, orange zest, or orange marmalade
Vermouth, Dry	White grape juice, white wine vinegar, or non-alcoholic white wine
Vermouth, Sweet	Apple juice, grape juice, balsamic vinegar, non-alcoholic sweet wine, or water with lemon juice
Whiskey	If a small amount is called for, it may be eliminated
White Burgundy	Non-alcoholic wine, white grape juice diluted with white wine vinegar
White Wine	Non-alcoholic wine, chicken broth, water
Vodka	White grape juice, apple cider with lime juice, water

Tom Collins

2 Tbsp gin

¼ cup lemonade

⅓ cup sugar

½ cup water, chilled

½ lemon - peeled and seeded

½ cup ice cubes

½ cup club soda

Directions: Add ingredients in order as directed above and secure the lid. Press **Speed Up** button until blender reaches speed 6. Allow the cycle to run for 15 seconds. When the timer reads 15 seconds, press any lower row button to stop.

Nutritional Information

Yields: 1 ¾ cups
Serving Size: ½ cup

Amount per serving

Calories: 209.5	Potassium: 12.91 mg
0.25% from Fat	Magnesium: 1.34 mg
0.41% from Protein	Zinc: .04mg
99.30% from Carb	Copper: .01 mg
Protein: .08 g	Manganese: 0.00 mg
Total Fat: .02 g	Vitamin A: 1.60 IU
Saturated Fat: 0.00 g	Vitamin E: 0.00 mg
Monosaturated Fat: 0.00 g	Thiamin: 0.00 mg
Polyunsaturated: .01 g	Riboflavin: 0.00 mg
Cholesterol: 0.00 mg	Niacin: .01 mg
Carbohydrates: 19.15 g	Pantothenic Acid: .01 mg
Fiber: .20 g	Vitamin B6: .01 mg
Calcium: 8.58 mg	Folate: .96 ug
Phosphorous: 3.30 mg	Vitamin B12: 0.00 ug
Iron: .06 mg	Vitamin C: 14.37 mg
Sodium: 7.75 mg	Selenium: .15 ug
Sugar: 18.64 mg	

Creamy Adult Mocha

½ cup coffee flavored liquor

½ cup milk

1 cup chocolate ice cream*

Directions: Add ingredients in order as directed above and secure the lid. Press **Speed Up** button until blender reaches speed 3. Allow the cycle to run for 10 seconds. When the timer reads 10 seconds, push any lower row button to stop.

*May substitute chocolate frozen yogurt

Nutritional Information

Yields: 2 cups
Serving Size: ½ cup

Amount per serving

Calories: 202.97	Potassium: 147.96 mg
23.60% from Fat,	Magnesium: 15.53 mg
6.40% from Protein	Zinc: .34 mg
70.00% from Carb	Copper: .06 mg
Protein: 2.50 g	Manganese: .05 mg
Total Fat: 4.09 g	Vitamin A: 199.70 IU
Saturated Fat: 2.50 g	Vitamin E: 57.04 mg
Monosaturated Fat: 1.17 g	Thiamin: .03 mg
Polyunsaturated: .19 g	Riboflavin: .13 mg
Cholesterol: 12.45 mg	Niacin: .16 mg
Carbohydrates: 27.29 g	Pantothenic Acid: .30 mg
Fiber: .40 g	Vitamin B6: .03 mg
Calcium: 79.98 mg	Folate: 7.13 ug
Phosphorous: 71.53 mg	Vitamin B12: .23 ug
Iron: .35 mg	Vitamin C: .60 mg
Sodium: 45.70 mg	Selenium: 1.73 ug
Sugar: 24.53 mg	

Daiquiri

½ cup water

1 (6 ounce) can frozen limeade concentrate

⅓ cup light rum

1 cup ice cubes

Directions: Add ingredients in order as directed above and secure the lid. Press the **Speed Up** button until blender reaches speed 6. Allow the cycle to run for 15 seconds. When the timer reads 15 seconds, press any lower row button to stop.

Arctic Mudslide Shake

1 ½ oz. vodka

1 ½ oz. irish cream

1 ½ oz. coffee liquor

8 cubes ice

1 ½ oz. of cream

1 scoop vanilla ice cream*

2 scoops chocolate ice cream

Directions: Add ingredients in order as directed above and secure the lid. Press the **Speed Up** button until blender reaches speed 6. Allow the cycle to run for 15 seconds. When the timer reads 15 seconds, press any lower row button to stop.

*May substitute vanilla frozen yogurt

Nutritional Information

Yields: 3 cups
Serving Size: ½ cup

Amount per serving

Calories: 79.85	Potassium: 19.24 mg
0.94% from Fat,	Magnesium: 1.42 mg
0.63% from Protein	Zinc: .03 mg
98.40% from Carb	Copper: .02 mg
Protein: .09 g	Manganese: .01 mg
Total Fat: .06 g	Vitamin A: 1.98 IU
Saturated Fat: .01 g	Vitamin E: 0.00 mg
Monosaturated Fat: 0.00 g	Thiamin: .01 mg
Polyunsaturated: .02 g	Riboflavin: .03 mg
Cholesterol: 0.00 mg	Niacin: .02 mg
Carbohydrates: 13.35 g	Pantothenic Acid: .02 mg
Fiber: .06 g	Vitamin B6: .01 mg
Calcium: 1.98mg	Folate: 1.42 ug
Phosphorous: 3.17 mg	Vitamin B12: 0.00ug
Iron: .22 mg	Vitamin C: 5.02 mg
Sodium: 1.26 mg	Selenium: .11 ug
Sugar: 12.77 mg	

Nutritional Information

Yields: 2 cups
Serving Size: ½ cup

Amount per serving

Calories: 202.04	Potassium: 97.16 mg
60.40% from Fat,	Magnesium: 10.74 mg
5.09% from Protein	Zinc: .25 mg
34.60% from Carb	Copper: .06 mg
Protein: 2.07 g	Manganese: .05 mg
Total Fat: 10.90 g	Vitamin A: 425.39 IU
Saturated Fat: 6.75 g	Vitamin E: 117.70 mg
Monosaturated Fat: 3.14 g	Thiamin: .02 mg
Polyunsaturated: .42 g	Riboflavin: .09 mg
Cholesterol: 38.12 mg	Niacin: .10 mg
Carbohydrates: 14.05 g	Pantothenic Acid: .23 mg
Fiber: .40 g	Vitamin B6: .02 mg
Calcium: 46.28 mg	Folate: 6.13 ug
Phosphorous: 52.96 mg	Vitamin B12.34 mg
Iron: .34 mg	Selenium: .96 ug
Sodium: 48.79 mg	
Sugar: 10.39 mg	

Sunburn

½ cup pineapple juice

½ cup orange juice

¼ cup rum

1 Tbsp amaretto liquor

3 Tbsp grenadine syrup

3 cups ice

Directions: Add ingredients in order as directed above and secure the lid. Press the **Speed Up** button until blender reaches speed 6. Allow the cycle to run for 15 seconds. When the timer reads 15 seconds, press any lower row button to stop.

Nutritional Information

Yields: 4 cups
Serving Size: ½ cup

Amount per serving

Calories: 58.91	Potassium: 53.40 mg
from Fat 1.37%	Magnesium: 4.11 mg
from Protein 1.76%	Zinc: .04 mg
from Carb 96.90%	Copper: .03 mg
Protein: .18 g	Manganese: .16 mg
Total Fat: .06 g	Vitamin A: 12.92 IU
Saturated Fat: .01 g	Vitamin E: 0.00 mg
Monosaturated Fat: .01 g	Thiamin: .03 mg
Polyunsaturated: .02 g	Riboflavin: .01 mg
Cholesterol: 0.00 mg	Niacin: .09 mg
Carbohydrates: 9.73 g	Pantothenic Acid: .05 mg
Fiber: .06 g	Vitamin B6: .02 mg
Calcium: 4.68 mg	Folate: 6.39 ug
Phosphorous: 3.74 mg	Vitamin B12: 0.00 ug
Iron: .08 mg	Vitamin C: 6.79 mg
Sodium: 2.58 mg	Selenium: .08 ug
Sugar: 8.13 mg	

Spicy Pirate

¾ cup orange juice

3 oz. light rum

¼ cup cream of coconut

⅛ tsp cinnamon

2 cups ice cubes

Directions: Add ingredients in order as directed above and secure the lid. Press the **Speed Up** button until blender reaches speed 5. Allow the blender to run for 10 seconds. When the timer reads 10 seconds, press any lower row button to stop.

Nutritional Information

Yields: 2 cups
Serving Size: ½ cup

Amount per serving

Calories: 119.34	Potassium: 138.24 mg
64.30% from Fat,	Magnesium: 9.38 mg
4.93% from Protein,	Zinc: .18mg
30.80% from Carb	Copper: .09 mg
Protein: .92 g	Manganese: .22 mg
Total Fat: 5.33 g	Vitamin A: 36.61 IU
Saturated Fat: 4.63 g	Vitamin E: 0.00 mg
Monosaturated Fat: .24 g	Thiamin: .06 mg
Polyunsaturated: .09 g	Riboflavin: .01mg
Cholesterol: 0.00 mg	Niacin: .27 mg
Carbohydrates: 5.75 g	Pantothenic Acid: .13 mg
Fiber: .46 g	Vitamin B6: .03 mg
Calcium: 7.19 mg	Folate: 11.87 ug
Phosphorous: 24.54 mg	Vitamin B12: 0.00 ug
Iron: .47 mg	Vitamin C: 15.80 mg
Sodium: 1.30 mg	Selenium: .05 ug
Sugar: 0.00 mg	

Purple Pleasure

2 oz. melon liquor

¾ cup strawberries - remove stems

2 oz. pineapple juice

2 oz. cream of coconut

3 oz. blue Curacao

Directions: Add ingredients in order as directed above and secure the lid. Press the **Speed Up** button until blender reaches speed 6. Allow the cycle to run for 10 seconds. When the timer read 10 seconds, press any lower row button to stop.

Nutritional Information

Yields: 2 cups
Serving Size: ½ cup

Amount per serving

Calories: 176.95	Potassium: 119.30 mg
37.30% from Fat	Magnesium: 10.58 mg
2.55% from Protein	Zinc: .20mg
60.10% from Carb	Copper: .09 mg
Protein: .79 g	Manganese: .44 mg
Total Fat: 5.12 g	Vitamin A: 4.13 IU
Saturated Fat: 4.40 g	Vitamin E: 0.00 mg
Monosaturated Fat: .23 g	Thiamin: .02 mg
Polyunsaturated: .14 g	Riboflavin: .01mg
Cholesterol: 0.00 mg	Niacin: .32 mg
Carbohydrates: 18.57 g	Pantothenic Acid: .09mg
Fiber: .91 g	Vitamin B6: .03 mg
Calcium: 8.88 mg	Folate: 13.36 ug
Phosphorous: 27.39 mg	Vitamin B12: 0.00 ug
Iron: .50 mg	Vitamin C: 18.67 mg
Sodium: 3.83 mg	Selenium: .25 ug
Sugar: 9.83 mg	

Pina Colada

1 cup cream of coconut

¾ cup pineapple juice

½ cup light rum

1 Tbsp milk*

1 (8 ounce) can pineapple - with juice

2 ½ cups ice

Directions: Add ingredients in order as directed above and secure the lid. Press **Speed Up** button until blender reaches speed 6. Allow the cycle to run for 15 seconds. When the timer reads 15 seconds, press any lower row button to stop.

*May substitute any type of milk (i.e., low-fat, skim, soy)

Nutritional Information

Yields: 4 cups
Serving Size: ½ cup

Amount per serving

Calories: 155.00	Potassium: 171.70 mg
71.80% from Fat	Magnesium: 17.29 mg
4.18% from Protein	Zinc: .37 mg
24.00% from Carb	Copper: .17 mg
Protein: 1.37 g	Manganese: .97 mg
Total Fat: 10.47 g	Vitamin A: 16.76 IU
Saturated Fat: 9.24 g	Vitamin E: 1.17 mg
Monosaturated Fat: .45 g	Thiamin: .05 mg
Polyunsaturated: .13 g	Riboflavin: .02 mg
Cholesterol: .08 mg	Niacin: .42mg
Carbohydrates: 7.88 g	Pantothenic Acid: .14 mg
Fiber: .95 g	Vitamin B6: .06 mg
Calcium: 14.63 mg	Folate: 13.94 ug
Phosphorous: 42.53 mg	Vitamin B12: .01 ug
Iron: .89 mg	Vitamin C: 5.74 mg
Sodium: 3.00 mg	Selenium: .19 ug
Sugar: 5.49 mg	

Tangy Melon Ball

¾ cup orange juice
½ cup melon flavored liquor
1 ½ oz. vodka
1 ½ cup ice cubes

Directions: Add ingredients in order as directed above and secure the lid. Press the **Speed Up** button until blender reaches speed 6. Allow the cycle to run for 15 seconds. When the timer reads 15 seconds, press any lower row button to stop.

Nutritional Information

Yields: 3 cups
Serving Size: ½ cup

Amount per serving

Calories: 97.87	Potassium: 65.91 mg
47.50% from Fat	Magnesium: 3.84 mg
5.25% from Protein	Zinc: .05 mg
47.20% from Carb	Copper: .02 mg
Protein: .83 g	Manganese: .01 mg
Total Fat: 3.34 g	Vitamin A: 152.82 IU
Saturated Fat: 2.01 g	Vitamin E: 35.45 mg
Monosaturated Fat: .94 g	Thiamin: .04 mg
Polyunsaturated: .16 g	Riboflavin: .02 mg
Cholesterol: 12.03 mg	Niacin: .10 mg
Carbohydrates: 7.46 g	Pantothenic Acid: .08mg
Fiber: .06 g	Vitamin B6: .02 mg
Calcium: 6.43 mg	Folate: 6.02 ug
Phosphorous: 14.07 mg	Vitamin B12: .02 ug
Iron: .08 mg	Vitamin C: 10.28 mg
Sodium: 19.46 mg	Selenium: .11 ug
Sugar: 1.96 mg	

Strawberry Daiquiri

6 oz. can lemonade concentrate - thawed
⅓ cup sugar or sugar substitute
3 cups strawberries - remove stems
½ cup light or dark rum
1 ½ cup ice cubes

Directions: Place ingredients in blender jar in the order listed and secure the lid. Press the **Speed Up** button and hold down until blender reaches speed 6. Allow the blender to run for 15 seconds. When the timer reads 15 seconds, press any lower row button to stop.

Nutritional Information

Yields: 3 ½ cups
Serving Size: ½ cup

Amount per serving

Calories: 138.68	Potassium: 116.48 mg
2.03% from Fat,	Magnesium: 9.68 mg
1.88% from Protein	Zinc: .12mg
96.10% from Carb	Copper: .05 mg
Protein: .51 g	Manganese: .26 mg
Total Fat: .24 g	Vitamin A: 9.52 IU
Saturated Fat: .02 g	Vitamin E: 0.00 mg
Monosaturated Fat: .03 g	Thiamin: .02 mg
Polyunsaturated: .12 g.	Riboflavin: .04 mg
Cholesterol: 0.00 mg	Niacin: .27 mg
Carbohydrates: 26.05 g	Pantothenic Acid: .10 mg
Fiber: 1.35 g	Vitamin B6: .04mg
Calcium: 12.22 mg	Folate: 16.85
Phosphorous: 18.62 mg	Vitamin B12: 0.00
Iron: .47 mg	Vitamin C: 42.61 ug
Sodium: 1.78 mg	Selenium: .42 ug
Sugar: 23.57 mg	

Caribbean Splash

1⅓ cup pineapple juice

½ cup light rum

1 banana - peeled and broken in half

1 Tbsp sugar or sugar substitute

1 ½ cup ice cubes

Directions: Place ingredients in jar in order listed above and secure the lid. Press **Speed Up** button until blender reaches speed 6. Allow the blender to run for 15 seconds. When the timer reads 15 seconds, press any lower row button to stop.

Nutritional Information

Yields: 3 ½ cups
Serving Size: ½ cup

Amount per serving

Calories: 89.40	Potassium: 140.88 mg
1.76% from Fat	Magnesium: 11.98 mg
2.78% from Protein	Zinc: .10 mg
95.50% from Carb	Copper: .07 mg
Protein: .39 g	Manganese: .53 mg
Total Fat: .11 g	Vitamin A: 16.10 IU
Saturated Fat: .03 g	Vitamin E: 0.00 mg
Monosaturated Fat: .01 g	Thiamin: .03 mg
Polyunsaturated: .03 g	Riboflavin: .03 mg
Cholesterol: 0.00 mg	Niacin: .27 mg
Carbohydrates: 13.26 g	Pantothenic Acid: .12 mg
Fiber: .65 g	Vitamin B6: .12 mg
Calcium: 9.18 mg	Folate: 15.24 ug
Phosphorous: 9.32 mg	Vitamin B12: 0.00 ug
Iron: .20 mg	Vitamin C: 6.96 mg
Sodium: .85 mg	Selenium: .27 ug
Sugar: 10.89 mg	

Zombie

2 Tbsp Rum

2 Tbsp Amaretto

1 orange - peeled, seeded and quartered

Juice of ½ medium lemon

¼ cup canned pineapple chunks - with juice

¼ cup sugar

¼ cup water

Directions: Place ingredients in jar in order listed above and secure the lid. Press **Speed Up** button until blender reaches speed 5. Allow the blender to run for 15 seconds. When the timer reads 15 seconds, press any lower row button to stop.

Nutritional Information

Yields: 2 cups
Serving Size: ½ cup

Amount per serving

Calories: 158.70	Potassium: 35.59 mg
0.67% from Fat	Magnesium: 5.29 mg
1.87% from Protein	Zinc: .04 mg
97.50% from Carb	Copper: .03 mg
Protein: .63 g	Manganese: .02 mg
Total Fat: .10 g	Vitamin A: 102.71 IU
Saturated Fat: .02 g	Vitamin E: 0.00 mg
Monosaturated Fat: .01 g	Thiamin: .04 mg
Polyunsaturated: .03 g	Riboflavin: .02 mg
Cholesterol: 0.00 mg	Niacin: .15 mg
Carbohydrates: 32.83 g	Pantothenic Acid: .13 mg
Fiber: 1.27 g	Vitamin B6: .03 mg
Calcium: 19.94 mg	Folate: 14.23 ug
Phosphorous: 8.23 mg	Vitamin B12: 0.00 ug
Iron: .10 mg	Vitamin C: 27.45 mg
Sodium: 4.50 mg	Selenium: .36 ug
Sugar: 28.58 mg	

Grasshopper

1 Tbsp white creme de cocoa

1 Tbsp green creme de menthe

½ cup vanilla ice cream

⅓ cup lowfat milk

¼ cup ice cubes

Directions: Place ingredients in jar in order listed above and secure the lid. Press the **Speed Up** button until blender reaches speed 4. Allow the blender to run for 10 seconds. When the timer reads 10 seconds, press any lower row button to stop.

Nutritional Information

Yields: 1 cup
Serving Size: ½ cup

Amount per serving

Calories: 151.52	Potassium: 132.39 mg
32.90% from Fat	Magnesium: 9.50 mg
8.76% from Protein	Zinc: .43 mg
58.30% from Carb	Copper: .03 mg
Protein: 2.63 g	Manganese: .01 mg
Total Fat: 4.39 g	Vitamin A: 231.10 IU
Saturated Fat: 2.70 g	Vitamin E: 65.20 mg
Monosaturated Fat: 1.18 g	Thiamin: .02 mg
Polyunsaturated: .20 g	Riboflavin: .16 mg
Cholesterol: 17.82 mg	Niacin: .08 mg
Carbohydrates: 17.48 g	Pantothenic Acid: .36 mg
Fiber: .25 g	Vitamin B6: .03 mg
Calcium: 94.31 mg	Folate: 3.83 ug
Phosphorous: 76.30 mg	Vitamin B12: .32 ug
Iron: .06 mg	Vitamin C: .22 mg
Sodium: 47.43 mg	Selenium: 2.05 ug
Sugar: 16.72 mg	

Brandy Alexander

2 Tbsp brandy

1 cup chocolate ice cream

¼ cup low-fat chocolate milk

¼ cup ice cubes

Directions: Place ingredients in jar in order listed above and secure the lid. Press the **Milkshake** button.

Nutritional Information

Yields: 2 cups
Serving Size: ½ cup

Amount per serving

Calories: 98.50	Potassium: 108.80 mg
40.10% from Fat	Magnesium: 11.60 mg
8.29% from Protein	Zinc: .26 mg
51.60% from Carb	Copper: .06 mg
Protein: 1.76 g	Manganese: .06 mg
Total Fat: 3.79 g	Vitamin A: 167.90 IU
Saturated Fat: 2.34 g	Vitamin E: 47.34 mg
Monosaturated Fat: 1.11 g	Thiamin: .02 mg
Polyunsaturated: .14 g	Riboflavin: .09 mg
Cholesterol: 11.69 mg	Niacin: .10 mg
Carbohydrates: 10.94 g	Pantothenic Acid: .23 mg
Fiber: .47 g	Vitamin B6: .02 mg
Calcium: 53.94 mg	Folate: 6.06 ug
Phosphorous: 51.61 mg	Vitamin B12: .15 ug
Iron: .35 mg	Vitamin C: .37 mg
Sodium: 34.61 mg	Selenium: 1.12 ug
Sugar: 9.92 mg	

Frosty Cider

1 ¾ cups apple cider

¼ cup Apple Schnapps*

½ large apple - seeded,cored and cut into fourths

½ large orange - peeled and halved

1 ¼ cups vanilla ice cream

½ tsp cinnamon

½ tsp nutmeg

Directions: Place ingredients in jar in order listed above and secure the lid. Press the **Milkshake** button.

*May substitute with Triple Sec

Margarita

3 Tbsp Margarita

1 Tbsp Triple Sec

1 Tbsp sweetened lime juice

¼ cup lemonade

1 ½ cup ice cubes

Directions: Place ingredients in jar in order listed above and secure the lid. Press the **Speed Up** button until blender reaches speed 5. Allow the blender to run for 10 seconds. When the timer reads 10 seconds, press any lower row button to stop.

Nutritional Information

Yields: 4 cups
Serving Size: ½ cup

Amount per serving

Calories: 416.31 8.25% from Fat	Magnesium: 5.74 mg
1.17% from Protein	Zinc: .19 mg
90.60% from Carb	Copper: .02 mg
Protein: 1.20 g	Manganese: .04 mg
Total Fat: 3.78 g	Vitamin A: 185.26 IU
Saturated Fat: 2.32 g	Vitamin E: 39.30 mg
Monosaturated Fat: 1.02 g	Thiamin: .03 mg
Polyunsaturated: .16 g	Riboflavin: .08 mg
Cholesterol: 14.38 mg	Niacin: .10 mg
Carbohydrates: 93.39 g	Pantothenic Acid: .19 mg
Fiber: .89 g	Vitamin B6: .03 mg
Calcium: 429.82 mg	Folate: 6.49 ug
Phosphorous: 140.52 mg	Vitamin B12: .09 ug
Iron: .16 mg	Vitamin C: 314.50 mg
Sodium: 104.95 mg	Selenium: 1.03 ug
Sugar: 76.15 mg	
Potassium: 94.03 mg	

Nutritional Information

Yields: 1 cup
Serving Size: ½ cup

Amount per serving

Calories: 94.91	Potassium: 6.52 mg
1.25% from Fat	Magnesium: .87 mg
0.25% from Protein	Zinc: .03 mg
98.50% from Carb	Copper: .02 mg
Protein: .02 g	Manganese: .01 mg
Total Fat: .04 g	Vitamin A: 1.23 IU
Saturated Fat: .01 g	Vitamin E: 0.00 mg
Monosaturated Fat: 0.00 g	Thiamin: 0.00 mg
Polyunsaturated: .02 g	Riboflavin: 0.00 mg
Cholesterol: 0.00 mg	Niacin: .02 mg
Carbohydrates: 7.60 g	Pantothenic Acid: .01 mg
Fiber: .03 g	Vitamin B6: 0.00 mg
Calcium: 4.58 mg	Folate: .62 ug
Phosphorous: 1.94 mg	Vitamin B12: 0.00 ug
Iron: .04 mg	Vitamin C: 4.75 mg
Sodium: 4.19 mg	Selenium: .07 ug
Sugar: 3.60 mg	

COFFEE

For coffee drinks, ice is used as a thickener. If you would like the drink to be thicker, add more ice than indicated in recipe. If you would like your drink to be thinner add less ice than is indicated in recipe. It is generally safe to increase and decrease amounts of ice by ¼ cup. When recipes call for ice cream, pack the ice cream around the blade at the bottom of the jar with a spatula or spoon. When recipe asks for brewed coffee, you may use hot chocolate. If recipe asks for instant coffee, you may use sweetened cocoa powder instead. Check individual recipes for amounts when substituting. For a creamier drink when the recipe calls for milk, use half & half.

Peanut Butter Cappuccino

2 cups ice cream

2 cups low-fat milk

2 Tbsp chocolate syrup

½ cup peanut butter

2-3 tsp instant coffee*

Directions: Pack ice cream around blade and place other ingredients into blender jar. Secure the lid, press the **Milkshake** button.

*May use 3 Tbsp sweetened cocoa powder

Fruit & Cream Café

1 cup strong brewed coffee*

½ cup low-fat milk**

2 Tbsp sugar

½ cup any fruit or juice - frozen or unfrozen
(i.e., peaches, bananas, strawberries, raspberries)

2 cups ice

Directions: Place ingredients into blender jar and secure the lid. Press the **Milkshake** button.

*May substitute 1 cup hot chocolate
**May substitute half & half

Nutritional Information

Yield: 4 cups
Serving Size: ½ cup

Amount per serving

Calories: 202.40	Potassium: 298.83 mg
53.80% from Fat,	Magnesium: 41.38 mg
13.90% from Protein	Zinc: .96mg
32.30% from Carb	Copper: .11 mg
Protein: 7.33 g	Manganese: .32 mg
Total Fat: 12.63 g	Vitamin A: 276.37 IU
Saturated Fat: 4.37 g	Vitamin E: 77.14 mg
Monosaturated Fat: 5.05 g	Thiamin: .06 mg
Polyunsaturated: 2.47 g	Riboflavin: .21 mg
Cholesterol: 18.24 mg	Niacin: 2.32 mg
Carbohydrates: 17.08 g	Pantothenic Acid: .57 mg
Fiber: 1.40 g	Vitamin B6: .12 mg
Calcium: 13.42 mg	Folate: 19.76 ug
Phosphorous: 154.22 mg	Vitamin B12: .37 ug
Iron: .44 mg	Vitamin C: .83 mg
Sodium: 65.63 mg	Selenium: .33 ug
Sugar: 10.46 mg	

Nutritional Information

Yield: 3 cups
Serving Size: ½ cup

Amount per serving

Calories: 32.27	Potassium: 87.67 mg
5.87% from Fat,	Magnesium: 7.25 mg
9.90% from Protein	Zinc: .11 mg
84.20% from Carb	Copper: .02 mg
Protein: .83 g	Manganese: .06 mg
Total Fat: .22 g	Vitamin A: 49.94 IU
Saturated Fat: .13 g	Vitamin E: 11.84 mg
Monosaturated Fat: .06 g	Thiamin: .01 mg
Polyunsaturated: .02 g	Riboflavin: .04 mg
Cholesterol: .82 mg	Niacin: .19 mg
Carbohydrates: 7.05 g	Pantothenic Acid: .09 mg
Fiber: .39 g	Vitamin B6: .01 mg
Calcium: 29.91 mg	Folate: 4.15 ug
Phosphorous: 23.21 mg	Vitamin B12: .08 ug
Iron: .417 mg	Vitamin C: 7.79 mg
Sodium: 11.38 mg	Selenium: .66 ug
Sugar: 5.04 mg	

Coffee Shop Style Cappuccino

¾ cup double strength coffee - chilled

1 cup low-fat milk

3 Tbsp granulated sugar

2 cups ice

Whipped cream

Directions: Place ingredients (except whipped cream) into blender jar and secure the lid. Press the **Milkshake** button. When cycle is complete, pour into cup and top with whipped cream.

Optional: To make a Caramel Cappuccino, add 3 Tbsp of caramel before pressing **Milkshake** button. To make Mocha Cappuccino, add 3 Tbsp chocolate syrup before pressing **Milkshake** button.

Nutritional Information

Yield: 4 cups
Serving Size: ½ cup

Amount per serving

Calories: 31.90	Potassium: 65.04 mg
8.26% from Fat,	Magnesium: 5.62 mg
13.40% from Protein	Zinc: .12 mg
78.30% from Carb	Copper: .01 mg
Protein: 1.09 g	Manganese: .01 mg
Total Fat: .30 g	Vitamin A: 62.47 IU
Saturated Fat: .19 g	Vitamin E: 17.76 mg
Monosaturated Fat: .09 g	Thiamin: .01 mg
Polyunsaturated: .01 g	Riboflavin: .05 mg
Cholesterol: 1.23 mg	Niacin: .08 mg
Carbohydrates: 6.33 g	Pantothenic Acid: .10 mg
Fiber: 0.00 g	Vitamin B6: .01 mg
Calcium: 39.69 mg	Folate: 1.53 ug
Phosphorous: 30.85 mg	Vitamin B12: .12 ug
Iron: .03 mg	Vitamin C: .31 mg
Sodium: 16.15 mg	Selenium: .75 ug
Sugar: 4.72 mg	

Cappuccino Cooler

2 cups coffee - chilled

2 cups vanilla ice cream

½ cup chocolate syrup

Ice

Whipped cream

Directions: Place ingredients (except ice and whipped cream) into blender jar and secure the lid. Press the **Milkshake** button. Place ice in cup(s) and pour blended mixture over ice. Top with whipped cream.

Nutritional Information

Yield: 4 cups
Serving Size: ½ cup

Amount per serving

Calories: 109.10	Potassium: 141.02 mg
33.10% from Fat	Magnesium: 16.92 mg
5.69% from Protein	Zinc: .35 mg
61.30% from Carb	Copper: .08 mg
Protein: 1.58 g	Manganese: .07 mg
Total Fat: 4.09 g	Vitamin A: 151.52 IU
Saturated Fat: 2.50 g	Vitamin E: 41.62 mg
Monosaturated Fat: 1.10 g	Thiamin: .02 mg
Polyunsaturated: .17 g	Riboflavin: .09 mg
Cholesterol: 15.78 mg	Niacin: .21 mg
Carbohydrates: 17.06 g	Pantothenic Acid: .21 mg
Fiber: .58 g	Vitamin B6: .02 mg
Calcium: 48.90 mg	Folate: 2.05 ug
Phosphorous: .54.82 mg	Vitamin B12: .14 ug
Iron: .33 mg	Vitamin C: .24 mg
Sodium: 38.53 mg	Selenium: .95 ug
Sugar: 13.98 mg	

Iced Latte

1 cup club soda

½ cup vanilla syrup

1 cup non-fat powdered milk

¼ cup coffee

1 cup ice

Directions: Place ingredients into blender jar and secure the lid. Press the **Milkshake** button.

Cocoa Cappuccino

2 cups vanilla ice cream

1 cup low-fat milk

2 Tbsp chocolate syrup

3 tsp instant coffee or 3 Tbsp sweetened cocoa

Directions: Place ingredients into blender jar and secure the lid. Press the **Milkshake** button.

Nutritional Information

Yield: 3 ½ cups
Serving Size: ½ cup

Amount per serving

Calories: 70.55	Potassium: 314.06 mg
1.69% from Fat,	Magnesium: 19.85 mg
35.30% from Protein	Zinc: .74 mg
63.00% from Carb	Copper: .01 mg
Protein: 6.21 g	Manganese: .01 mg
Total Fat: .13 g	Vitamin A: 3.77 IU
Saturated Fat: .09 g	Vitamin E: 1.03 mg
Monosaturated Fat: .03 g	Thiamin: .07 mg
Polyunsaturated: .01 g	Riboflavin: .27 mg
Cholesterol: 3.43 mg	Niacin: .20 mg
Carbohydrates: 11.08 g	Pantothenic Acid: .61 mg
Fiber: 0.00 g	Vitamin B6: .06 mg
Calcium: 217.79 mg	Folate: 8.57 ug
Phosphorous: 166.03 mg	Vitamin B12: .69 ug
Iron: .07 mg	Vitamin C: 1.17 mg
Sodium: 99.35 mg	Selenium: 4.69 ug
Sugar: 11.05 mg	

Nutritional Information

Yield: 3 cups
Serving Size: ½ cup

Amount per serving

Calories: 181.20	Potassium: 474.18 mg
26.80% from Fat,	Magnesium: 32.46 mg
19.70% from Protein	Zinc: 1.18 mg
53.60% from Carb	Copper: .04 mg
Protein: 9.03 g	Manganese: .03 mg
Total Fat: 5.47 g	Vitamin A: 206.30IU
Saturated Fat: .3.37 g	Vitamin E: 56.59 mg
Monosaturated Fat: 1.47 g	Thiamin: .10 mg
Polyunsaturated: .22 g	Riboflavin: .43 mg
Cholesterol: 25.05mg	Niacin: .34 mg
Carbohydrates: 24.59 g	Pantothenic Acid: .99 mg
Fiber: .45 g	Vitamin B6: 1.0 mg
Calcium: 313.65 mg	Folate: 812.48 ug
Phosphorous: 250.25 mg	Vitamin B12: .99 ug
Iron: .21 mg	Vitamin C: 1.66 mg
Sodium: 148.46 mg	Selenium: 6.44 ug
Sugar: 22.67 mg	

Mocha Cocoa Mint Cappuccino

2 cups vanilla ice cream

1 cup strong coffee - brewed and chilled

½ cup low-fat milk

¼ tsp mint extract

Directions: Place ingredients into blender jar and secure the lid. Press the **Milkshake** button.

Spicy Creamy Café

¾ cup low-fat milk

2 ½ Tbsp sweet white chocolate - melted

¼ cup French vanilla nondairy creamer

1 ½ tsp instant coffee*

Optional, 2 tsp sugar

½ tsp cinnamon

¼ tsp nutmeg

1½-2 cups ice

Directions: Place ingredients into blender jar and secure the lid. Press the **Milkshake** button.

*May substitute 3 Tbsp sweetened cocoa powder

Nutritional Information

Yield: 3 cups
Serving Size: ½ cup

Amount per serving

Calories: 133.15	Potassium: 301.97 mg
35.30% from Fat,	Magnesium: 20.08 mg
15.70% from Protein	Zinc: .74 mg
49.00% from Carb	Copper: .02 mg
Protein: 5.33 g	Manganese: .02 mg
Total Fat: 5.34 g	Vitamin A: 205.00 IU
Saturated Fat: .3.30 g	Vitamin E: 56.09 mg
Monosaturated Fat: 1.44 g	Thiamin: .06 mg
Polyunsaturated: .22 g	Riboflavin: .27 mg
Cholesterol: 23.05 mg	Niacin: .24 mg
Carbohydrates: 16.65 g	Pantothenic Acid: .64 mg
Fiber: .34 g	Vitamin B6: .06 mg
Calcium: 187.77 mg	Folate: 7.42 ug
Phosphorous: 147.44 mg	Vitamin B12: .65 ug
Iron: .10 mg	Vitamin C: 1.97 mg
Sodium: 92.17 mg	Selenium: 3.63 ug
Sugar: 15.35 mg	

Nutritional Information

Yield: 2 cups
Serving Size: ½ cup

Amount per serving

Calories: 161.71	Potassium: 459.73 mg
27.20% from Fat	Magnesium: 31.99 mg
23.10% from Protein	Zinc: 1.07 mg
49.70% from Carb	Copper: .05 mg
Protein: 9.40 g	Manganese: .12 mg
Total Fat: 4.91 g	Vitamin A: 105.36 IU
Saturated Fat: .2.77 g	Vitamin E: 28.05 mg
Monosaturated Fat: 1.46 g	Thiamin: .11 mg
Polyunsaturated: .35 g	Riboflavin: .39 mg
Cholesterol: 14.40 mg	Niacin: .41 mg
Carbohydrates: 20.22 g	Pantothenic Acid: .93 mg
Fiber: .18 g	Vitamin B6: .11 mg
Calcium: 309.32 mg	Folate: 12.70 ug
Phosphorous: 246.72 mg	Vitamin B12: .94 ug
Iron: .42 mg	Vitamin C: 1.979 mg
Sodium: 187.09 mg	Selenium: 6.28 ug
Sugar: 11.76 mg	

Cappuccino

2 Tbsp sweet white chocolate

1 tsp instant coffee

1 tsp sugar or other sweetener (to taste)

¾ cup low-fat milk, hot

1 tsp cappuccino syrup

Directions: Place ingredients into blender jar and secure the lid. Press the **Speed Up** button until blender reaches speed 7, then press any lower row button to stop after 10 seconds or until smooth.

Nutritional Information

Yield: 1 cup
Serving Size: ¼ cup

Amount per serving

Calories: 120.62	Potassium: 429.03 mg
10.20% from Fat,	Magnesium: 28.67 mg
28.90% from Protein	Zinc: .99 mg
60.90% from Carb	Copper: .03 mg
Protein: 8.71 g	Manganese: .05 mg
Total Fat: 1.37 g	Vitamin A: 5.66 IU
Saturated Fat: .66 g	Vitamin E: 1.35 mg
Monosaturated Fat: .43 g	Thiamin: .10 mg
Polyunsaturated: .16 g	Riboflavin: .36 mg
Cholesterol: 4.50 mg	Niacin: .34 mg
Carbohydrates: 18.36 g	Pantothenic Acid: .86 mg
Fiber: 0.00 g	Vitamin B6: .09 mg
Calcium: 288.56 mg	Folate: 11.90 ug
Phosphorous: 229.18 mg	Vitamin B12: .91 ug
Iron: .23 mg	Vitamin C: 1.57 mg
Sodium: 162.24 mg	Selenium: 6.19 ug
Sugar: 13.16 mg	

Colada Café

½ cup pineapple chunks - with juice

⅓ cup cream of coconut

⅓ cup strong brewed coffee at room temperature

2 cups ice

Directions: Place ingredients into blender jar and secure the lid. Press the **Milkshake** button.

Nutritional Information

Yield: 2 cups
Serving Size: ½ cup

Amount per serving

Calories: 76.23	Potassium: 117.68 mg
76.40% from Fat,	Magnesium: 12.32 mg
4.28% from Protein	Zinc: .23 mg
19.30% from Carb	Copper: .11 mg
Protein: .88 g	Manganese: .61 mg
Total Fat: 6.96 g	Vitamin A: 11.69 IU
Saturated Fat: 6.15 g	Vitamin E: 0.00 mg
Monosaturated Fat: .30 g	Thiamin: .03 mg
Polyunsaturated: .09 g	Riboflavin: .01 mg
Cholesterol: 0.00 mg	Niacin: .31 mg
Carbohydrates: 3.96 g	Pantothenic Acid: .08mg
Fiber: 069 g	Vitamin B6: .03 mg
Calcium: 7.21 mg	Folate: 6.14 ug
Phosphorous: 25.83 mg	Vitamin B12: 0.00 ug
Iron: .59 mg	Vitamin C: 2.93 mg
Sodium: 1.31 mg	Selenium: 6.14 ug
Sugar: 2.31 mg	

MILKSHAKES

To make great shakes, use the **Milkshake** button. If the ingredients have not blended on first Milkshake cycle, press the **Milkshake** button again, and allow the blender to run another cycle. If in the middle of the second cycle, the milkshake looks completed, you may press any lower row button to stop. For a thicker milkshake, optionally add ½ cup ice cream or ½ cup ice more than recipe calls for. For a thinner milkshake, add more milk (approximately ¼ cup). You may also run the Milkshake cycle more than once to create a thinner consistency.

1 cup vanilla nonfat frozen yogurt

½ cup milk

1 medium peach - peeled

1 Tbsp sugar

Directions: Place ingredients in blender jar in order as listed, and secure the lid. Press the **Milkshake** button.

SUBSTITUTIONS

When a recipe asks for milk, you may use any kind of desired milk, i.e. whole, skim, soy, etc. If the recipe asks for vanilla coffee creamer, you can substitute with any type of milk plus 2 tsps of vanilla extract.

When recipe asks for fruit, you may use either frozen or fresh. Your milkshake will have a sweeter taste if you use fresh fruit. For a chunky fruit milkshake, use frozen fruit that has not been thawed.

When recipe asks for ice cream, you may substitute with nonfat frozen yogurt of the same flavor.

When the recipe calls for sugar you may substitute any desired sweetener. If you use honey as sweetener, use 1/3 of the amount.

TIPS

• When using ice cream in a recipe, make sure to pack the ice cream around the bottom of jar.

• For the best consistency, when placing ingredients into the jar, always add ice cream first and milk second.

• If the ice cream you are using is soft, reduce the amount of milk by ¼ cup. For example, if the recipe asks for ¾ cup milk, and the ice cream is soft, use only ½ cup milk.

• Whenever possible, do not use ice that has been left out. Ice that has been melting will make milkshakes runny.

Nutritional Information

Yields: 1 ½ cups
Serving Size: ½ cup

Amount per serving

Calories: 118.33	Potassium: 274.51 mg
24.50% from Fat,	Magnesium: 17.99 mg
13.20% from Protein	Zinc: .48 mg
62.30% from Carb	Copper: .06 mg
Protein: 4.01 g	Manganese: .04 mg
Total Fat: 3.30 g	Vitamin A: 355.60 IU
Saturated Fat: 1.95 g	Vitamin E: 52.85 mg
Monosaturated Fat: .94 g	Thiamin: .05 mg
Polyunsaturated: .16 g	Riboflavin: .20 mg
Cholesterol: 2.60 mg	Niacin: .60 mg
Carbohydrates: 18.87 g	Pantothenic Acid: .54 mg
Fiber: .79 g	Vitamin B6: .07 mg
Calcium: 130.00 mg	Folate: 7.43 ug
Phosphorous: 117.90 mg	Vitamin B12: .32 ug
Iron: .30 mg	Vitamin C: 4.33 mg
Sodium: 65.54 mg	Selenium: 2.66 ug
Sugar: 15.91 mg	

Raspberry Shake

1 ½ cups vanilla ice cream
½ cup low-fat milk
½ cup raspberries
1 Tbsp sugar

Directions: Place ingredients in blender jar in order listed, and secure the lid. Press the **Milkshake** button.

Sweet Blueberry Shake

½ cup vanilla ice cream
¾ cup low-fat milk
¾ cup blueberries
1 Tbsp sugar
½ cup ice

Directions: Place ingredients in blender jar in order listed, and secure the lid. Press the **Milkshake** button.

Nutritional Information

Yields: 2 cups
Serving Size: ½ cup

Amount per serving

Calories: 130.92	Potassium: 185.65 mg
42.40% from Fat,	Magnesium: 15.84 mg
9.68% from Protein	Zinc: .57 mg
47.90% from Carb	Copper: .03 mg
Protein: 3.28 g	Manganese: .11 mg
Total Fat: 6.38 g	Vitamin A: 294.58 IU
Saturated Fat: 3.88 g	Vitamin E: 81.18 mg
Monosaturated Fat: 1.71 g	Thiamin: .04 mg
Polyunsaturated: .31 g	Riboflavin: .19 mg
Cholesterol: 24.91 mg	Niacin: .19 mg
Carbohydrates: 16.23 g	Pantothenic Acid: .48 mg
Fiber: 1.38 g	Vitamin B6: .05 mg
Calcium: 116.39 mg	Folate: 7.76 ug
Phosphorous: 95.09 mg	Vitamin B12: .34 ug
Iron: .17 mg	Vitamin C: 4.72 mg
Sodium: 61.04 mg	Selenium: 1.77 ug
Sugar: 12.10 mg	

Nutritional Information

Yields: 2 cups
Serving Size: ½ cup

Amount per serving

Calories: 85.88	Potassium: 139.72 mg
26.20% from Fat,	Magnesium: 11.52 mg
11.80% from Protein	Zinc: .37 mg
62.00% from Carb	Copper: .02 mg
Protein: 2.64 g	Manganese: .09 mg
Total Fat: 2.60 g	Vitamin A: 184.01 IU
Saturated Fat: 1.56 g	Vitamin E: 48.94 mg
Monosaturated Fat: .70 g	Thiamin: .04 mg
Polyunsaturated: .14 g	Riboflavin: .14 mg
Cholesterol: 9.74 mg	Niacin: .18 mg
Carbohydrates: 13.87 g	Pantothenic Acid: .31 mg
Fiber: .78 g	Vitamin B6: .05 mg
Calcium: 90.12 mg	Folate: 5.30 ug
Phosphorous: 73.30 mg	Vitamin B12: .27 ug
Iron: .11 mg	Vitamin C: 3.30 mg
Sodium: 41.37 mg	Selenium: 1.52 ug
Sugar: 9.66 mg	

Strawberry Shake

½ cup vanilla ice cream

¾ cup low-fat milk

1 cup strawberries

1 Tbsp sugar

¼ cup ice cubes

Directions: Place ingredients in blender jar in order listed, and secure the lid. Press the **Milkshake** button.

Nutritional Information

Yields: 2 cups
Serving Size: ½ cup

Amount per serving

Calories: 82.54	Potassium: 176.92 mg
27.60% from Fat,	Magnesium: 14.83 mg
12.60% from Protein	Zinc: .38 mg
59.90% from Carb	Copper: .03 mg
Protein: 2.70 g	Manganese: .15 mg
Total Fat: 2.63 g	Vitamin A: 173.89 IU
Saturated Fat: 1.56 g	Vitamin E: 48.94 mg
Monosaturated Fat: .70 g	Thiamin: .04 mg
Polyunsaturated: .16 g	Riboflavin: .14 mg
Cholesterol: 9.74 mg	Niacin: .21 mg
Carbohydrates: 12.85 g	Pantothenic Acid: .32 mg
Fiber: .89 g	Vitamin B6: .05 mg
Calcium: 94.57 mg	Folate: 12.78 ug
Phosphorous: 79.15 mg	Vitamin B12: .27 ug
Iron: .20 mg	Vitamin C: 23.01 mg
Sodium: 41.48 mg	Selenium: 1.65 ug
Sugar: 8.72 mg	

Strawberry Banana Shake

1 cup vanilla ice cream

½ cup low-fat milk

½ cup strawberries

½ banana

1 Tbsp sugar

Directions: Place ingredients in jar in order listed, and secure the lid. Press the **Milkshake** button.

Nutritional Information

Yields: 2 cups
Serving Size: ½ cup

Amount per serving

Calories: 1221.83	Potassium: 223.00 mg
31.30% from Fat	Magnesium: 17.48 mg
8.79% from Protein	Zinc: .44 mg
59.90% from Carb	Copper: .04 mg
Protein: 2.80 g	Manganese: .13 mg
Total Fat: 4.42 g	Vitamin A: 228.10 IU
Saturated Fat: 2.68 g	Vitamin E: 60.37 mg
Monosaturated Fat: 1.18 g	Thiamin: .04 mg
Polyunsaturated: .22 g	Riboflavin: .16 mg
Cholesterol: 17.01 mg	Niacin: .27 mg
Carbohydrates: 19.05 g	Pantothenic Acid: .41 mg
Fiber: 1.12 g	Vitamin B6: .11 mg
Calcium: 93.59 mg	Folate: 11.95 ug
Phosphorous: 80.49 mg	Vitamin B12: .27 ug
Iron: .18 mg	Vitamin C: 13.39 mg
Sodium: 46.91 mg	Selenium: 1.70 ug
Sugar: 13.94 mg	

Orange Shake

⅓ cup orange soda

½ cup unsweetened pineapple juice

1 ½ cup orange sherbet

⅓ cup ice cubes

Directions: Place ingredients in jar in order listed, and secure the lid. Press the **Milkshake** button.

Pina Colada Shake

1 ½ cups vanilla ice cream

½ cup low-fat milk

½ cup pineapple chunks - do not drain

½ tsp coconut extract*

Directions: Place ingredients in jar in order listed, and secure the lid. Press the **Milkshake** button.

*May substitute 1 Tbsp cream of coconut

Nutritional Information

Yields: 2 cups
Serving Size: ½ cup

Amount per serving

Calories: 158.42	Potassium: 126.82 mg
6.25% from Fat	Magnesium: 8.50 mg
1.74% from Protein	Zinc: .31 mg
92.00% from Carb	Copper: .05 mg
Protein: .71 g	Manganese: .32 mg
Total Fat: 1.13 g	Vitamin A: 359.87 IU
Saturated Fat: .65 g	Vitamin E: 4.99 mg
Monosaturated Fat: .30 g	Thiamin: .03 mg
Polyunsaturated: .05 g	Riboflavin: .17 mg
Cholesterol: 0.00 mg	Niacin: 1.46 mg
Carbohydrates: 37.58 g	Pantothenic Acid: .15 mg
Fiber: 1.94 g	Vitamin B6: .18 mg
Calcium: 96.78 mg	Folate: 11.07 ug
Phosphorous: 52.87 mg	Vitamin B12: .07 ug
Iron: .17 mg	Vitamin C: 46.56 mg
Sodium: 27.18 mg	Selenium: .75 ug
Sugar: 32.77 mg	

Nutritional Information

Yields: 2 cups
Serving Size: ½ cup

Amount per serving

Calories: 134.24	Potassium: 202.27 mg
41.70% from Fat	Magnesium: 18.12 mg
9.34% from Protein	Zinc: .55 mg
49.00% from Carb	Copper: .05 mg
Protein: 3.24 g	Manganese: .36 mg
Total Fat: 6.44 g	Vitamin A: 301.20 IU
Saturated Fat: 4.00 g	Vitamin E: 81.18 mg
Monosaturated Fat: 1.171 g	Thiamin: .06 mg
Polyunsaturated: .27 g	Riboflavin: .20 mg
Cholesterol: 24.91 mg	Niacin: .19 mg
Carbohydrates: 17.01 g	Pantothenic Acid: .46 mg
Fiber: .64 g	Vitamin B6: .06 mg
Calcium: 117.17 mg	Folate: 6.18 ug
Phosphorous: 92.04 mg	Vitamin B12: .34 ug
Iron: .19 mg	Vitamin C: 3.07 mg
Sodium: 61.58 mg	Selenium: 1.90 ug
Sugar: 13.77 mg	

Chocolate Shake

2 cups vanilla ice cream
½ cup low-fat milk
¼ cup chocolate syrup

Directions: Place ingredients in jar in order as listed and secure the lid.
Press the **Milkshake** button.

Mocha Mint Frosty

1 cup vanilla nonfat frozen yogurt
½ cup milk
¼ cup decaffeinated coffee - chilled
2 Tbsp chocolate syrup
¼ tsp mint extract

Directions: Place ingredients in blender jar in order as listed, and secure the lid. Press the **Milkshake** button.

Nutritional Information

Yields: 2 cups
Serving Size: ½ cup

Amount per serving

Calories: 194.78	Potassium: 226.88 mg
37.90% from Fat	Magnesium: 23.31 mg
8.00% from Protein	Zinc: .73 mg
54.10% from Carb	Copper: .09 mg
Protein: 3.49 g	Manganese: .06 mg
Total Fat: 8.40 g	Vitamin A: 365.34 IU
Saturated Fat: 5.16 g	Vitamin E: 101.99 mg
Monosaturated Fat: 2.27 g	Thiamin: .04 mg
Polyunsaturated: .34 g	Riboflavin: .24 mg
Cholesterol: 32.80 mg	Niacin: .16 mg
Carbohydrates: 26.98 g	Pantothenic Acid: .53 mg
Fiber: .84 g	Vitamin B6: .05 mg
Calcium: 137.30 mg	Folate: 5.69 ug
Phosphorous: 126.03 mg	Vitamin B12: .41 ug
Iron: .35 mg	Vitamin C: .83 mg
Sodium: 84.47 mg	Selenium: 2.30 ug
Sugar: 21.60 mg	

Nutritional Information

Yields: 2 cups
Serving Size: ½ cup

Amount per serving

Calories: 91.66	Potassium: 152.73 mg
24.00% from Fat	Magnesium: 14.90 mg
12.20% from Protein	Zinc: .34 mg
63.80% from Carb	Copper: .05 mg
Protein: 2.80 g	Manganese: .03 mg
Total Fat: 2.45 g	Vitamin A: 140.22 IU
Saturated Fat: 1.49 g	Vitamin E: 39.64 mg
Monosaturated Fat: .69 g	Thiamin: .03 mg
Polyunsaturated: .09 g	Riboflavin: .15 mg
Cholesterol: 1.95 mg	Niacin: .20 mg
Carbohydrates: 14.66 g	Pantothenic Acid: .35 mg
Fiber: .17 g	Vitamin B6: .04 mg
Calcium: 96.57 mg	Folate: 4.17 ug
Phosphorous: 89.47 mg	Vitamin B12: .24 ug
Iron: .27 mg	Vitamin C: .68 mg
Sodium: 54.08 mg	Selenium: 2.11 ug
Sugar: 11.83mg	

Chocolate Mint Shake

1 ½ cup vanilla nonfat frozen yogurt

½ cup low-fat milk

¼ cup chocolate syrup

⅛ tsp peppermint extract*

Directions: Place ingredients in blender jar in order as listed, and secure the lid. Press the **Milkshake** button.

*May substitute mint extract

Nutritional Information

Yields: 2 cups
Serving Size: ½ cup

Amount per serving

Calories: 138.60	Potassium: 198.13 mg
22.90% from Fat	Magnesium: 20.84 mg
10.50% from Protein	Zinc: .46 mg
66.60% from Carb	Copper: .09 mg
Protein: 3.64 g	Manganese: .06 mg
Total Fat: 3.53 g	Vitamin A: 177.74 IU
Saturated Fat: 2.14 g	Vitamin E: 50.08 mg
Monosaturated Fat: 1.00 g	Thiamin: .03 mg
Polyunsaturated: .13 g	Riboflavin: .19 mg
Cholesterol: 2.31 mg	Niacin: .23 mg
Carbohydrates: 23.12 g	Pantothenic Acid: .46 mg
Fiber: .33 g	Vitamin B6: .06 mg
Calcium: 122.72 mg	Folate: 5.36 ug
Phosphorous: 120.36 mg	Vitamin B12: .29 ug
Iron: .45 mg	Vitamin C: .83 mg
Sodium: 74.06 mg	Selenium: 2.79 ug
Sugar: 19.33 mg	

Cookie Delight

2 cups vanilla nonfat frozen yogurt

1 cup low-fat milk

5 chocolate sandwich cookies

Directions: Place ingredients in blender jar in order as listed, and secure the lid. Press the **Milkshake** button.

Optional: To make a Mint Cookie Delight, add 1/8 tsp mint extract

Nutritional Information

Yields: 2 ½ cups
Serving Size: ½ cup

Amount per serving

Calories: 164.70	Potassium: 227.60 mg
31.70% from Fat	Magnesium: 20.44 mg
11.30% from Protein	Zinc: .54 mg
57.00% from Carb	Copper: .06 mg
Protein: 4.71 g	Manganese: .06 mg
Total Fat: 5.86 g	Vitamin A: 222.19 IU
Saturated Fat: 2.69 g	Vitamin E: 63.42 mg
Monosaturated Fat: 1.94 g	Thiamin: .05 mg
Polyunsaturated: .87 g	Riboflavin: .24 mg
Cholesterol: 3.12 mg	Niacin: .42 mg
Carbohydrates: 23.69 g	Pantothenic Acid: .57 mg
Fiber: .32 g	Vitamin B6: .07 mg
Calcium: 154.83 mg	Folate: 11.51 ug
Phosphorous: 138.72 mg	Vitamin B12: .38 ug
Iron: .59 mg	Vitamin C: 1.05 mg
Sodium: 139.05 mg	Selenium: 3.63 ug
Sugar: 17.46 mg	

S'More Shake

1 ½ cup vanilla ice cream*

¾ cup milk

3 Tbsp marshmallow cream

1 ½ Tbsp peanut butter

1 ½ Tbsp chocolate syrup

1 ½ graham cracker - break into pieces

Directions: Place ingredients in blender jar in order as listed, and secure the lid. Make sure cream is dabbed onto ice cream and does not stick to side of jar. Press the **Milkshake** button.

For a thicker shake, use 2-2½ cups vanilla ice cream

Nutritional Information

Yields: 2 cups
Serving Size: ½ cup

Amount per serving

Calories: 218.37	Potassium: 263.47 mg
43.70% from Fat,	Magnesium: 32.39 mg
10.40% from Protein	Zinc: .94 mg
45.90% from Carb	Copper: .08 mg
Protein: 5.87 g	Manganese: .14 mg
Total Fat: 10.91 g	Vitamin A: 340.04 IU
Saturated Fat: 5.10 g	Vitamin E: 95.73 mg
Monosaturated Fat: 3.64 g	Thiamin: .07 mg
Polyunsaturated: 1.18 g	Riboflavin: .25 mg
Cholesterol: 27.66 mg	Niacin: 1.24 mg
Carbohydrates: 25.75 g	Pantothenic Acid: .55 mg
Fiber: 1.16 g	Vitamin B6: .09 mg
Calcium: 146.30 mg	Folate: 14.65 ug
Phosphorous: 150.73 mg	Vitamin B12: .42 ug
Iron: .60 mg	Vitamin C: .89 mg
Sodium: 127.38 mg	Selenium: 2.71 ug
Sugar: 16.01 mg	

Chocolate Peanut Butter Shake

1 cup vanilla frozen yogurt

¾ cup milk

¼ cup peanut butter

½ cup chocolate syrup

Directions: Place ingredients in blender jar in order as listed, and secure the lid. Press the **Milkshake** button

Nutritional Information

Yields: 2 cups
Serving Size: ½ cup

Amount per serving

Calories: 211.60	Potassium: 308.19 mg
44.20% from Fat	Magnesium: 46.40 mg
13.50% from Protein	Zinc: .90 mg
42.20% from Carb	Copper: .17 mg
Protein: 7.40 g	Manganese: .35 mg
Total Fat: 10.75 g	Vitamin A: 170.08 IU
Saturated Fat: 3.18 g	Vitamin E: 49.02 mg
Monosaturated Fat: 4.56 g	Thiamin: .06 mg
Polyunsaturated: 2.38 g	Riboflavin: .19 mg
Cholesterol: 2.57 mg	Niacin: 2.40 mg
Carbohydrates: 23.09 g	Pantothenic Acid: .56 mg
Fiber: 1.40 g	Vitamin B6: .13 mg
Calcium: 125.39 mg	Folate: 20.02 ug
Phosphorous: 165.31 mg	Vitamin B12: .30 ug
Iron: .71 mg	Vitamin C: .87 mg
Sodium: 70.05 mg	Selenium: 3.79 ug
Sugar: 16.27 mg	

Chocolate Strawberry Shake

2 cups chocolate ice cream

²/₃ cup milk

1 cup strawberries - remove stems

Directions: Place ingredients in blender jar in order listed, and secure the lid. Press the **Milkshake** button.

Vanilla Shake

1 ½ cup vanilla ice cream

½ cup low-fat milk

¾ tsp vanilla

Directions: Place ingredients in jar in order listed, and secure the lid. Press the **Milkshake** button.

Nutritional Information

Yields: 2 ½ cups
Serving Size: ½ cup

Amount per serving

Calories: 139.52	Potassium: 237.02 mg
38.60% from Fat	Magnesium: 24.51 mg
9.54% from Protein	Zinc: .50 mg
51.90% from Carb	Copper: .09 mg
Protein: 3.50 g	Manganese: .19 mg
Total Fat: 6.28 g	Vitamin A: 289.88 IU
Saturated Fat: 13.83 g	Vitamin E: 81.26 mg
Monosaturated Fat: 1.82 g	Thiamin: .04 mg
Polyunsaturated: .28 g	Riboflavin: .17 mg
Cholesterol: 19.26 mg	Niacin: .27 mg
Carbohydrates: 19.03 g	Pantothenic Acid: .45 mg
Fiber: 1.24 g	Vitamin B6: .06 mg
Calcium: 108.99 mg	Folate: 17.71 ug
Phosphorous: 100.20 mg	Vitamin B12: .29 ug
Iron: .64 mg	Vitamin C: 18.64 mg
Sodium: 59.46 mg	Selenium: 2.26 ug
Sugar: 14.81 mg	

Nutritional Information

Yields: 1 cup
Serving Size: ½ cup

Amount per serving

Calories: 250.53	Potassium: 327.28 mg
44.50% from Fat,	Magnesium: 25.10 mg
9.75% from Protein	Zinc: 1.02 mg
45.70% from Carb	Copper: .03 mg
Protein: 6.18 g	Manganese: .101 mg
Total Fat: 12.56 g	Vitamin A: 579.02 IU
Saturated Fat: 7.76 g	Vitamin E: 162.36 mg
Monosaturated Fat: 3.40 g	Thiamin: .07 mg
Polyunsaturated: .51 g	Riboflavin: .38 mg
Cholesterol: 49.81 mg	Niacin: .19 mg
Carbohydrates: 29.00 g	Pantothenic Acid: .486 mg
Fiber: .75 g	Vitamin B6: .08 mg
Calcium: 225.27 mg	Folate: 9.07 ug
Phosphorous: 181.37 mg	Vitamin B12: .68 ug
Iron: .14 mg	Vitamin C: 1.38 mg
Sodium: 121.92 mg	Selenium: 3.47 ug
Sugar: 23.04 mg	

Candy Bar Shake

2 ½ cups vanilla ice cream

¾ cup milk

2 mini candy bars

Directions: Break candy bars in half, place ingredients in jar in order listed, and secure the lid. Press the **Milkshake** button.

*May use any candy bar

Eggnog Milkshake

2 cups vanilla frozen yogurt

¾ cup eggnog

⅛ tsp nutmeg

Directions: Place ingredients in jar in order listed, and secure the lid. Press the **Milkshake** button.

Nutritional Information

Yields: 2 ½ cups
Serving Size: ½ cup

Amount per serving

Calories: 208.65	Potassium: 242.95 mg
44.60% from Fat	Magnesium: 24.22 mg
9.56% from Protein	Zinc: .77 mg
45.80% from Carb	Copper: .06 mg
Protein: 5.13 g	Manganese: .11 mg
Total Fat: 10.65 g	Vitamin A: 377.69 IU
Saturated Fat: 6.68 g	Vitamin E: 105.74 mg
Monosaturated Fat: 2.67 g	Thiamin: .06 mg
Polyunsaturated: .52 g	Riboflavin: .26 mg
Cholesterol: 33.05 mg	Niacin: .69 mg
Carbohydrates: 24.60 g	Pantothenic Acid: .61 mg
Fiber: .78 g	Vitamin B6: .06 mg
Calcium: 150.72 mg	Folate: 10.97 ug
Phosphorous: 135.75 mg	Vitamin B12: .45 ug
Iron: .13 mg	Vitamin C: .87 mg
Sodium: 97.04 mg	Selenium: 2.29 ug
Sugar: 20.23 mg	

Nutritional Information

Yields: 2 ½ cups
Serving Size: ½ cup

Amount per serving

Calories: 167.12	Potassium: 177.30 mg
48.20% from Fat,	Magnesium: 15.38 mg
8.08% from Protein	Zinc: .57 mg
43.70% from Carb	Copper: .02 mg
Protein: 3.46 g	Manganese: .01 mg
Total Fat: 9.19 g	Vitamin A: 303.25 IU
Saturated Fat: 5.61 g	Vitamin E: 83.73 mg
Monosaturated Fat: 2.56 g	Thiamin: .04 mg
Polyunsaturated: .39 g	Riboflavin: .21 mg
Cholesterol: 47.74 mg	Niacin: .11 mg
Carbohydrates: 18.73 g	Pantothenic Acid: .49 mg
Fiber: .41 g	Vitamin B6: .05 mg
Calcium: 123.11 mg	Folate: 3.30 ug
Phosphorous: 101.92 mg	Vitamin B12: .40 ug
Iron: .13 mg	Vitamin C: .92 mg
Sodium: 66.50 mg	Selenium: 2.63 ug
Sugar: 15.40 mg	

Healthy Breakfast Shake

1 ¼ cups milk

½ cup vanilla yogurt

½ cup peanut butter

3 Tbsp wheat germ

1 banana - peeled

2 cups ice

Directions: Place ingredients in blender jar in order as listed, and secure the lid. Press the **Milkshake** button.

Nutritional Information

Yields: 4 cups
Serving Size: ½ cup

Amount per serving

Calories: 91.82	Potassium: 216.39 mg
34.50% from Fat	Magnesium: 23.33 mg
16.20% from Protein	Zinc: .50 mg
49.40% from Carb	Copper: .05 mg
Protein: 3.93 g	Manganese: .17 mg
Total Fat: 3.72 g	Vitamin A: 96.61 IU
Saturated Fat: 1.00 g	Vitamin E: 25.28 mg
Monosaturated Fat: 1.61 g	Thiamin: .04 mg
Polyunsaturated: .89 g	Riboflavin: .13 mg
Cholesterol: 2.30 mg	Niacin: 1.01 mg
Carbohydrates: 12.00 g	Pantothenic Acid: .35 mg
Fiber: .89 g	Vitamin B6: .12 mg
Calcium: 84.34 mg	Folate: 13.36 ug
Phosphorous: 86.74 mg	Vitamin B12: .25 ug
Iron: .21 mg	Vitamin C: 2.23 mg
Sodium: 33.72 mg	Selenium: 2.37 ug
Sugar: 7.05 mg	

Banana Split Shake

8 oz. sweetened condensed milk

2 Tbsp chocolate syrup

2 bananas - peeled

3 cups ice

Directions: Place ingredients in blender jar in order as listed, and secure the lid. Press the **Milkshake** button.

Nutritional Information

Yields: 4 cups
Serving Size: ½ cup

Amount per serving

Calories: 133.33	Potassium: 246.62 mg
17.00% from Fat	Magnesium: 19.58 mg
7.83% from Protein	Zinc: .35 mg
75.10% from Carb	Copper: .05 mg
Protein: 2.72 g	Manganese: .12 mg
Total Fat: 2.63 g	Vitamin A: 99.73 IU
Saturated Fat: 1.61 g	Vitamin E: 20.70 mg
Monosaturated Fat: .71 g	Thiamin: .04 mg
Polyunsaturated: .12 g	Riboflavin: .15 mg
Cholesterol: 9.64 mg	Niacin: .32 mg
Carbohydrates: 26	Pantothenic Acid: .34 mg
Fiber: 1.06 g	Vitamin B6: .15 mg
Calcium: 82.84 mg	Folate: 10.68 ug
Phosphorous: 84.11 mg	Vitamin B12: .12 ug
Iron: .22 mg	Vitamin C: 4.01 mg
Sodium: 38.69 mg	Selenium: 4.63 ug
Sugar: 21.60 mg	

KIDS' SHAKES

Mud Shake

1 ½ cup chocolate ice cream

¼ cup lowfat milk

Directions: Place ingredients in jar in order listed above and secure the lid. Press the **Milkshake** button.

½ cup crushed chocolate sandwich cookies

Gummy Worms

Whipped Topping

Directions: Place 1 Tbsp crushed cookies in bottom of glass. Add drink and a layer of whipped topping. Cover with remaining cookie crumbs and insert gummy worms.

Nutritional Information

Yields: 1 ½ cups
Serving Size: ½ cup

Amount per serving

Calories: 248.11	Potassium: 200.54 mg
40.10% from Fat	Magnesium: 29.57 mg
5.93% from Protein	Zinc: .59 mg
54.00% from Carb	Copper: .17 mg
Protein: 3.82 g	Manganese: .22 mg
Total Fat: 11.46 g	Vitamin A: 237.70 IU
Saturated Fat: 4.51 g	Vitamin E: 66.80 mg
Monosaturated Fat: 4.07 g	Thiamin: .05 mg
Polyunsaturated: .2.26g	Riboflavin: .18 mg
Cholesterol: 17.44 mg	Niacin: .72 mg
Carbohydrates: 34.74 g	Pantothenic Acid: .38 mg
Fiber: 1.50 g	Vitamin B6: .04 mg
Calcium: 83.16 mg	Folate: 23.30 ug
Phosphorous: 97.81 mg	Vitamin B12: .22 ug
Iron: 1.57 mg	Vitamin C: .53 mg
Sodium: 217.77 mg	Selenium: 3.04 ug
Sugar: 22.87 mg	

Fruity Gumball Shake

1 cup vanilla ice cream

¼ cup strawberries

¼ cup pineapple chunks - with juice

½ banana - peeled

Directions: Place ingredients in blender jar in order listed above and secure the lid. Press the **Milkshake** button.

Gumballs

Whipped Topping

Directions: Pour drink into cup, and add whipped topping. Place gumballs on top.

Nutritional Information

Yields: 2 cups
Serving Size: ½ cup

Amount per serving

Calories: 123.38	Magnesium: 13.98 mg
40.60% from Fat,	Zinc: .28 mg
6.61% from Protein	Copper: .05 mg
52.80% from Carb	Manganese: .26 mg
Protein: 2.09 g	Vitamin A: 272.39 IU
Total Fat: 5.70 g	Vitamin E: 68.37 mg
Saturated Fat: 3.24 g	Thiamin: .04 mg
Monosaturated Fat: 1.51 g	Riboflavin: .10 mg
Polyunsaturated: .23 g	Niacin: .25 mg
Cholesterol: 39.13 mg	Pantothenic Acid: .31 mg
Carbohydrates: 16.68 g	Vitamin B6: .11 mg
Fiber: 1.10 g	Folate: 10.69 ug
Calcium: 60.99 mg	Vitamin B12: .22 ug
.24 mg	Vitamin C: 8.74 mg
Sodium: 26.67 mg	Selenium: 1.58 ug
Sugar: 13.83 mg	
Potassium: 174.31 mg	

Pink Drink

1 ½ cups strawberry ice cream

¼ cup strawberries - remove stems

¼ cup low-fat milk

Directions: With spatula or spoon, pack ice cream around the blade. Add remaining ingredients and secure the lid. Press the **Milkshake** button. Pour into cup and add sprinkles of desired color.

StrawBearyShake

1 ¼ cup vanilla ice cream

¼ cup strawberries - remove stems

¼ cup low-fat milk

Directions: With spatula or spoon, pack ice cream around the blade. Add remaining ingredients and secure the lid. Press the Milkshake button.

Whipped Topping

Gummy Bears

Pour drink into cup and add whipped topping. Place gummy bears on top.

Nutritional Information

Yields: 2 cups
Serving Size: ½ cup

Amount per serving

Calories: 105.46	Potassium: 135.27
36.00% from Fat	Magnesium: 10.63
8.24% from Protein	Zinc: .25g
55.80% from Carb	Copper: .02mg
Protein: 2.25 g	Manganese: .08g
Total Fat: 4.37 g	Vitamin A: 190.75 IU
Saturated Fat: 2.68 g	Vitamin E: 56.90 mg
Monosaturated Fat: .06 g	Thiamin: .03 mg
Polyunsaturated: .02 g	Riboflavin: .16 mg
Cholesterol: 14.97 mg	Niacin: .14 mg
Carbohydrates: 15.24 g	Pantothenic Acid: .43 mg
Fiber: .64 g	Vitamin B6: .04 mg
Calcium: 82.75 mg	Folate: 9.14 ug
Phosphorous: 68.85 mg	Vitamin B12: .21 ug
Iron: .15 mg	Vitamin C: 9.58 mg
Sodium: 38.71 mg	Selenium: 1.36 ug
Sugar: .44 mg	

Nutritional Information

Yields: 2 cups
Serving Size: ½ cup

Amount per serving

Calories: 177.71	Potassium: 124.8 mg
59.70% from Fat	Magnesium: 12.79 mg
8.05% from Protein	Zinc: .32 mg
32.20% from Carb	Copper: .09 mg
Protein: 3.66 g	Manganese: .20 mg
Total Fat: 12.07 g	Vitamin A: 227.17 IU
Saturated Fat: 4.84 g	Vitamin E: 62.16 mg
Monosaturated Fat: 4.86 g	Thiamin: .18 mg
Polyunsaturated: 1.29 g	Riboflavin: .16 mg
Cholesterol: 48.91 mg	Niacin: 1.27 mg
Carbohydrates: 14.67 g	Pantothenic Acid: .25 mg
Fiber: 1.06 g	Vitamin B6: .03 mg
Calcium: 81.47 mg	Folate: 41.47 ug
Phosphorous: 105.04 mg	Vitamin B12: .17 ug
Iron: .38 mg	Vitamin C: 1.41 mg
Sodium: 95.88 mg	Selenium: 14.67 g
Sugar: 12.21 mg	

Frosty Cola

1 ½ cup vanilla ice cream

⅓ cup cola

Directions: Place ingredients in jar in order listed above and secure the lid. Press the **Milkshake** button.

Whipped Topping

Gummy Cola Bottles

Pour drink into cup and add whipped topping. Place gummy cola bottles on top.

Blueberry Breeze

1 ¼ cups vanilla ice cream

¼ cup blueberries

2 Tbsp blueberry syrup

Directions: Place ingredients in jar in order listed above and secure the lid. Press the **Milkshake** button.

Whipped Topping

Purple Sugar Crystals

Pour drink into a cup and add whipped topping. Place the sugar crystals on top.

Nutritional Information

Yields: 2 cups
Serving Size: ½ cup

Amount per serving

Calories: 143.19	Potassium: 114.95 mg
52.60% from Fat	Magnesium: 7.94 mg
7.38% from Protein	Zinc: .34 mg
40.00% from Carb	Copper: .02 mg
Protein: 2.64 g	Manganese: .01 mg
Total Fat: 8.39 g	Vitamin A: 379.90 IU
Saturated Fat: 4.82 g	Vitamin E: 102.56 mg
Monosaturated Fat: 2.25 g	Thiamin: .03 mg
Polyunsaturated: .29 g	Riboflavin: .12 mg
Cholesterol: 58.69 mg	Niacin: .06 mg
Carbohydrates: 14.34 g	Pantothenic Acid: .33 mg
Fiber: .45 g	Vitamin B6: .03 mg
Calcium: 85.28 mg	Folate: 5.80 ug
Phosphorous: 76.99 mg	Vitamin B12: .32 ug
Iron: .14 mg	Vitamin C: .52 mg
Sodium: 42.50 mg	Selenium: 1.95 ug
Sugar: 13.65 mg	

Nutritional Information

Yields: ½ cup
Serving Size: ¼ cup

Amount per serving

Calories: 311.98	Potassium: 216.67 mg
39.90% from Fat	Magnesium: 15.76 mg
5.74% from Protein	Zinc: .59 mg
54.40% from Carb	Copper: .05 mg
Protein: 4.54 g	Manganese: .08 mg
Total Fat: 14.03 g	Vitamin A: 642.96 IU
Saturated Fat: 8.05 g	Vitamin E: 170.93 mg
Monosaturated Fat: 3.76 g	Thiamin: .06 mg
Polyunsaturated: .51 g	Riboflavin: .21 mg
Cholesterol: 97.82 mg	Niacin: .18 mg
Carbohydrates: 43.06 g	Pantothenic Acid: .57 mg
Fiber: 1.19 g	Vitamin B6: .06 mg
Calcium: 146.45 mg	Folate: 11.35 ug
Phosphorous: 128.46 mg	Vitamin B12: .54 ug
Iron: .42 mg	Vitamin C: 2.62 mg
Sodium: 79.78 mg	Selenium: 3.40 ug
Sugar: 24.55 mg	

MILK SUBSTITUTES

To blend Milk Substitutes, you will use the Speed buttons. See each specific recipe for varying instructions. Whenever any recipe calls for milk, any nondairy "milk" alternative can be substituted in its place. When using soybeans in milk substitute, do not use milk more than one year old. Old soybeans produce a thick starchy milk that becomes difficult to drain and or press.

Nut Milk

¾ cup nut of choice

Directions: Make sure jar is completely dry. Add ingredient and secure the lid. Press the Speed Button until blender reaches speed 10. Allow the cycle to run for 30 seconds. When the display reads 30 seconds, press any lower row button to stop. You may need to use a rubber spatula to scrap the ingredients off the sides of the jar. Move ingredients towards the center of the jar, and if necessary hold down the Pulse button for 10 seconds until peanuts are blended to a paste.

3 ¾ cups purified water - room temperature
3 tsps molasses
1 ½ tsps vanilla
¼ tsp salt

Directions: Add above ingredients to jar and secure the lid. Press the **Whole Juice** button. Allow the blender to run a complete cycle.

Note: If a smoother consistency is desired, strain through a 4 layer cheesecloth.

Oat Milk

¾ cup whole oats

Directions: Make sure jar is completely dry. Add ingredient and secure the lid. Press the **Speed Up** button until blender reaches Speed 10. Allow the blender to run for 20 seconds. When the display reads 20 seconds, press any lower row button to stop.

3 ¾ cup purified water - room temperature
1 medium apple - cored and quartered
3 tsps molasses
1 ½ tsps vanilla
¼ tsp salt

Directions: Add ingredients to jar and secure the lid. Press the **Whole Juice** button. Allow the blender to run a complete cycle. Chill and let rest in refrigerator for at least 5 minutes.

Note: If smoother consistency is desired, strain through 4 layer cheesecloth.

Nutritional Information

Yields: 4 cups
Serving Size: ½ cup

Amount per serving

Calories: 87.59	Potassium: 136.28 mg
66.00% from Fat,	Magnesium: 30.58 mg
15.40% from Protein	Zinc: .46 mg
18.60% from Carb	Copper: .18 mg
Protein: 3.53 g	Manganese: .31 mg
Total Fat: 6.74 g	Vitamin A: 0.00 IU
Saturated Fat: .94 g	Vitamin E: 0.00 mg
Monosaturated Fat: 3.34g	Thiamin: .09 mg
Polyunsaturated: 2.13 g	Riboflavin: .02 mg
Cholesterol: 0.00 mg	Niacin: 1.68 mg
Carbohydrates: 4.28 g	Pantothenic Acid: .26 mg
Fiber: 1.16 g	Vitamin B6: .07 mg
Calcium: 20.35 mg	Folate: 32.85ug
Phosphorous: 52.33 mg	Vitamin B12: 0.00 ug
Iron: .75 mg	Vitamin C: 0.00 mg
Sodium: 79.41 mg	Selenium: 1.45 ug
Sugar: 2.11 mg	

Nutritional Information

Yields: 4 cups
Serving Size: ½ cup

Amount per serving

Calories: 66.87	Potassium: 102.52 mg
13.80% from Fat	Magnesium: 33.47 mg
15.00% from Protein	Zinc: .59 mg
71.20% from Carb	Copper: .11 mg
Protein: 2.47 g	Manganese: .761 mg
Total Fat: 1.01 g	Vitamin A: 0.00 IU
Saturated Fat: .18 g	Vitamin E: 0.00 mg
Monosaturated Fat: .32 g	Thiamin: .11 mg
Polyunsaturated: .37 g	Riboflavin: .02 mg
Cholesterol: 0.00 mg	Niacin: .17 mg
Carbohydrates: 11.76 g	Pantothenic Acid: .22 mg
Fiber: 1.55 g	Vitamin B6: .04 mg
Calcium: 15.65 mg	Folate: 8.19 ug
Phosphorous: 77.35 mg	Vitamin B12: 0.00 ug
Iron: .82 mg	Vitamin C: 0.00 mg
Sodium: 77.24 mg	Selenium: .47 ug
Sugar: 1.56 mg	

Seed Milk

¾ cup seed of choice

Directions: Make sure jar is completely dry. Add ingredient to jar and secure the lid. Press the **Speed Up** button until blender reaches speed 10. Allow the blender to run for 15 seconds. When the display reads 15 seconds, press any lower row button to stop. It may be necessary to scrape the ingredient off the sides with a rubber spatula and move towards the center of the jar. If necessary, press the Pulse button for 10 seconds until seeds are blended into a paste.

3 ¾ cups purified water - room temperature

3 tsps molasses

1 ½ tsp vanilla

¼ tsp salt

Directions: Add ingredients to jar and secure the lid. Press the **Whole Juice** button. Allow the blender to run a complete cycle.

Nutritional Information

Yields: 4 cups
Serving Size: ½ cup

Amount per serving

Calories: 87.33	Potassium: 102.96 mg
13.80% from Fat,	Magnesium: 54.97 mg
15.00% from Protein	Zinc: 1.05 mg
71.20% from Carb	Copper: .57 mg
Protein: 2.39 g	Manganese: .37 mg
Total Fat: 6.71 g	Vitamin A: 1.22 IU
Saturated Fat: .94 g	Vitamin E: 0.00 mg
Monosaturated Fat: 2.53 g	Thiamin: .11 mg
Polyunsaturated: 2.94 g	Riboflavin: .03 mg
Cholesterol: 0.00 mg	Niacin: .64 mg
Carbohydrates: 5.24 g	Pantothenic Acid: .03 mg
Fiber: 1.59 g	Vitamin B6: .12 mg
Calcium: 139.38 mg	Folate: 13.10 ug
Phosphorous: 85.78 mg	Vitamin B12: 0.00 ug
Iron: 2.09 mg	Vitamin C: 0.00 mg
Sodium: 78.44 mg	Selenium: 1.24 ug
Sugar: 1.60 mg	

Wheat Milk

¾ cup whole wheat

Directions: Make sure jar is completely dry. Place ingredients in jar and secure the lid. Press the **Speed Up** button until blender reaches speed 10. Allow the blender to complete the cycle.

3 1/3 cups purified water - room temperature

3 tsps molasses

1 ½ tsp vanilla

¼ tsp salt

Directions: Add ingredients to jar and secure the lid. Press the **Whole Juice** button. Chill and rest in refrigerator for at least 5 minutes.

Nutritional Information

Yields: 4 cups
Serving Size: ½ cup

Amount per serving

Calories: 48.12	Potassium: 85.34 mg
3.92% from Fat	Magnesium: 22.00 mg
12.60% from Protein	Zinc: .34 mg
83.50% from Carb	Copper: .06 mg
Protein: 1.54 g	Manganese: .47 mg
Total Fat: 6.21 g	Vitamin A: 1.01 IU
Saturated Fat: .04 g	Vitamin E: 0.00 mg
Monosaturated Fat: .03 g	Thiamin: .05 mg
Polyunsaturated: .09 g	Riboflavin: .03 mg
Cholesterol: 0.00 mg	Niacin: .74 mg
Carbohydrates: 10.24 g	Pantothenic Acid: .13 mg
Fiber: 1.37 g	Vitamin B6: .06mg
Calcium: 9.36 mg	Folate: 4.95 ug
Phosphorous: 39.79 mg	Vitamin B12: 0.00 ug
Iron: 2.56 mg	Vitamin C: 0.00 mg
Sodium: 75.29 mg	Selenium: 8.42 ug
Sugar: 1.61 mg	

Rice Milk

½ cup cooked rice

2 cups water

½ Tbsp sugar

¼ tsp salt

Directions: Place ingredients in blender jar and secure the lid. Press the **Whole Juice** button.

Nutritional Information

Yields: 2 cups
Serving Size: ½ cup

Amount per serving

Calories: 31.03	Potassium: 8.16 mg
1.74% from Fat,	Magnesium: 3.18 mg
6.58% from Protein	Zinc: .07 mg
91.70% from Carb	Copper: .03 mg
Protein: .50 g	Manganese: .06 mg
Total Fat: .06 g	Vitamin A: 0.00 IU
Saturated Fat: .02 g	Vitamin E: 0.00 mg
Monosaturated Fat: .02 g	Thiamin: .05 mg
Polyunsaturated: .02 g	Riboflavin: 0.00 mg
Cholesterol: 0.00 mg	Niacin: .31 mg
Carbohydrates: 6.98 g	Pantothenic Acid: 0.07 mg
Fiber: .09 g	Vitamin B6: 0.00 mg
Calcium: 6.63 mg	Folate: 16.63 ug
Phosphorous: 9.19 mg	Vitamin B12: 0.00 ug
Iron: .25 mg	Vitamin C: 0.00 mg
Sodium: 150.39 mg	Selenium: 1.80 ug
Sugar: 1.60 mg	

Soy Milk

6 oz. tofu

2 cups hot water

4 tsps sugar

2 tsps vanilla

⅛ tsp salt

Directions: Place ingredients in blender jar and secure the lid. Press the **Speed Up** button until blender reaches speed 5. Allow the blender to run a complete cycle.

Nutritional Information

Yields: 2 ½ cups
Serving Size: ½ cup

Amount per serving

Calories: 38.75	Potassium: 43.47 mg
30.60% from Fat,	Magnesium: 10.34 mg
24.10% from Protein	Zinc: .22 mg
45.30% from Carb	Copper: .06 mg
Protein: 2.23 g	Manganese: .14 mg
Total Fat: 1.26 g	Vitamin A: 2.38 IU
Saturated Fat: .18 g	Vitamin E: 0.00 mg
Monosaturated Fat: .28 g	Thiamin: .02 mg
Polyunsaturated: .71 g	Riboflavin: .01 mg
Cholesterol: 0.00 mg	Niacin: .19mg
Carbohydrates: 4.19 g	Pantothenic Acid: .02 mg
Fiber: .07 g	Vitamin B6: .02 mg
Calcium: 39.92 mg	Folate: 14.97 ug
Phosphorous: 31.40 mg	Vitamin B12: 0.00 ug
Iron: .38 mg	Vitamin C: 0.07 mg
Sodium: 63.72 mg	Selenium: 3.05 ug
Sugar: 3.81 mg	

SMOOTHIES

You may use any desired sweetener: (i.e. Splenda™, honey) in place of sugar for smoothies. When substituting with honey, only add 1/3 of sugar measurement. For example, if recipe calls for 1 cup sugar, substitute with 1/3 cup of honey.

You may leave stems and seeds on fruit unless recipe specifically instructs to remove.

When the recipe asks for grapes, you may substitute with any kind of juice. Wash all fruit before placing in blender. You may use either fresh or frozen fruit; however, if you are using frozen fruit, you must allow it to thaw before placing in blender. The smoothie may not be as sweet if using frozen fruit. To correct this, add addtional sugar or sugar substitute.

Protein Powders:

You may add any type or flavor of protein powder to your smoothies. For best results, add the powder after blending the smoothie and press the Pulse button for approximately 5 seconds or until protein powder has been blended into smoothie.

For every 4 cups of smoothie, you should add approximately 2 scoops of protein powder (However, if you have Diabetes Mellitus (Type I or II), hypoglycemia, kidney disease, or any other health condition affecting the renal system, we strongly recommend consulting your physician for the correct amount of smoothie intake and/or protein powder).

Fresh Fruit Smoothie

2 cups grapes

1 cup strawberries

1 cup watermelon

½ cup cantaloupe – remove seeds

½ cup pineapple

½ banana – peeled

1 ½ cup ice

Directions: Place ingredients in jar in order as listed and secure the lid. Press the **Smoothie** button.

Nutritional Information

Yields: 3 cups
Serving Size: ½ cup

Amount per serving

Calories: 53.21	Potassium: 271.53 mg
3.29% from Fat,	Magnesium: 14.08 mg
4.99% from Protein	Zinc: .14 mg
91.70% from Carb	Copper: .06 mg
Protein: .74 g	Manganese: .42 mg
Total Fat: .22 g	Vitamin A: 692.03 IU
Saturated Fat: .05 g	Vitamin E: 0.00 mg
Monosaturated Fat: .02 g	Thiamin: .05 mg
Polyunsaturated: .07 g	Riboflavin: .04 mg
Cholesterol: 0.00 mg	Niacin: .52 mg
Carbohydrates: 13.62 g	Pantothenic Acid: .18 mg
Fiber: 1.65 g	Vitamin B6: .11 mg
Calcium: 13.47 mg	Folate: 15.18 ug
Phosphorous: 15.14 mg	Vitamin B12: 0.00 ug
Iron: .48 mg	Vitamin C: 29.04 mg
Sodium: 3.91 mg	Selenium: .57 ug
Sugar: 9.65 mg	

Papaya Banana Smoothie

2 cups grapes

1 cup watermelon

½ cup cantaloupe - remove seeds

½ banana – peeled

1 cup frozen strawberries

1 ½ cup ice

Directions: Place ingredients in jar in order as listed and secure the lid. Press the **Smoothie** button.

Soy Sensation

1 cup soy milk

½ ripe banana

2 Tbsp chocolate syrup

1 ½ cups ice

Directions: Place ingredients in jar in order as listed and secure the lid. Press the **Smoothie** button.

Nutritional Information

Yields: 2 cups
Serving Size: ½ cup

Amount per serving

Calories: 63.50	Potassium: 305.01 mg
5.65% from Fat,	Magnesium: 17.98 mg
8.86% from Protein	Zinc: .23 mg
85.50% from Carb	Copper: .04 mg
Protein: 1.53 g	Manganese: .11 mg
Total Fat: .43 g	Vitamin A: 606.16 IU
Saturated Fat: 0.22 g	Vitamin E: 2.14 mg
Monosaturated Fat: .10 g	Thiamin: .03 mg
Polyunsaturated: .05 g	Riboflavin: .08 mg
Cholesterol: 0.92 mg	Niacin: .44 mg
Carbohydrates: 14.79 g	Pantothenic Acid: .33 mg
Fiber: 1.92 g	Vitamin B6: .16 mg
Calcium: 42.50 mg	Folate: 29.13 ug
Phosphorous: 32.92 mg	Vitamin B12: 0.09 ug
Iron: .16 mg	Vitamin C: 35.83 mg
Sodium: 12.67 mg	Selenium: 1.20 ug
Sugar: 8.76 mg	

Nutritional Information

Yields: 2 ½ cups
Serving Size: ½ cup

Amount per serving

Calories: 51.68	Potassium: 134.29 mg
18.50% from Fat,	Magnesium: 16.70 mg
15.40% from Protein	Zinc: .17 mg
66.10% from Carb	Copper: .10 mg
Protein: 2.11 g	Manganese: .14 mg
Total Fat: 1.13 g	Vitamin A: 25.33 IU
Saturated Fat: 0.15 g	Vitamin E: 0.00 mg
Monosaturated Fat: .18 g	Thiamin: .08 mg
Polyunsaturated: .42 g	Riboflavin: .05 mg
Cholesterol: 0.00 mg	Niacin: .19 mg
Carbohydrates: 9.04 g	Pantothenic Acid: .07 mg
Fiber: 1.16 g	Vitamin B6: .08 mg
Calcium: 3.43 mg	Folate: 4.08 ug
Phosphorous: 32.93 mg	Vitamin B12: 0.00 ug
Iron: .43 mg	Vitamin C: 1.31 mg
Sodium: 9.73 mg	Selenium: .88 ug
Sugar: 4.63 mg	

Lemon Strawberry Cooler

½ cup cold water

1 ½ cups strawberries – leave stems

1 banana – peeled, cut in half

6 ounce can frozen lemonade

Directions: Place ingredients in jar in order as listed and secure the lid. Press the **Smoothie** button.

Watermelon and Raspberry Smoothie

2 cups watermelon - seeded, diced

1 Tbsp frozen lemonade concentrate

¾ cup frozen raspberries

2 Tbsp sugar

½ cup ice

Directions: Place ingredients in jar in order as listed and secure the lid. Press the **Smoothie** button.

Nutritional Information

Yields: 4 cups
Serving Size: ½ cup

Amount per serving

Calories: 69.68	Potassium: 142.70 mg
1.79% from Fat,	Magnesium: 10.83 mg
2.37% from Protein	Zinc: .10 mg
95.80% from Carb	Copper: .05 mg
Protein: .45 g	Manganese: .18 mg
Total Fat: .15 g	Vitamin A: 32.14 IU
Saturated Fat: .03 g	Vitamin E: 0.00 mg
Monosaturated Fat: .01 g	Thiamin: .02 mg
Polyunsaturated: .05 g	Riboflavin: .05 mg
Cholesterol: 0.00 mg	Niacin: .33 mg
Carbohydrates: 18.08 g	Pantothenic Acid: .12 mg
Fiber: 1.40 g	Vitamin B6: .09 mg
Calcium: 9.35 mg	Folate: 11.86 ug
Phosphorous: 11.43 mg	Vitamin B12: 0.00 ug
Iron: .51 mg	Vitamin C: 22.47 mg
Sodium: 2.16 mg	Selenium: 56 ug
Sugar: 13.76 mg	

Nutritional Information

Yields: 2 cups
Serving Size: ½ cup

Amount per serving

Calories: 43.35	Potassium: 124.12 mg
5.11% from Fat	Magnesium: 13.00 mg
6.29% from Protein	Zinc: .18 mg
88.60% from Carb	Copper: .06 mg
Protein: .76 g	Manganese: .18 mg
Total Fat: .27 g	Vitamin A: 446.06 IU
Saturated Fat: .02 g	Vitamin E: 0.00 mg
Monosaturated Fat: .04 g	Thiamin: .03 mg
Polyunsaturated: .13 g	Riboflavin: .03 mg
Cholesterol: 0.00mg	Niacin: .28 mg
Carbohydrates: 10.72 g	Pantothenic Acid: .25 mg
Fiber: 1.82 g	Vitamin B6: .05 mg
Calcium: 11.48 mg	Folate: 7.38 ug
Phosphorous: 15.57 mg	Vitamin B12: 0.00 ug
Iron: .38 mg	Vitamin C: 13.09 mg
Sodium: 1.18 mg	Selenium: .37 ug
Sugar: 7.85 mg	

Orange Apricot Smoothie

2 cups oranges - peeled and cut in half

3 apricots - pitted

$\frac{1}{3}$ cup non-fat dry powdered milk

1 Tbsp sugar

2 cups ice

Directions: Place ingredients in jar in order as listed and secure the lid. Press the **Smoothie** button.

Cantaloupe Craze

¾ cup cantaloupe

2 cups orange – peeled *

$\frac{1}{3}$ cup non-fat dry powdered milk

1 Tbsp sugar

1 ½ cup ice

Directions: Place ingredients in jar in order listed and secure the lid. Press the **Smoothie** button.

*May substitute 1 ½ cup orange juice

Nutritional Information

Yields: 3 cups
Serving Size: ½ cup

Amount per serving

Calories: 56.55	Potassium: 248.54 mg
1.99% from Fat,	Magnesium: 13.89 mg
20.30% from Protein	Zinc: .32 mg
77.70% from Carb	Copper: .04 mg
Protein: 3.03 g	Manganese: .02 mg
Total Fat: .13 g	Vitamin A: 199.54 IU
Saturated Fat: .04 g	Vitamin E: .40 mg
Monosaturated Fat: .03 g	Thiamin: .08 mg
Polyunsaturated: .02 g	Riboflavin: .13 mg
Cholesterol: 1.33 mg	Niacin: .28 mg
Carbohydrates: 11.61 g	Pantothenic Acid: .40 mg
Fiber: 1.57 g	Vitamin B6: .06 mg
Calcium: 108.76 mg	Folate: 21.51 ug
Phosphorous: 74.18 mg	Vitamin B12: .27 ug
Iron: .13 mg	Vitamin C: 32.39 mg
Sodium: 35.84 mg	Selenium: 2.16 ug
Sugar: 10.01 mg	

Nutritional Information

Yields: 4 cups
Serving Size: ½ cup

Amount per serving

Calories: 44.89	Potassium: 215.46 mg
2.35% from Fat,	Magnesium: 11.99 mg
19.90% from Protein	Zinc: .27 mg
77.70% from Carb	Copper: .03 mg
Protein: 2.37 g	Manganese: .02 mg
Total Fat: .12 g	Vitamin A: 663.55 IU
Saturated Fat: .04 g	Vitamin E: .30 mg
Monosaturated Fat: .02 g	Thiamin: .07 mg
Polyunsaturated: .03 g	Riboflavin: .10 mg
Cholesterol: 1.00 mg	Niacin: .30 mg
Carbohydrates: 9.24 g	Pantothenic Acid: .31 mg
Fiber: 1.23 g	Vitamin B6: .06 mg
Calcium: 82.34 mg	Folate: 19.48 ug
Phosphorous: 57.19 mg	Vitamin B12: .20 ug
Iron: .10 mg	Vitamin C: 30.37 mg
Sodium: 29.41 mg	Selenium: 1.66 ug
Sugar: 8.11 mg	

Melon Melody Smoothie

¼ cup orange juice

½ cup cantaloupe – leave seeds

1 ½ cups watermelon - leave seeds

½ cup - honeydews - leave seeds

1 Tbsp sugar

1 ½ cups ice

Directions: Place ingredients in jar in order as listed, and secure the lid. Press the **Smoothie** button.

Nutritional Information

Yields: 2 ½ cups
Serving Size: ½ cup

Amount per serving

Calories: 31.73	Potassium: 163.01 mg
4.13% from Fat	Magnesium: 9.88 mg
7.12% from Protein	Zinc: .10 mg
88.70% from Carb	Copper: .04 mg
Protein: .63 g	Manganese: .03 mg
Total Fat: .16 g	Vitamin A: 880.05 IU
Saturated Fat: .03 g	Vitamin E: 0.00 mg
Monosaturated Fat: .02 g	Thiamin: .04 mg
Polyunsaturated: .06 g	Riboflavin: .02 mg
Cholesterol: 0.00 mg	Niacin: .32 mg
Carbohydrates: 7.79 g	Pantothenic Acid: .17 mg
Fiber: .51 g	Vitamin B6: .06 mg
Calcium: 7.13 mg	Folate: 10.71 ug
Phosphorous: 11.05 mg	Vitamin B12: 0.00 ug
Iron: .20 mg	Vitamin C: 17.52 mg
Sodium: 6.60 mg	Selenium: .39 ug
Sugar: 5.69 mg	

Fresh Lime Smoothie

2 cups green grapes

½ cup honeydew - remove rind and seeds

½ lime

1 Tbsp sugar

1 ½ cups ice

Directions: Place ingredients in jar in order as listed and secure the lid. Press the **Smoothie** button.

Nutritional Information

Yields: 3 cups
Serving Size: ½ cup

Amount per serving

Calories: 28.62 (3.82% from Fat, 3.90% from Protein, 92.30% from Carb)	Magnesium: .62 mg
	Zinc: .03 mg
	Copper: .02 mg
Protein: .32 g	Manganese: .22 mg
Total Fat: .14 g	Vitamin A: 43.17 IU
Saturated Fat: .04 g	Vitamin E: 0.00 mg
Monosaturated Fat: .01 g	Thiamin: .04 mg
Polyunsaturated: .04 g	Riboflavin: .02 mg
Cholesterol: 0.00 mg	Niacin: .16 mg
Carbohydrates: 7.52 g	Pantothenic Acid: .04 mg
Fiber: .44 g	Vitamin B6: 0.05 mg
Calcium: 6.10 mg	Folate: 4.85 ug
Phosphorous: 5.41 mg	Vitamin B12: 0.00 ug
Iron: .12 mg	Vitamin C: 6.88 mg
Sodium: 3.37 mg	Selenium: .14 ug
Sugar: 6.35 mg	
Potassium: 103.38 mg	

Ocean Fruit Smoothie

½ cup coconut milk

1 mango - peeled

1 pear – quartered, seeded

1 Tbsp sugar

1 banana - cut in half

1 cup ice

Directions: Place ingredients in jar in order as listed and secure the lid. Press the **Smoothie** button.

Nutritional Information

Yields: 3 cups
Serving Size: ½ cup

Amount per serving

Calories: 110.11	Potassium: 226.25 mg
31.70% from Fat	Magnesium: 20.95 mg
3.20% from Protein	Zinc: .19 mg
65.10% from Carb	Copper: .13 mg
Protein: .96 g	Manganese: .24 mg
Total Fat: 4.23 g	Vitamin A: 287.94 IU
Saturated Fat: 3.61 g	Vitamin E: 0.00 mg
Monosaturated Fat: .22 g	Thiamin: .04 mg
Polyunsaturated: .09 g	Riboflavin: .05 mg
Cholesterol: 0.00 mg	Niacin: .54 mg
Carbohydrates: 19.59 g	Pantothenic Acid: .18 mg
Fiber: 2.35 g	Vitamin B6: 0.15 mg
Calcium: 11.25 mg	Folate: 14.90 ug
Phosphorous: 31.21 mg	Vitamin B12: 0.00 ug
Iron: .79 mg	Vitamin C: 13.38 mg
Sodium: 3.74 mg	Selenium: .50 ug
Sugar: 13.68 mg	

Crunchy Blueberry Smoothie

½ cup milk

¾ cup vanilla yogurt

½ tsp salt

¼ tsp vanilla

½ Tbsp sugar

¼ cup pecans

1 cup frozen peaches - sliced

⅓ cup frozen blueberries

Directions: Place ingredients in jar in order as listed and secure the lid. Press the **Smoothie** button.

Nutritional Information

Yields: 3 cups
Serving Size: ½ cup

Amount per serving

Calories: 75.06	Potassium: 121.25 mg
45.30% from Fat	Magnesium: 13.11 mg
13.60% from Protein	Zinc: .55 mg
41.10% from Carb	Copper: .06 mg
Protein: 2.65 g	Manganese: .22 mg
Total Fat: 3.92 g	Vitamin A: 59.64 IU
Saturated Fat: .66 g	Vitamin E: 15.47 mg
Monosaturated Fat: 2.03 g	Thiamin: .05 mg
Polyunsaturated: 1.03 g	Riboflavin: .11 mg
Cholesterol: 2.55 mg	Niacin: .15 mg
Carbohydrates: 7.99 g	Pantothenic Acid: .29 mg
Fiber: .67 g	Vitamin B6: 0.04 mg
Calcium: 80.60 mg	Folate: 5.99 ug
Phosphorous: 74.25 mg	Vitamin B12: 0.25 ug
Iron: .16 mg	Vitamin C: .51 mg
Sodium: 225.74 mg	Selenium: 2.36 ug
Sugar: 7.26 mg	

Citrus Smoothie

¾ cup lemonade

¼ lemon yogurt

1 cup lime sherbet

½ cup ice

Directions: Place ingredients in jar in order as listed, and secure the lid. Press the **Smoothie** button.

Orange Strawberry Smoothie

1 orange - peel and remove seeds

⅓ cup nonfat vanilla yogurt

1 cup strawberries – leave stems

½ banana - peeled

1 cup ice

Directions: Place ingredients in jar in order as listed, and secure the lid. Press the **Smoothie** button.

Nutritional Information

Yields: 2 cups
Serving Size: ½ cup

Amount per serving

Calories: 100.17	Potassium: 62.74 mg
22.80% from Fat	Magnesium: 2.77 mg
11.10% from Protein	Zinc: .46 mg
66.10% from Carb	Copper: .01 mg
Protein: 1.23 g	Manganese: 0.00 mg
Total Fat: 1.13 g	Vitamin A: 52.18 IU
Saturated Fat: .71 g	Vitamin E: 1.70 mg
Monosaturated Fat: .32 g	Thiamin: .01 mg
Polyunsaturated: .04 g	Riboflavin: .05 mg
Cholesterol: 25.67 mg	Niacin: .05 mg
Carbohydrates: 7.34 g	Pantothenic Acid: .08 mg
Fiber: 0.00 g	Vitamin B6: .01 mg
Calcium: 55.45 mg	Folate: 5.01 ug
Phosphorous: 19.64 mg	Vitamin B12: .11 ug
Iron: .09 mg	Vitamin C: 7.46 mg
Sodium: 27.73 mg	Selenium: .74 ug
Sugar: 1.96 mg	

Nutritional Information

Yields: 2 ½ cups
Serving Size: ½ cup

Amount per serving

Calories: 189.10 1.34% from Fat,	Magnesium: 11.53 mg
2.28% from Protein	Zinc: .23 mg
96.40% from Carb	Copper: .04 mg
Protein: 1.16 g	Manganese: 0.17 mg
Total Fat: .30 g	Vitamin A: 836.51 IU
Saturated Fat: .15 g	Vitamin E: 1.96 mg
Monosaturated Fat: .07 g	Thiamin: .02 mg
Polyunsaturated: .04 g	Riboflavin: .33 mg
Cholesterol: .82 mg	Niacin: 3.52 mg
Carbohydrates: 49.08 g	Pantothenic Acid: .019 mg
Fiber: 1.44 g	Vitamin B6: .40 mg
Calcium: 183.35 mg	Folate: 12.31 ug
Phosphorous: 98.70 mg	Vitamin B12: .09 ug
Iron: .41 mg	Vitamin C: 115.65mg
Sodium: 15.01 mg	Selenium: 1.26 ug
Sugar: 1.96 mg	
Potassium: 230.89 mg	

Banana Smoothie

½ cup orange juice

2 Tbsp egg substitute

1 tsp vanilla

⅓ cup sugar

2 bananas – peeled and broken in half

3 cups ice

Directions: Place ingredients in jar in order as listed and secure the lid. Press the **Smoothie** button.

Blueberry Grape Smoothie

2 cups grapes

¾ cups blueberries

½ banana – peeled

1 Tbsp sugar

2 cups ice

Directions: Place ingredients in jar in order as listed, and secure the lid. Press the **Smoothie** button.

Nutritional Information

Yields: 4 cups
Serving Size: ½ cup

Amount per serving

Calories: 77.58	Potassium: 177.73 mg
3.28% from Fat,	Magnesium: 12.25 mg
4.95% from Protein	Zinc: .11 mg
91.80% from Carb	Copper: .04 mg
Protein: 1.00 g	Manganese: .11 mg
Total Fat: .30 g	Vitamin A: 50.26 IU
Saturated Fat: .07 g	Vitamin E: 0.00 mg
Monosaturated Fat: .05 g	Thiamin: .03 mg
Polyunsaturated: .10 g	Riboflavin: .04 mg
Cholesterol: .04 mg	Niacin: .30 mg
Carbohydrates: 18.62 g	Pantothenic Acid: .26 mg
Fiber: 1.01 g	Vitamin B6: .15 mg
Calcium: 5.65 mg	Folate: 10.89ug
Phosphorous: 14.74 mg	Vitamin B12: .01 ug
Iron: .21 mg	Vitamin C: 8.38mg
Sodium: 7.52 mg	Selenium: 1.42 ug
Sugar: 13.07 mg	

Nutritional Information

Yields: 3 ½ cups
Serving Size: ½ cup

Amount per serving

Calories: 35.62	Potassium: 97.53 mg
5.33% from Fat	Magnesium: 5.04 mg
3.57% from Protein	Zinc: .04 mg
91.10% from Carb	Copper: .02 mg
Protein: .35 g	Manganese: .24 mg
Total Fat: .23 g	Vitamin A: 40.78 IU
Saturated Fat: .05 g	Vitamin E: 0.00 mg
Monosaturated Fat: .02 g	Thiamin: .03 mg
Polyunsaturated: .08 g	Riboflavin: .03 mg
Cholesterol: 0.00 mg	Niacin: .24 mg
Carbohydrates: 8.98 g	Pantothenic Acid: .06 mg
Fiber: .96 g	Vitamin B6: .08 mg
Calcium: 5.54 mg	Folate: 4.36 ug
Phosphorous: 6.81 mg	Vitamin B12: 0.00 ug
Iron: .13 mg	Vitamin C: 2.40 mg
Sodium: .80 mg	Selenium: .15 ug
Sugar: 6.99 mg	

Grape Orange Grapefruit Smoothie

2 cups grapes

1 cup orange – peeled

½ cup grapefruit

1 Tbsp sugar

2 cups ice

Directions: Place ingredients in jar in order as listed, and secure the lid. Press the **Smoothie** button.

Nutritional Information

Yields: 3 ½ cups
Serving Size: ½ cup

Amount per serving

Calories: 118.63	Potassium: 102.22 mg
0.44% from Fat	Magnesium: 1.97 mg
0.58% from Protein	Zinc: .03 mg
99.00% from Carb	Copper: .02 mg
Protein: .19 g	Manganese: .10 mg
Total Fat: .06 g	Vitamin A: 736.86 IU
Saturated Fat: .02 g	Vitamin E: 0.00 mg
Monosaturated Fat: 0.00 g	Thiamin: .02 mg
Polyunsaturated: .02 g	Riboflavin: .21 mg
Cholesterol: 0.00 mg	Niacin: 2.37 mg
Carbohydrates: 31.70 g	Pantothenic Acid: .05 mg
Fiber: .38 g	Vitamin B6: .25 mg
Calcium: 109.24mg	Folate: 2.17 ug
Phosphorous: 50.91 mg	Vitamin B12: 0.00 ug
Iron: .07 mg	Vitamin C: 74.75 mg
Sodium: 2.55 mg	Selenium: .06 ug
Sugar: 29.05 mg	

Pineapple Grapefruit Smoothie

1 ½ cup grapes

½ cup grapefruit

¾ cup pineapple

1 Tbsp sugar

1 ½ cup ice

Directions: Place ingredients in jar in order as listed, and secure the lid. Press the **Smoothie** button.

Nutritional Information

Yields: 3 ½ cups
Serving Size: ½ cup

Amount per serving

Calories: 26.44	Potassium: 79.59 mg
3.22% from Fat	Magnesium: 4.29 mg
4.31% from Protein	Zinc: .04 mg
92.50% from Carb	Copper: .03 mg
Protein: .32 g	Manganese: .34 mg
Total Fat: .11 g	Vitamin A: 181.31 IU
Saturated Fat: .03 g	Vitamin E: 0.00 mg
Monosaturated Fat: .01 g	Thiamin: .04 mg
Polyunsaturated: .03 g	Riboflavin: .02 mg
Cholesterol: 0.00 mg	Niacin: .18 mg
Carbohydrates: 6.81 g	Pantothenic Acid: .09 mg
Fiber: .59 g	Vitamin B6: .05 mg
Calcium: 6.89 mg	Folate: 4.92 ug
Phosphorous: 4.61 mg	Vitamin B12: 0.00 ug
Iron: .12 mg	Vitamin C: 12.45 mg
Sodium: .56 mg	Selenium: .09 ug
Sugar: 5.89 mg	

Orange Raspberry Banana Grape Smoothie

2 cups oranges - peeled

1 cup grapes

½ banana

¾ cup raspberries

1 Tbsp sugar

2 cups ice

Directions: Place ingredients in jar in order as listed and secure the lid. Press the **Smoothie** button.

Grape Pineapple Berry Smoothie

2 cups grapes

1 cup pineapple

½ cup raspberries

1 Tbsp Sugar

2 cups ice

Directions: Place ingredients in jar in order as listed and secure the lid. Press the **Smoothie** button.

Nutritional Information

Yields: 4 cups
Serving Size: ½ cup

Amount per serving

Calories: 205.04	Potassium: 167.94 mg
0.59% from Fat	Magnesium: 5.64 mg
0.57% from Protein	Zinc: .09mg
98.80% from Carb	Copper: .03 mg
Protein: .31 g	Manganese: .19 mg
Total Fat: .15 g	Vitamin A: 1021.31 IU
Saturated Fat: .03 g	Vitamin E: 0.00 mg
Monosaturated Fat: .01 g	Thiamin: .02 mg
Polyunsaturated: .06 g	Riboflavin: .36 mg
Cholesterol: 0.00 mg	Niacin: 4.17 mg
Carbohydrates: 54.69 g	Pantothenic Acid: .07 mg
Fiber: 1.25 g	Vitamin B6: .45 mg
Calcium: 189.46 mg	Folate: 4.76 ug
Phosphorous: 91.06 mg	Vitamin B12: 0.00 ug
Iron: .17 mg	Vitamin C: 124.30 mg
Sodium: 4.44 mg	Selenium: .13 ug
Sugar: 48.63 mg	

Nutritional Information

Yields: 3 ¾ cups
Serving Size: ½ cup

Amount per serving

Calories: 30.62	Potassium: 83.01 mg
4.32% from Fat	Magnesium: 5.51 mg
4.27% from Protein	Zinc: .06 mg
91.40% from Carb	Copper: .04 mg
Protein: .36 g	Manganese: .47mg
Total Fat: .16 g	Vitamin A: 38.81 IU
Saturated Fat: .03 g	Vitamin E: 0.00 mg
Monosaturated Fat: .01 g	Thiamin: .04 mg
Polyunsaturated: .06 g	Riboflavin: .02 mg
Cholesterol: 0.00 mg	Niacin: .22 mg
Carbohydrates: 7.80 g	Pantothenic Acid: .08 mg
Fiber: 1.04 g	Vitamin B6: .05 mg
Calcium: 8.17 mg	Folate: 5.80 ug
Phosphorous: 6.48 mg	Vitamin B12: 0.00 ug
Iron: .19 mg	Vitamin C: 10.61 mg
Sodium: .78 mg	Selenium: .06 ug
Sugar: 6.26 mg	

Fresh Lime Grape Smoothie

2 cups green grapes

¼ lemon – peeled

¼ lime – peeled

¾ cup pineapple

¼ cup cherries

1 Tbsp sugar

2 cups ice

Directions: Place ingredients in jar in order as listed and secure the lid. Press the **Smoothie** button.

Grape Berry Pear Smoothie

2 cups green grapes

½ cup fresh raspberries*

⅛ lemon – peeled

½ pear - cored, cut in half

1 Tbsp sugar

2 cups ice

Directions: Place ingredients in jar in order as listed and secure the lid. Press the **Smoothie** button.

*May substitute blackberries instead

Nutritional Information

Yields: 4 cups
Serving Size: ½ cup

Amount per serving

Calories: 32.27	Potassium: 75.15 mg
2.86% from Fat	Magnesium: 3.65 mg
3.31% from Protein	Zinc: .03 mg
93.80% from Carb	Copper: .03 mg
Protein: .30 g	Manganese: .34 mg
Total Fat: .11 g	Vitamin A: 35.65 IU
Saturated Fat: .03 g	Vitamin E: 0.00 mg
Monosaturated Fat: .01 g	Thiamin: .04 mg
Polyunsaturated: .03 g	Riboflavin: .02 mg
Cholesterol: 0.00 mg	Niacin: .15 mg
Carbohydrates: 8.43 g	Pantothenic Acid: .05 mg
Fiber: .55 g	Vitamin B6: .05 mg
Calcium: 6.39 mg	Folate: 3.73 ug
Phosphorous: 4.77 mg	Vitamin B12: 0.00 ug
Iron: .13 mg	Vitamin C: 8.44 mg
Sodium: .68 mg	Selenium: .06 ug
Sugar: 7.23 mg	

Nutritional Information

Yields: 4 cups
Serving Size: ½ cup

Amount per serving

Calories: 34.11	Potassium: 76.00 mg
3.73% from Fat	Magnesium: 4.04 mg
3.44% from Protein	Zinc: .06 mg
92.80% from Carb	Copper: .03 mg
Protein: .33 g	Manganese: .22 mg
Total Fat: .16 g	Vitamin A: 29.32 IU
Saturated Fat: .03 g	Vitamin E: 0.00 mg
Monosaturated Fat: .01 g	Thiamin: .03 mg
Polyunsaturated: .06 g	Riboflavin: .02 mg
Cholesterol: 0.00 mg	Niacin: .14 mg
Carbohydrates: 8.79 g	Pantothenic Acid: .04 mg
Fiber: 1.21 g	Vitamin B6: .04 mg
Calcium: 7.25 mg	Folate: 3.84 ug
Phosphorous: 6.53 mg	Vitamin B12: 0.00 ug
Iron: .16 mg	Vitamin C: 5.36 mg
Sodium: .74 mg	Selenium: .08 ug
Sugar: 7.02 mg	

Orange Berry Pear Smoothie

2 cups oranges – peeled

1/3 cup raspberries*

1/2 pear – cored, cut in half

1/8 lemon – peeled

1 Tbsp sugar

2 cups ice

Directions: Place ingredients in jar in order as listed and secure the jar. Press the **Smoothie** button.

*May substitute blackberries

Lime Kiwi Smoothie

2 kiwis – peeled

1 large pear – seeded

1 Tbsp lime juice

2 Tbsp sugar

1/3 cup water

1 cup ice

Directions: Place ingredients in jar in order as listed and secure the lid. Press the **Smoothie** button.

Nutritional Information

Yields: 4 cups
Serving Size: ½ cup

Amount per serving

Calories: 38.51	Potassium: 109.65 mg
2.40% from Fat	Magnesium: 6.83 mg
5.38% from Protein	Zinc: .07 mg
92.20% from Carb	Copper: .04 mg
Protein: .57 g	Manganese: .05 mg
Total Fat: .11 g	Vitamin A: 106.73 IU
Saturated Fat: .01 g	Vitamin E: 0.00 mg
Monosaturated Fat: .02 g	Thiamin: .04 mg
Polyunsaturated: .04 g	Riboflavin: .02 mg
Cholesterol: 0.00 mg	Niacin: .18 mg
Carbohydrates: 9.82 g	Pantothenic Acid: .14 mg
Fiber: 1.92 g	Vitamin B6: .04 mg
Calcium: 21.39 mg	Folate: 15.88 ug
Phosphorous: 9.79 mg	Vitamin B12: 0.00 ug
Iron: .12 mg	Vitamin C: 27.71 mg
Sodium: .25 mg	Selenium: .27 ug
Sugar: 7.38 mg	

Nutritional Information

Yields: 2 cups
Serving Size: ½ cup

Amount per serving

Calories: 83.25	Potassium: 207.15 mg
3.05% from Fat,	Magnesium: 11.66 mg
3.20% from Protein	Zinc: .12 mg
93.80% from Carb	Copper: .10 mg
Protein: .73 g	Manganese: .07 mg
Total Fat: .31 g	Vitamin A: 52.22 IU
Saturated Fat: .02 g	Vitamin E: 0.00 mg
Monosaturated Fat: .04 g	Thiamin: .02 mg
Polyunsaturated: .15 g	Riboflavin: .03 mg
Cholesterol: 0.00 mg	Niacin: .24 mg
Carbohydrates: 21.30 g	Pantothenic Acid: .11 mg
Fiber: 3.00 g	Vitamin B6: .04 mg
Calcium: 20.70 mg	Folate: 15.34 ug
Phosphorous: 21.60 mg	Vitamin B12: 0.00 ug
Iron: .24 mg	Vitamin C: 44.62 mg
Sodium: 2.50 mg	Selenium: .18 ug
Sugar: 15.56 mg	

Fruit Combo Smoothie

½ cup pineapple chunks - with juice

½ pear – remove core

½ apple – remove seeds and core

½ orange – peeled

1 Tbsp sugar

1 cup ice

Directions: Place ingredients in jar in order as listed and secure the jar. Press the **Smoothie** button.

Nutritional Information

Yields: 2 cups
Serving Size: ½ cup

Amount per serving

Calories: 55.76	Potassium: 73.77 mg
1.12% from Fat,	Magnesium: 4.79 mg
1.63% from Protein	Zinc: .05 mg
97.30% from Carb	Copper: .05 mg
Protein: .25 g	Manganese: .25 mg
Total Fat: .08 g	Vitamin A: 85.44 IU
Saturated Fat: .01 g	Vitamin E: 0.00 mg
Monosaturated Fat: .01 g	Thiamin: .02 mg
Polyunsaturated: .02 g	Riboflavin: .04 mg
Cholesterol: 0.00 mg	Niacin: .40 mg
Carbohydrates: 14.75 g	Pantothenic Acid: .06 mg
Fiber: 1.30 g	Vitamin B6: .06 mg
Calcium: 17.23 mg	Folate: 4.74 ug
Phosphorous: 11.47 mg	Vitamin B12: 0.00 ug
Iron: .11 mg	Vitamin C: 16.25 mg
Sodium: .90 mg	Selenium: .06 ug
Sugar: 11.94 mg	

Fruit Blend

½ cup plain non-fat yogurt

½ orange

1 banana

¼ cup frozen peaches

½ cup frozen strawberries

½ cup ice cubes

Directions: Place ingredients in jar in order as listed and secure the lid. Press the **Smoothie** button.

Nutritional Information

Yields: 2 ½ cups
Serving Size: ½ cup

Amount per serving

Calories: 61.84	Potassium: 198.98 mg
12.60% from Fat	Magnesium: 14.24 mg
8.06% from Protein	Zinc: .23 mg
79.30% from Carb	Copper: .04 mg
Protein: 1.35 g	Manganese: .15mg
Total Fat: .94 g	Vitamin A: 131.11 IU
Saturated Fat: .55 g	Vitamin E: 6.61 mg
Monosaturated Fat: .24 g	Thiamin: .02 mg
Polyunsaturated: .06 g	Riboflavin: .08 mg
Cholesterol: 3.18 mg	Niacin: .59 mg
Carbohydrates: 13.28 g	Pantothenic Acid: .23 mg
Fiber: 1.38 g	Vitamin B6: .15 mg
Calcium: 44.42 mg	Folate: 11.81 ug
Phosphorous: 38.67 mg	Vitamin B12: .09 ug
Iron: .28 mg	Vitamin C: 18.40 mg
Sodium: 12.21 mg	Selenium: 1.00 ug
Sugar: 8.79 mg	

Berry Blast Smoothie

2 cups grapes

½ cup strawberries

½ cup raspberries

½ cup blackberries

½ cup blueberries

2 cups ice

Directions: Place ingredients in jar in order as listed and secure the lid. Press the **Smoothie** button.

"Just Peachy" Smoothie

1 ½ orange – peeled

1 ½ ripe peaches - pitted

½ cup plain lowfat yogurt

2 cups ice

Directions: Place ingredients in jar in order as listed and secure the lid. Press the **Smoothie** button.

Nutritional Information

Yields: 4 cups
Serving Size: ½ cup

Amount per serving

Calories: 66.10	Potassium: 191.58 mg
6.16% from Fat	Magnesium: 13.29 mg
5.03% from Protein	Zinc: .23 mg
88.80% from Carb	Copper: .08 mg
Protein: .92 g	Manganese: .66 mg
Total Fat: .50 g	Vitamin A: 110.94 IU
Saturated Fat: .07 g	Vitamin E: 0.00 mg
Monosaturated Fat: .05 g	Thiamin: .06 mg
Polyunsaturated: .22 g	Riboflavin: .05 mg
Cholesterol: 0.00 mg	Niacin: .57 mg
Carbohydrates: 16.33 g	Pantothenic Acid: .17 mg
Fiber: .54 g	Vitamin B6: .08 mg
Calcium: 21.47 mg	Folate: 15.62 ug
Phosphorous: 18.74 mg	Vitamin B12: 0.00 ug
Iron: .59 mg	Vitamin C: 21.51 mg
Sodium: 2.00 mg	Selenium: .36 ug
Sugar: 11.93 mg	

Nutritional Information

Yields: 4 cups
Serving Size: ½ cup

Amount per serving

Calories: 37.04	Potassium: 142.11 mg
13.70% from Fat	Magnesium: 7.94 mg
11.10% from Protein	Zinc: .16 mg
75.20% from Carb	Copper: .04 mg
Protein: 1.12 g	Manganese: .03 mg
Total Fat: .61 g	Vitamin A: 188.75 IU
Saturated Fat: .33 g	Vitamin E: 4.13 mg
Monosaturated Fat: .16 g	Thiamin: .04 mg
Polyunsaturated: .05 g	Riboflavin: .04 mg
Cholesterol: 1.99 mg	Niacin: .35 mg
Carbohydrates: 7.58 g	Pantothenic Acid: .19 mg
Fiber: 1.27 g	Vitamin B6: .03 mg
Calcium: 34.09 mg	Folate: 12.60 ug
Phosphorous: 25.26 mg	Vitamin B12: .06 ug
Iron: .12 mg	Vitamin C: 20.37 mg
Sodium: 7.04 mg	Selenium: .54 ug
Sugar: 6.41 mg	

Basic Fruit Smoothie

1 cup soy milk

2 Tbsp pineapple juice frozen concentrate*

½ banana peeled

1 cup ice

Directions: Place ingredients in jar in order as listed and secure the lid. Press the **Smoothie** button.

*May substitute any kind of frozen juice concentrate

Nutritional Information

Yields: 2 cups
Serving Size: ½ cup

Amount per serving

Calories: 55.65	Potassium: 177.09 mg
20.20% from Fat	Magnesium: 18.45 mg
17.20% from Protein	Zinc: .19 mg
62.60% from Carb	Copper: .10 mg
Protein: 2.57g	Manganese: .33 mg
Total Fat: 1.34 g	Vitamin A: 34.10 IU
Saturated Fat: .15 g	Vitamin E: 0.00 mg
Monosaturated Fat: .21 g	Thiamin: .12 mg
Polyunsaturated: .53 g	Riboflavin: .06 mg
Cholesterol: 0.00 mg	Niacin: .26 mg
Carbohydrates: 9.34g	Pantothenic Acid: .11 mg
Fiber: 1.32 g	Vitamin B6: .11 mg
Calcium: 5.34 mg	Folate: 6.82 ug
Phosphorous: 35.54 mg	Vitamin B12: 0.00 ug
Iron: .45 mg	Vitamin C: 3.73 mg
Sodium: 7.69 mg	Selenium: 1.00 ug
Sugar: 4.78 mg	

Tofu Dessert Smoothie

¼ cup water

¼ cup soft tofu

½ banana

1 Tbsp Splenda™

½ cup strawberries

½ cup ice cubes

Directions: Place ingredients in jar in order as listed and secure the lid. Press the **Smoothie** button.

Nutritional Information

Yields: 2 cups
Serving Size: ½ cup

Amount per serving

Calories: 48.00	Potassium: 126.67 mg
11.40% from Fat	Magnesium: 12.43 mg
10.20% from Protein	Zinc: .16 mg
78.30% from Carb	Copper: .05 mg
Protein: 1.34 g	Manganese: .19 mg
Total Fat: .66 g	Vitamin A: 25.52 IU
Saturated Fat: .11 g	Vitamin E: 0.00 mg
Monosaturated Fat: .14 g	Thiamin: .02 mg
Polyunsaturated: .35 g	Riboflavin: .03 mg
Cholesterol: 0.00 mg	Niacin: .34 mg
Carbohydrates: 10.23 g	Pantothenic Acid: .10 mg
Fiber: 1.10 g	Vitamin B6: .08 mg
Calcium: 22.89 mg	Folate: 15.27 ug
Phosphorous: 21.98 mg	Vitamin B12: 0.00 ug
Iron: .43 mg	Vitamin C: 13.04 mg
Sodium: 2.28 mg	Selenium: 1.78ug
Sugar: 6.81mg	

Healthy Pineapple Smoothie

1 ¾ cup canned pineapple - with juice, chilled
¾ cup soft tofu
2 cups ice

Directions: Place ingredients in jar in order as listed and secure the lid. Press the **Smoothie** button.

Nutritional Information

Yields: 2 ½ cups
Serving Size: ½ cup

Amount per serving

Calories: 48.73	Potassium: 107.03 mg
24.00% from Fat	Magnesium: 16.55 mg
20.20% from Protein	Zinc: .29 mg
55.80% from Carb	Copper: .11 mg
Protein: 2.73 g	Manganese: .78 mg
Total Fat: 1.44 g	Vitamin A: 32.98 IU
Saturated Fat: .20 g	Vitamin E: 0.00 mg
Monosaturated Fat: .31 g	Thiamin: .06 mg
Polyunsaturated: .80 g	Riboflavin: .03 mg
Cholesterol: 0.00 mg	Niacin: .46 mg
Carbohydrates: 7.52 g	Pantothenic Acid: .13 mg
Fiber: .83 g	Vitamin B6: .08 mg
Calcium: 48.34 mg	Folate: 24.51 ug
Phosphorous: 38.56 mg	Vitamin B12: 0.00 ug
Iron: .56 mg	Vitamin C: 19.71 mg
Sodium: 3.52 mg	Selenium: 3.37 ug
Sugar: 5.20 mg	

Country Orange Banana Berry Smoothie

2 cups grapes
2 cups oranges - peeled
⅓ cup raspberries
½ ripe banana
Optional, 1 Tbsp sugar
2 cups ice

Directions: Place ingredients in jar in order as listed and secure the lid. Press the **Smoothie** button.

Nutritional Information

Yields: 4 cups
Serving Size: ½ cup

Amount per serving

Calories: 39.86	Potassium: 144.72 mg
3.23% from Fat	Magnesium: 8.73 mg
5.98% from Protein	Zinc: .07 mg
90.80% from Carb	Copper: .04 mg
Protein: .66 g	Manganese: .15 mg
Total Fat: .16 g	Vitamin A: 120.44 IU
Saturated Fat: .03 g	Vitamin E: 0.00 mg
Monosaturated Fat: .02 g	Thiamin: .05 mg
Polyunsaturated: .05 g	Riboflavin: .03 mg
Cholesterol: 0.00 mg	Niacin: .25 mg
Carbohydrates: 10.01 g	Pantothenic Acid: .16 mg
Fiber: 1.76 g	Vitamin B6: .08 mg
Calcium: 21.36 mg	Folate: 16.91 ug
Phosphorous: 11.00 mg	Vitamin B12: 0.00 ug
Iron: .14 mg	Vitamin C: 26.56 mg
Sodium: .38 mg	Selenium: .34 ug
Sugar: 7.45 mg	

Orange Kiwi Grape Smoothie

1 ½ cups grapes

1 cup oranges - peeled

2 cups kiwi - peeled

2 cups ice

Directions: Place ingredients in jar in order as listed and secure the lid. Press the **Smoothie** button.

Nutritional Information

Yields: 4 cups
Serving Size: ½ cup

Amount per serving

Calories: 49.13	Potassium: 211.73 mg
5.24% from Fat	Magnesium: 10.64 mg
6.05% from Protein	Zinc: .08 mg
88.70% from Carb	Copper: .07 mg
Protein: .82 g	Manganese: .17 mg
Total Fat: .32 g	Vitamin A: 106.37 IU
Saturated Fat: .04 g	Vitamin E: 0.00 mg
Monosaturated Fat: .03 g	Thiamin: .05 mg
Polyunsaturated: .15 g	Riboflavin: .03 mg
Cholesterol: 0.00 mg	Niacin: .27 mg
Carbohydrates: 12.09 g	Pantothenic Acid: .14 mg
Fiber: 2.02 g	Vitamin B6: .06 mg
Calcium: 26.46 mg	Folate: 18.50 ug
Phosphorous: 19.92 mg	Vitamin B12: 0.00 ug
Iron: .21 mg	Vitamin C: 53.68 mg
Sodium: 1.67 mg	Selenium: .22 ug
Sugar: 8.88 mg	

Kiwi Strawberry Smoothie

¼ cup pineapple juice

5 strawberries

1 kiwi - peeled

½ banana

3 Tbsp sugar

1 cup ice

Directions: Place ingredients in jar in order as listed and secure the lid. Press the **Smoothie** button.

Nutritional Information

Yields: 2 cups
Serving Size: ½ cup

Amount per serving

Calories: 78.54 (2.06% from Fat, 2.61% from Protein, 95.30% from Carb)	Magnesium: 11.98 mg
	Zinc: .12 mg
	Copper: .07 mg
Protein: .55 g	Manganese: .34 mg
Total Fat: .19 g	Vitamin A: 45.44 IU
Saturated Fat: .01 g	Vitamin E: 0.00 mg
Monosaturated Fat: .02 g	Thiamin: .03 mg
Polyunsaturated: .10 g	Riboflavin: .03 mg
Cholesterol: 0.00 mg	Niacin: .37 mg
Carbohydrates: 19.98 g	Pantothenic Acid: .12 mg
Fiber: 1.87 g	Vitamin B6: .04 mg
Calcium: 19.33 mg	Folate: 18.67 ug
Phosphorous: 16.17 mg	Vitamin B12: 0.00 ug
Iron: .53 mg	Vitamin C: 45.52 mg
Sodium: 1.94 mg	Selenium: .50 ug
Sugar: 16.13 mg	
Potassium: 173.88 mg	

Coco Mint Smoothie

¼ cup cream of coconut

⅛ cup milk

½ tsp mint extract

¼ cup pineapple

1 ½ cup ice

Directions: Place ingredients in jar in order as listed and secure the lid. Press the **Smoothie** button.

Strawberry Strength Smoothie

1 cup strawberries

¼ cup strawberry low-fat yogurt

2 Tbsp sugar

¼ cup vanilla non-fat frozen yogurt

½ cup ice

Directions: Place ingredients in jar in order as listed and secure the lid. Press the **Smoothie** button.

Nutritional Information

Yields: 2 cups
Serving Size: ½ cup

Amount per serving

Calories: 57.40 (77.40% from Fat, 5.57% from Protein, 17.00% from Carb)	Magnesium: 6.25 mg
	Zinc: .19 mg
	Copper: .07 mg
Protein: .86 g	Manganese: .31 mg
Total Fat: 5.29 g	Vitamin A: 23.20 IU
Saturated Fat: 4.66 g	Vitamin E: 4.42 mg
Monosaturated Fat: .24 g	Thiamin: .01 mg
Polyunsaturated: .06 g	Riboflavin: .02 mg
Cholesterol: 0.38mg	Niacin: .19 mg
Carbohydrates: 2.61 g	Pantothenic Acid: .09 mg
Fiber: .47 g	Vitamin B6: .02 mg
Calcium: 12.15 mg	Folate: 5.36 ug
Phosphorous: 26.37 mg	Vitamin B12: .03 ug
Iron: .37 mg	Vitamin C: 3.95 mg
Sodium: 4.07mg	Selenium: .26 ug
Sugar: 1.29 mg	
Potassium: 71.71 mg	

Nutritional Information

Yields: 1 cup
Serving Size: ½ cup

Amount per serving

Calories: 148.01	Potassium: 261.49 mg
8.49% from Fat	Magnesium: 19.27 mg
6.55% from Protein	Zinc: .45 mg
85.00% from Carb	Copper: .09 mg
Protein: 2.53 g	Manganese: .34 mg
Total Fat: 1.46 g	Vitamin A: 98.91 IU
Saturated Fat: .84 g	Vitamin E: 13.50 mg
Monosaturated Fat: .39 g	Thiamin: .04 mg
Polyunsaturated: .11 g	Riboflavin: .14 mg
Cholesterol: 1.59 mg	Niacin: .59 mg
Carbohydrates: 32.88 g	Pantothenic Acid: .39 mg
Fiber: 2.32 g	Vitamin B6: .06 mg
Calcium: 90.10 mg	Folate: 22.62 ug
Phosphorous: 74.03 mg	Vitamin B12: .20 ug
Iron: .91 mg	Vitamin C: 45.88 mg
Sodium: 35.63 mg	Selenium: 2.39 ug
Sugar: 27.78 mg	

Coco Peach Smoothie

1 cup peaches

¼ cup coconut milk

¼ cup pineapple*

¼ cup low-fat milk

1 cup ice

Directions: Place ingredients in jar in order as listed and secure the lid.
Press the **Smoothie** button.

*May substitute canned pineapple with juice

Sweet 'n Tropical Smoothie

1 cup milk

½ cup pineapple juice

1 Tbsp maple syrup

2 Tbsp non-fat dry powdered milk

½ Tbsp coconut milk

1 frozen banana – peeled, broken into 1-inch pieces

1 ½ cups ice

Directions: Place ingredients in jar in order as listed and secure the lid.
Press the **Smoothie** button.

Nutritional Information

Yields: 2 cups
Serving Size: ½ cup

Amount per serving

Calories: 55.46	Potassium: 145.84 mg
8.49% from Fat	Magnesium: 13.16 mg
6.55% from Protein	Zinc: .23 mg
85.00% from Carb	Copper: .07 mg
Protein: 1.24 g	Manganese: .25 mg
Total Fat: 3.28 g	Vitamin A: 173.87 IU
Saturated Fat: 2.78 g	Vitamin E: 8.85 mg
Monosaturated Fat: .20 g	Thiamin: .02 mg
Polyunsaturated: .08 g	Riboflavin: .04 mg
Cholesterol: .76 mg	Niacin: .49 mg
Carbohydrates: 6.44 g	Pantothenic Acid: .16 mg
Fiber: .77 g	Vitamin B6: .03 mg
Calcium: 24.50 mg	Folate: 5.89 ug
Phosphorous: 37.32 mg	Vitamin B12: .07 ug
Iron: .60 mg	Vitamin C: 6.45 mg
Sodium: 8.64 mg	Selenium: .56 ug
Sugar: 5.26 mg	

Nutritional Information

Yields: 3 cups
Serving Size: ½ cup

Amount per serving

Calories: 71.13 (9.34% from Fat, 14.20% from Protein, 76.50% from Carb)	Magnesium: 17.69 mg
	Zinc: .48 mg
	Copper: .05 mg
Protein: 2.64 g	Manganese: .40 mg
Total Fat: .77 g	Vitamin A: 97.30 IU
Saturated Fat: .52 g	Vitamin E: 23.74 mg
Monosaturated Fat: .14 g	Thiamin: .04 mg
Polyunsaturated: .04 g	Riboflavin: .14 mg
Cholesterol: 2.53 mg	Niacin: .29 mg
Carbohydrates: 14.20 g	Pantothenic Acid: .34 mg
Fiber: .69 g	Vitamin B6: .14 mg
Calcium: 87.07 mg	Folate: 13.24 ug
Phosphorous: 71.20 mg	Vitamin B12: .28 ug
Iron: .22 mg	Vitamin C: 4.59 mg
Sodium: 32.18 mg	Selenium: 2.32 ug
Sugar: 11.30 mg	
Potassium: 232.71 mg	

Apple Smoothie

1 cup apple juice
½ cup frozen peach slices
½ cup frozen strawberries
1 banana - peeled
⅛ tsp cinnamon
1 ½ cups ice

Directions: Place ingredients in jar in order as listed and secure the lid. Press the **Smoothie** button.

Tomato Lime Cooler

½ cup water
1 Tbsp lime juice
1 large tomato - quartered
2 Tbsp sugar
½ cup ice

Directions: Place ingredients in jar in order as listed and secure the lid. Press the **Smoothie** button.

Nutritional Information

Yields: 2 ½ cups
Serving Size: ½ cup

Amount per serving

Calories: 80.55	Potassium: 233.12 mg
2.14% from Fat	Magnesium: 14.20 mg
3.01% from Protein	Zinc: .11 mg
94.80% from Carb	Copper: .05 mg
Protein: .65 g	Manganese: .19 mg
Total Fat: .21 g	Vitamin A: 100.30 IU
Saturated Fat: .05 g	Vitamin E: 0.00 mg
Monosaturated Fat: .03 g	Thiamin: .02 mg
Polyunsaturated: .06 g	Riboflavin: .05 mg
Cholesterol: 0.00 mg	Niacin: .48 mg
Carbohydrates: 20.43 g	Pantothenic Acid: .19 mg
Fiber: 1.77 g	Vitamin B6: .14 mg
Calcium: 9.35 mg	Folate: 10.52 ug
Phosphorous: 15.60 mg	Vitamin B12: 0.00 ug
Iron: .48 mg	Vitamin C: 35.57 mg
Sodium: 5.60 mg	Selenium: .60 ug
Sugar: 15.45 mg	

Nutritional Information

Yields: 2 cups
Serving Size: ½ cup

Amount per serving

Calories: 31.89	Potassium: 91.29 mg
2.20% from Fat,	Magnesium: 4.66 mg
3.95% from Protein	Zinc: .07 mg
93.90% from Carb	Copper: .03 mg
Protein: .34 g	Manganese: .04 mg
Total Fat: .08 g	Vitamin A: 310.91 IU
Saturated Fat: .02 g	Vitamin E: 0.00 mg
Monosaturated Fat: .02 g	Thiamin: .02 mg
Polyunsaturated: .05 g	Riboflavin: .01 mg
Cholesterol: 0.00 mg	Niacin: .23 mg
Carbohydrates: 8.02 g	Pantothenic Acid: .04 mg
Fiber: .46 g	Vitamin B6: .03 mg
Calcium: 4.84 mg	Folate: 5.89 ug
Phosphorous: 9.32 mg	Vitamin B12: 0.00 ug
Iron: .11 mg	Vitamin C: 4.98 mg
Sodium: 3.07 mg	Selenium: .04 ug
Sugar: 7.33 mg	

Orange Frosty

⅔ cup milk

⅔ cup water

¼ cup sugar

6 oz. frozen orange juice concentrate

1 tsp vanilla

2 cups ice

Directions: Place ingredients in jar in order as listed and secure the lid. Press the **Smoothie** button.

Note: You may also throw in a whole orange (peeled and halved) to add flavor.

Fruit 'n Yogurt Blend

1 cup vanilla yogurt

1 Tbsp frozen orange juice concentrate

¾ cup peaches – peeled

1 cup strawberries

1 banana – peeled

1 cup ice

Directions: Place ingredients in jar in order as listed and secure the lid. Press the **Smoothie** button.

Nutritional Information

Yields: 4 cups
Serving Size: ½ cup

Amount per serving

Calories: 95.95	Potassium: 323.64 mg
1.14% from Fat	Magnesium: 18.49 mg
17.10% from Protein	Zinc: .45 mg
81.70% from Carb	Copper: .04 mg
Protein: 4.12 g	Manganese: .01 mg
Total Fat: .12 g	Vitamin A: 82.78 IU
Saturated Fat: .06 g	Vitamin E: .60 mg
Monosaturated Fat: .03 g	Thiamin: .10 mg
Polyunsaturated: .01 g	Riboflavin: .17 mg
Cholesterol: 2.00 mg	Niacin: .25 mg
Carbohydrates: 19.68g	Pantothenic Acid: .48 mg
Fiber: .17 g	Vitamin B6: .07 mg
Calcium: 133.02 mg	Folate: 37.96 ug
Phosphorous: 108.95 mg	Vitamin B12: .40 ug
Iron: .11 mg	Vitamin C: .30 mg
Sodium: 54.85 mg	Selenium: 2.85 ug
Sugar: 19.51mg	

Nutritional Information

Yields: 3 cups
Serving Size: ½ cup

Amount per serving

Calories: 76.89	Potassium: 188.75 mg
7.10% from Fat,	Magnesium: 12.39 mg
12.20% from Protein	Zinc: .40 mg
80.70% from Carb	Copper: .03 mg
Protein: 2.45 g	Manganese: .11 mg
Total Fat: .63 g	Vitamin A: 120.56 IU
Saturated Fat: .34 g	Vitamin E: 4.90 mg
Monosaturated Fat: .17 g	Thiamin: .04 mg
Polyunsaturated: .08 g	Riboflavin: .10 mg
Cholesterol: 2.04 mg	Niacin: .37 mg
Carbohydrates: 16.20 g	Pantothenic Acid: .31 mg
Fiber: 1.09 g	Vitamin B6: .04 mg
Calcium: 75.76 mg	Folate: 16.09 ug
Phosphorous: 66.33 mg	Vitamin B12: .22 ug
Iron: .26 mg	Vitamin C: 48.74 mg
Sodium: 29.17 mg	Selenium: 2.24 ug
Sugar: 14.85 mg	

Orange Strawberry Grape Smoothie

2 cups red grapes

½ cup orange juice

1 cup frozen strawberries

1 cup ice

Directions: Place ingredients in jar in order as listed and secure the lid. Press the **Smoothie** button.

Coconut 'n Banana Smoothie

⅓ cup coconut milk

¼ cup milk

½ cup pineapple

1 banana – peeled, broken in half

1 cup ice

Directions: Place ingredients in jar in order as listed and secure the lid. Press the **Smoothie** button.

Nutritional Information

Yields: 2 cups
Serving Size: ½ cup

Amount per serving

Calories: 48.44	Potassium: 184.84 mg
3.82% from Fat	Magnesium: 10.65 mg
4.76% from Protein	Zinc: .09mg
91.40% from Carb	Copper: .05 mg
Protein: .63 g	Manganese: .33 mg
Total Fat: .23 g	Vitamin A: 72.14 IU
Saturated Fat: .04 g	Vitamin E: 0.00 mg
Monosaturated Fat: .03 g	Thiamin: .07 mg
Polyunsaturated: .07 g	Riboflavin: .04 mg
Cholesterol: 0.00 mg	Niacin: .41 mg
Carbohydrates: 12.12 g	Pantothenic Acid: .12 mg
Fiber: 1.43 g	Vitamin B6: .06 mg
Calcium: 15.17 mg	Folate: 15.91 ug
Phosphorous: 12.91 mg	Vitamin B12: 0.00 ug
Iron: .53 mg	Vitamin C: 33.92 mg
Sodium: 1.88 mg	Selenium: .44 ug
Sugar: 6.26 mg	

Nutritional Information

Yields: 2 cups
Serving Size: ½ cup

Amount per serving

Calories: 106.93	Potassium: 332.51 mg
33.30% from Fat	Magnesium: 29.36 mg
12.60% from Protein	Zinc: .49 mg
54.10% from Carb	Copper: .09 mg
Protein: 3.61 g	Manganese: .48 mg
Total Fat: 4.22 g	Vitamin A: 36.50 IU
Saturated Fat: 3.64 g	Vitamin E: .45 mg
Monosaturated Fat: .20 g	Thiamin: .06 mg
Polyunsaturated: .08 g	Riboflavin: .15 mg
Cholesterol: 1.50 mg	Niacin: .54 mg
Carbohydrates: 15.44 g	Pantothenic Acid: .46 mg
Fiber: 1.25 g	Vitamin B6: .19 mg
Calcium: 102.06 mg	Folate: 16.79 ug
Phosphorous: 100.48 mg	Vitamin B12: .30 ug
Iron: .80 mg	Vitamin C: 10.97 mg
Sodium: 43.14 mg	Selenium: 2.44 ug
Sugar: 10.28 mg	

CranRazzle

⅔ cup cranberry juice cocktail

⅓ cup canned cranberries

½ cup strawberries

½ cup raspberry sherbet

1 cup ice

Directions: Place ingredients in jar in order as listed and secure the lid. Press the **Smoothie** button.

Mango Paradise

1 ½ cup mango juice

⅓ cup vanilla yogurt

⅓ cup strawberries

⅓ cup peaches

¾ cup rainbow sherbet

½ cups ice

Directions: Place ingredients in jar in order as listed and secure the lid. Press the **Smoothie** button.

Nutritional Information

Yields: 2 ½ cups
Serving Size: ½ cup

Amount per serving

Calories: 48.25	Potassium: 53.33 mg
8.24% from Fat,	Magnesium: 3.55 mg
3.04% from Protein	Zinc: .15 mg
88.70% from Carb	Copper: .02 mg
Protein: .27 g	Manganese: .16 mg
Total Fat: .32 g	Vitamin A: 27.98 IU
Saturated Fat: .16 g	Vitamin E: 0.00 mg
Monosaturated Fat: .08 g	Thiamin: .01 mg
Polyunsaturated: .04 g	Riboflavin: .02 mg
Cholesterol: 6.66 mg	Niacin: .13 mg
Carbohydrates: 7.77 g	Pantothenic Acid: .06 mg
Fiber: .84 g	Vitamin B6: .02 mg
Calcium: 11.99 mg	Folate: 4.75 ug
Phosphorous: 4.50 mg	Vitamin B12: .01 ug
Iron: .25 mg	Vitamin C: 22.28 mg
Sodium: 5.23 mg	Selenium: .16 ug
Sugar: 5.86 mg	

Nutritional Information

Yields: 4 cups
Serving Size: ½ cup

Amount per serving

Calories: 64.60	Potassium: 80.75 mg
10.20% from Fat	Magnesium: 4.68 mg
8.02% from Protein	Zinc: .24 mg
81.70% from Carb	Copper: .02 mg
Protein: .40 g	Manganese: .03 mg
Total Fat: .51 g	Vitamin A: 69.45 IU
Saturated Fat: .31 g	Vitamin E: 1.23 mg
Monosaturated Fat: .15 g	Thiamin: .19 mg
Polyunsaturated: .03 g	Riboflavin: .23 mg
Cholesterol: 9.87mg	Niacin: 2.46 mg
Carbohydrates: 9.18 g	Pantothenic Acid: .11 mg
Fiber: .30 g	Vitamin B6: .24 mg
Calcium: 29.94 mg	Folate: 6.13 ug
Phosphorous: 18.26 mg	Vitamin B12: .77 ug
Iron: .17 mg	Vitamin C: 11.71 mg
Sodium: 13.44mg	Selenium: .57 ug
Sugar: 8.24 mg	

JUICES

To blend whole juices, press the **Whole Juice** button. This cycle runs for 50 seconds. You may press the button, walk away from your machine, and in 50 seconds your juice will be ready to drink. Using the **Whole Juice** button, you may leave stems and seeds in and on your vegetables unless otherwise indicated by the recipe. You may add ½ to 1 whole banana to create a thicker more smoothie like texture to your juice.

A common mistake in making whole vegetable juices is overloading with low water content vegetables and underloading with high water content vegetables and fruits. Most vegetables have low water content. If you are only using vegetables with low water content, it helps to add approximately ¼ to ½ cup water or juice before adding any ingredients into the jar. You may also want to add ¼ cup water at the beginning of the recipe, if you would like your whole vegetable juice to have a thinner consistency.

The recipes included in this recipe book will recommend adding water at the beginning of the recipe if the drink has a thick consistency. You may add as much ice to the whole vegetable juice as you would like, not to exceed 1 cup per recipe. The more ice you add to your juice, the cooler your juice will be. Some of the recipes in this book recommend adding ice to obtain the perfect temperature for your juice.

Any vegetable juice can be turned into soup. After the vegetable juice is completely blended into desired consistency, press the "Soup" button.

Strawberry Grape Juice

2 cups grapes

1 cup strawberries

Optional, add ½ cup ice

Directions: Place ingredients in jar in order listed and secure the lid. Press the **Whole Juice** button.

Nutritional Information

Yields: 2 cups
Serving Size: ½ cup

Amount per serving

Calories: 50.16	Potassium: 169.63 mg
3.57% from Fat	Magnesium: 8.38 mg
3.78% from Protein	Zinc: .09 mg
92.60% from Carb	Copper: .05 mg
Protein: .53 g	Manganese: .49 mg
Total Fat: .22 g	Vitamin A: 70.86 IU
Saturated Fat: .06 g	Vitamin E: 0.00 mg
Monosaturated Fat: .01 g	Thiamin: .05 mg
Polyunsaturated: .08 g	Riboflavin: .05 mg
Cholesterol: 0.00 mg	Niacin: .39 mg
Carbohydrates: 12.93 g	Pantothenic Acid: .07 mg
Fiber: 1.57 g	Vitamin B6: .07 mg
Calcium: 15.28 mg	Folate: 11.23 ug
Phosphorous: 11.78 mg	Vitamin B12: 0.00 ug
Iron: .55 mg	Vitamin C: 24.60 mg
Sodium: 2.03 mg	Selenium: .43 ug
Sugar: 9.99mg	

Tropical Juice Blend

1 cup cranberry juice cocktail

¼ lemon - peeled

1 cup pineapple

1 cup papaya

1 cup mango

½ banana

Optional, ½ cup ice

Directions: Place ingredients in jar in order listed and secure the lid. Press the **Whole Juice** button.

Creamy Berry Grape Orange Juice

½ cup low-fat plain yogurt

1 cup grapes

2 medium oranges - peeled

1 cup frozen blackberries

Optional, ½ cup ice

Directions: Place ingredients in jar in order listed and secure the lid. Press the **Whole Juice** button.

Nutritional Information

Yields: 4 cups
Serving Size: ½ cup

Amount per serving

Calories: 55.59	Potassium: 139.87 mg
2.08% from Fat,	Magnesium: 9.23 mg
2.90% from Protein	Zinc: .07 mg
95.00% from Carb	Copper: .06 mg
Protein: .44 g	Manganese: .27 mg
Total Fat: .14 g	Vitamin A: 369.60 IU
Saturated Fat: .03 g	Vitamin E: 0.00 mg
Monosaturated Fat: .03 g	Thiamin: .04 mg
Polyunsaturated: .03 g	Riboflavin: .03 mg
Cholesterol: 0.00 mg	Niacin: .34 mg
Carbohydrates: 14.36 g	Pantothenic Acid: .19 mg
Fiber: 1.28 g	Vitamin B6: .09 mg
Calcium: 11.28 mg	Folate: 14.52 ug
Phosphorous: 7.36 mg	Vitamin B12: 0.00 ug
Iron: .16 mg	Vitamin C: 28.41 mg
Sodium: 2.20 mg	Selenium: .35 ug
Sugar: 7.07 mg	

Nutritional Information

Yields: 3 cups
Serving Size: ½ cup

Amount per serving

Calories: 60.85	Potassium: 231.24 mg
3.84% from Fat,	Magnesium: 15.58 mg
13.20% from Protein	Zinc: .37 mg
83.00% from Carb	Copper: .08 mg
Protein: 2.18 g	Manganese: .28 mg
Total Fat: .28 g	Vitamin A: 206.12 IU
Saturated Fat: .05 g	Vitamin E: .41 mg
Monosaturated Fat: .04 g	Thiamin: .08 mg
Polyunsaturated: .10 g	Riboflavin: .09 mg
Cholesterol: .41 mg	Niacin: .40 mg
Carbohydrates: 13.71 g	Pantothenic Acid: .35 mg
Fiber: 2.88 g	Vitamin B6: .07 mg
Calcium: 74.27 mg	Folate: 27.46 ug
Phosphorous: 47.45 mg	Vitamin B12: .12 ug
Iron: .27 mg	Vitamin C: 38.47 mg
Sodium: 16.27 mg	Selenium: 1.15 ug
Sugar: 10.97 mg	

Grape Pineapple Berry Juice

2 cups grapes

2 cups pineapple

1 cup frozen raspberries*

Directions: Place ingredients in jar in order as listed and secure the lid. Press the **Whole Juice** button.

*May substitute blackberries or strawberries

Orange Strawberry Juice

2 oranges – peeled, halved

2 cups strawberries

½ cup ice

Directions: Place ingredients in jar in order as listed and secure the lid. Press the **Whole Juice** button.

Nutritional Information

Yields: 4 cups
Serving Size: ½ cup

Amount per serving

Calories: 43.68	Potassium: 129.38 mg
2.91% from Fat	Magnesium: 8.84 mg
3.88% from Protein	Zinc: .08 mg
93.20% from Carb	Copper: .06 mg
Protein: .47 g	Manganese: .70 mg
Total Fat: .16 g	Vitamin A: 57.13 IU
Saturated Fat: .03 g	Vitamin E: 0.00 mg
Monosaturated Fat: .01 g	Thiamin: .06 mg
Polyunsaturated: .05 g	Riboflavin: .04 mg
Cholesterol: 0.00 mg	Niacin: .39 mg
Carbohydrates: 11.36 g	Pantothenic Acid: .11 mg
Fiber: 1.33 g	Vitamin B6: .08 mg
Calcium: 12.68 mg	Folate: 11.43 ug
Phosphorous: 8.99 mg	Vitamin B12: 0.00 ug
Iron: .38 mg	Vitamin C: 26.33 mg
Sodium: 1.40 mg	Selenium: .26 ug
Sugar: 8.59 mg	

Nutritional Information

Yields: 3 cups
Serving Size: ½ cup

Amount per serving

Calories: 45.04	Potassium: 188.53 mg
4.05% from Fat	Magnesium: 12.72 mg
7.32% from Protein	Zinc: .11 mg
88.60% from Carb	Copper: .05 mg
Protein: .92 g	Manganese: .21 mg
Total Fat: .23 g	Vitamin A: 144.08 IU
Saturated Fat: .02 g	Vitamin E: 0.00 mg
Monosaturated Fat: .04 g	Thiamin: .07 mg
Polyunsaturated: .09 g	Riboflavin: .04 mg
Cholesterol: 0.00 mg	Niacin: .37 mg
Carbohydrates: 11.10 g	Pantothenic Acid: .22 mg
Fiber: 2.49 g	Vitamin B6: .06 mg
Calcium: 32.64 mg	Folate: 30.56 ug
Phosphorous: 20.75 mg	Vitamin B12: 0.00 ug
Iron: .27 mg	Vitamin C: 62.42 mg
Sodium: .51 mg	Selenium: .51 ug
Sugar: 8.10 mg	

Orange Apple Juice

¼ cup cold water

2 oranges - peeled, halved

1 apple - cored and cut into eighths

Optional, ½ cup ice

Directions: Place ingredients in jar in order as listed and secure the lid. Press the **Whole Juice** button.

Mixed Berry Banana Drink

¼ cup light vanilla soy milk

2 Tbsp apple sauce

2 Tbsp frozen orange pineapple juice concentrate

½ banana – peeled

¼ cup mixed blackberries and raspberries

Optional, ¼ cup ice

Directions: Place ingredients in jar in order listed and secure the lid. Press the **Whole Juice** button.

Nutritional Information

Yields: 2 cups
Serving Size: ½ cup

Amount per serving

Calories: 58.60	Potassium: 195.32 mg
2.11% from Fat	Magnesium: 10.63 mg
5.88% from Protein	Zinc: .08 mg
92.00% from Carb	Copper: .05 mg
Protein: .95 g	Manganese: .04 mg
Total Fat: .15 g	Vitamin A: 219.16 IU
Saturated Fat: .02 g	Vitamin E: 0.00 mg
Monosaturated Fat: .02 g	Thiamin: .09 mg
Polyunsaturated: .03 g	Riboflavin: .05 mg
Cholesterol: 0.00 mg	Niacin: .29 mg
Carbohydrates: 14.89 g	Pantothenic Acid: .25 mg
Fiber: 2.62 g	Vitamin B6: .07 mg
Calcium: 38.70 mg	Folate: 27.60 ug
Phosphorous: 16.40 mg	Vitamin B12: 0.00 ug
Iron: .11 mg	Vitamin C: 50.22 mg
Sodium: .30 mg	Selenium: .46 ug
Sugar: 11.83 mg	

Nutritional Information

Yields: 1 cup
Serving Size: ½ cup

Amount per serving

Calories: 98.72	Potassium: 290.12 mg
8.24% from Fat	Magnesium: 20.27 mg
6.86% from Protein	Zinc: .22 mg
84.90% from Carb	Copper: .10 mg
Protein: 1.82 g	Manganese: .28 mg
Total Fat: .97 g	Vitamin A: 57.35 IU
Saturated Fat: .13 g	Vitamin E: 0.00 mg
Monosaturated Fat: .16 g	Thiamin: .14 mg
Polyunsaturated: .38 g	Riboflavin: .08 mg
Cholesterol: 0.00 mg	Niacin: .43 mg
Carbohydrates: 22.51 g	Pantothenic Acid: .20 mg
Fiber: 2.58 g	Vitamin B6: .16 mg
Calcium: 31.21 mg	Folate: 17.43 ug
Phosphorous: 42.00 mg	Vitamin B12: 0.00 ug
Iron: .48 mg	Vitamin C: 50.34 mg
Sodium: 12.92 mg	Selenium: .93 ug
Sugar: 12.91 mg	

Homemade Fruit Cocktail

½ cup cold water

1 orange – peeled and quartered

1 cup strawberries

1 cup peaches - peeled and quartered

1 Tbsp sugar

½ banana – peeled

Optional, ½ cup ice

Directions: Place ingredients in jar in order listed and secure the lid. Press the **Whole Juice** button.

Apple Apricot Refresher

1 cup apple juice

8 oz. plain yogurt

4 apricots – pitted and quartered

1 Tbsp sugar

1 apple – cored and cut into eighths

½ banana – peeled

Directions: Place ingredients in jar in order listed and secure the lid. Press the **Whole Juice** button.

Nutritional Information

Yields: 3 cups
Serving Size: ½ cup

Amount per serving

Calories: 45.53	Potassium: 145.26 mg
3.36% from Fat	Magnesium: 9.42 mg
4.48% from Protein	Zinc: .10 mg
92.20% from Carb	Copper: .04 mg
Protein: .56 g	Manganese: .15 mg
Total Fat: .19 g	Vitamin A: 186.74 IU
Saturated Fat: .02 g	Vitamin E: 0.00 mg
Monosaturated Fat: .03 g	Thiamin: .02 mg
Polyunsaturated: .07 g	Riboflavin: .05 mg
Cholesterol: 0.00 mg	Niacin: .74mg
Carbohydrates: 11.60 g	Pantothenic Acid: .12 mg
Fiber: 1.27 g	Vitamin B6: .10 mg
Calcium: 22.15 mg	Folate: 9.71 ug
Phosphorous: 21.54 mg	Vitamin B12: 0.00 ug
Iron: .21 mg	Vitamin C: 27.85 mg
Sodium: 1.11 mg	Selenium: .25 ug
Sugar: 8.84 mg	

Nutritional Information

Yields: 4 cups
Serving Size: ½ cup

Amount per serving

Calories: 51.59	Potassium: 149.92 mg
16.80% from Fat,	Magnesium: 8.63 mg
9.08% from Protein	Zinc: .21 mg
74.10% from Carb	Copper: .03 mg
Protein: 1.23 g	Manganese: .06 mg
Total Fat: 1.01 g	Vitamin A: 103.24 IU
Saturated Fat: .61 g	Vitamin E: 7.66 mg
Monosaturated Fat: .26 g	Thiamin: .02 mg
Polyunsaturated: .05 g	Riboflavin: .06 mg
Cholesterol: 3.69 mg	Niacin: .16 mg
Carbohydrates: 10.05 g	Pantothenic Acid: .18 mg
Fiber: .61 g	Vitamin B6: .06 mg
Calcium: 38.36 mg	Folate: 4.04 ug
Phosphorous: 34.11 mg	Vitamin B12: .10 ug
Iron: .17 mg	Vitamin C: 1.79 mg
Sodium: 15.41 mg	Selenium: .79 ug
Sugar: 8.29 mg	

Orange Banana Strawberry Juice

1 orange – peeled and quartered

1 cup strawberries

1 banana – peeled and broken in half

Optional, ½ cup ice

Directions: Place ingredients in jar in order listed and secure the lid. Press the **Whole Juice** button.

Pineapple Juice

2 ½ cups pineapple

1 tsp sugar

1 cup ice

Directions: Cut the pineapple into pieces no bigger than 2 inches square. Place the pineapple down towards the blade, at the bottom of the jar. Place other ingredients in jar in order listed and secure the lid. Press the **Whole Juice** button.

Nutritional Information

Yields: 2 ½ cups
Serving Size: ½ cup

Amount per serving

Calories: 54.73	Potassium: 163.41 mg
2.84% from Fat,	Magnesium: 12.05 mg
3.52% from Protein	Zinc: .09 mg
93.60% from Carb	Copper: .04 mg
Protein: 1.53 g	Manganese: .20 mg
Total Fat: .19 g	Vitamin A: 122.85 IU
Saturated Fat: .04 g	Vitamin E: 0.00 mg
Monosaturated Fat: .02 g	Thiamin: .02 mg
Polyunsaturated: .07 g	Riboflavin: .06 mg
Cholesterol: 0.00 mg	Niacin: .72 mg
Carbohydrates: 14.11 g	Pantothenic Acid: .14 mg
Fiber: 1.40 g	Vitamin B6: .16 mg
Calcium: 24.81 mg	Folate: 13.30 ug
Phosphorous: 22.35 mg	Vitamin B12: 0.00 ug
Iron: .21 mg	Vitamin C: 32.48 mg
Sodium: 1.00 mg	Selenium: .42 ug
Sugar: 9.60 mg	

Nutritional Information

Yields: 2 cups
Serving Size: ½ cup

Amount per serving

Calories: 46.50	Potassium: 111.41 mg
2.01% from Fat	Magnesium: 11.63 mg
4.02% from Protein	Zinc: .10 mg
94.00% from Carb	Copper: .10 mg
Protein: .52 g	Manganese: 1.14 mg
Total Fat: .12 g	Vitamin A: 54.25 IU
Saturated Fat: .01 g	Vitamin E: 0.00 mg
Monosaturated Fat: .01 g	Thiamin: .08 mg
Polyunsaturated: .04 g	Riboflavin: .03 mg
Cholesterol: 0.00 mg	Niacin: .47 mg
Carbohydrates: 12.24 g	Pantothenic Acid: .20 mg
Fiber: 1.36 g	Vitamin B6: .11 mg
Calcium: 12.59 mg	Folate: 14.53 ug
Phosphorous: 7.75 mg	Vitamin B12: 0.00 ug
Iron: .27 mg	Vitamin C: 35.07 mg
Sodium: .97 mg	Selenium: .10 ug
Sugar: 8.97 mg	

Citrus Punch

¾ cup cranberry juice cocktail

½ cup club soda

½ orange – peeled

¼ cup pineapple

¼ cup strawberries

¼ banana – peeled

½ cup ice

Directions: Place ingredients in jar in order listed and secure the lid. Press the **Whole Juice** button.

Nutritional Information

Yields: 3 cups
Serving Size: ½ cup

Amount per serving

Calories: 36.34	Potassium: 49.54 mg
1.84% from Fat	Magnesium: 4.12 mg
1.51% from Protein	Zinc: .07 mg
96.70% from Carb	Copper: .02 mg
Protein: .15 g	Manganese: .18 mg
Total Fat: .08 g	Vitamin A: 51.31 IU
Saturated Fat: .01 g	Vitamin E: 0.00 mg
Monosaturated Fat: .01 g	Thiamin: .01 mg
Polyunsaturated: .03 g	Riboflavin: .02 mg
Cholesterol: 0.00 mg	Niacin: .28 mg
Carbohydrates: 9.33 g	Pantothenic Acid: .06 mg
Fiber: .42 g	Vitamin B6: .06 mg
Calcium: 11.79 mg	Folate: 3.74 ug
Phosphorous: 7.57 mg	Vitamin B12: 0.00 ug
Iron: .11 mg	Vitamin C: 22.80 mg
Sodium: 5.13 mg	Selenium: .09 ug
Sugar: 7.81mg	

Cran Grape Juice

½ medium grapefruit – peeled and quartered

½ cup cranberry juice cocktail

1 cup ginger ale

1 Tbsp sugar

½ cup ice

Directions: Place ingredients in jar in order listed and secure the lid. Press the **Whole Juice** button.

Nutritional Information

Yields: 2 ½ cups
Serving Size: ½ cup

Amount per serving

Calories: 41.64	Potassium: 51.19 mg
1.20% from Fat	Magnesium: 3.65mg
1.91% from Protein	Zinc: .07 mg
96.90% from Carb	Copper: .03 mg
Protein: .21 g	Manganese: .06 mg
Total Fat: .06 g	Vitamin A: 308.78 IU
Saturated Fat: .01 g	Vitamin E: 0.00 mg
Monosaturated Fat: .01 g	Thiamin: .01 mg
Polyunsaturated: .02 g	Riboflavin: .01 mg
Cholesterol: 0.00 mg	Niacin: .09 mg
Carbohydrates: 10.61 g	Pantothenic Acid: .11 mg
Fiber: .39 g	Vitamin B6: .02 mg
Calcium: 6.21 mg	Folate: 3.32 ug
Phosphorous: 3.16 mg	Vitamin B12: 0.00 ug
Iron: .16 mg	Vitamin C: 20.38 mg
Sodium: 3.92 mg	Selenium: .15 ug
Sugar: 9.98 mg	

Cider Burst

¼ cup apple cider

½ orange – peeled, halved

½ cup pineapple

½ apple – quartered

½ tsp honey

1 cup ice

Directions: Place ingredients in jar in order listed and secure the lid. Press the **Whole Juice** button.

Nutritional Information

Yields: 2 ½ cups
Serving Size: ½ cup

Amount per serving

Calories: 100.72	Potassium: 35.81 mg
0.31% from Fat	Magnesium: 2.39 mg
0.47% from Protein	Zinc: .02 mg
99.20% from Carb	Copper: .02 mg
Protein: .12 g	Manganese: .19 mg
Total Fat: .04 g	Vitamin A: 63.54 IU
Saturated Fat: 0.00 g	Vitamin E: 0.00 mg
Monosaturated Fat: 0.00 g	Thiamin: .01 mg
Polyunsaturated: .01 g	Riboflavin: .03 mg
Cholesterol: 0.00 mg	Niacin: .29 mg
Carbohydrates: 25.60 g	Pantothenic Acid: .04 mg
Fiber: .41 g	Vitamin B6: .04 mg
Calcium: 101.20 mg	Folate: 2.34 ug
Phosphorous: 31.86 mg	Vitamin B12: 0.00 ug
Iron: .07 mg	Vitamin C: 81.82 mg
Sodium: 18.62 mg	Selenium: .14 ug
Sugar: 21.11 mg	

Citrus Grape Juice

1 ½ oranges – peeled, halved

2 Tbsp frozen orange juice concentrate

¾ cup pineapple*

⅓ cup white grape juice

⅓ cup club soda

½ cup ice

Directions: Place ingredients in jar in order listed and secure the lid. Press the **Whole Juice** button.

*Pineapple should be cut into pieces no bigger than 2 inches square.

Nutritional Information

Yields: 3 ½ cups
Serving Size: ½ cup

Amount per serving

Calories: 39.04	Potassium: 142.87 mg
1.91% from Fat	Magnesium: 8.95 mg
6.08% from Protein	Zinc: .08 mg
92.00% from Carb	Copper: .05 mg
Protein: .64 g	Manganese: .21 mg
Total Fat: .09 g	Vitamin A: 118.06 IU
Saturated Fat: .01 g	Vitamin E: 0.00 mg
Monosaturated Fat: .01 g	Thiamin: .07 mg
Polyunsaturated: .02 g	Riboflavin: .03 mg
Cholesterol: 0.00 mg	Niacin: .26 mg
Carbohydrates: 9.72 g	Pantothenic Acid: .18 mg
Fiber: 1.23 g	Vitamin B6: .05 mg
Calcium: 20.94 mg	Folate: 23.36 ug
Phosphorous: 11.03 mg	Vitamin B12: 0.00 ug
Iron: .13 mg	Vitamin C: 37.42 mg
Sodium: 2.80 mg	Selenium: .25 ug
Sugar: 8.16 mg	

Apple Juice

⅓ cup cold water

4 medium apples – cored and cut into eighths

2 double layers of cheesecloth

Directions: Place ingredients in jar in order listed and secure the lid. Press the **Whole Juice** button. Transfer apple juice to a bowl lined with cheesecloth. Grab hold of cheesecloth and twist until juice is extracted into bowl. Place juice in pitcher and refrigerate for at least 5 minutes.

Sweetened Orange Juice

¼ cup water

2 oranges – peeled and quartered

¼ tsp vanilla extract

1 Tbsp sugar

¾ cup ice

Directions: Place ingredients in jar in order as listed and secure the lid. Press the **Whole Juice** button.

Nutritional Information

Yields: 3 cups
Serving Size: ½ cup

Amount per serving

Calories: 40.96	Potassium: 76.80 mg
2.20% from Fat	Magnesium: 3.55 mg
2.03% from Protein	Zinc: .04 mg
95.80% from Carb	Copper: .03 mg
Protein: .23 g	Manganese: .03 mg
Total Fat: .11 g	Vitamin A: 32.43 IU
Saturated Fat: .02 g	Vitamin E: 0.00 mg
Monosaturated Fat: 0.00 g	Thiamin: .02 mg
Polyunsaturated: .03 g	Riboflavin: .02 mg
Cholesterol: 0.00 mg	Niacin: .08 mg
Carbohydrates: 10.89 g	Pantothenic Acid: .06 mg
Fiber: 1.11 g	Vitamin B6: .03 mg
Calcium: 4.53 mg	Folate: 0.00 ug
Phosphorous: 9.39 mg	Vitamin B12: 0.00 ug
Iron: .06 mg	Vitamin C: 3.41 mg
Sodium: .26 mg	Selenium: 0.00 ug
Sugar: 8.62 mg	

Nutritional Information

Yields: 2 cups
Serving Size: ½ cup

Amount per serving

Calories: 44.02	Potassium: 166.92 mg
2.08% from Fat	Magnesium: 9.38 mg
7.23% from Protein	Zinc: .06 mg
90.70% from Carb	Copper: .04 mg
Protein: .86 g	Manganese: .02 mg
Total Fat: .11 g	Vitamin A: 207.00 IU
Saturated Fat: .01 g	Vitamin E: 0.00 mg
Monosaturated Fat: .02 g	Thiamin: .08 mg
Polyunsaturated: .02 g	Riboflavin: .04 mg
Cholesterol: 0.00 mg	Niacin: .26 mg
Carbohydrates: 10.84 g	Pantothenic Acid: .23 mg
Fiber: 2.21 g	Vitamin B6: .06 mg
Calcium: 37.13 mg	Folate: 27.60 ug
Phosphorous: 12.90 mg	Vitamin B12: 0.00 ug
Iron: .09 mg	Vitamin C: 48.94 mg
Sodium: .32 mg	Selenium: .46 ug
Sugar: 8.64 mg	

Grape Juice

4 cups grapes*

Optional, ½ cup ice

Directions: Place ingredient(s) in jar in order as listed and secure the lid. Press the **Whole Juice** button.

*Grapes may contain seeds, or may be seedless

Nutritional Information

Yields: 4 cups
Serving Size: ½ cup

Amount per serving

Calories: 30.82	Potassium: 87.86 mg
4.24% from Fat	Magnesium: 2.30 mg
3.39% from Protein	Zinc: .02 mg
92.40% from Carb	Copper: .02 mg
Protein: .29 g	Manganese: .33 mg
Total Fat: .16 g	Vitamin A: 46.00 IU
Saturated Fat: .05 g	Vitamin E: 0.00 mg
Monosaturated Fat: .01 g	Thiamin: .04 mg
Polyunsaturated: .05 g	Riboflavin: .03 mg
Cholesterol: 0.00 mg	Niacin: .14 mg
Carbohydrates: 7.89 g	Pantothenic Acid: .01 mg
Fiber: .41 g	Vitamin B6: .05 mg
Calcium: 6.44 mg	Folate: 1.84 ug
Phosphorous: 4.60 mg	Vitamin B12: 0.00 ug
Iron: .13 mg	Vitamin C: 1.84 mg
Sodium: .92 mg	Selenium: .05 ug
Sugar: 7.47 mg	

Kiwi Grape Juice

2 cups grapes

1 cup kiwi – peeled

Optional, ½ cup ice

Directions: Place ingredients in jar in order as listed and secure the lid. Press the **Whole Juice** button.

Nutritional Information

Yields: 3 cups
Serving Size: ½ cup

Amount per serving

Calories: 59.09	Potassium: 209.19 mg
5.05% from Fat	Magnesium: 8.08 mg
4.41% from Protein	Zinc: .07 mg
90.50% from Carb	Copper: .06 mg
Protein: .72 g	Manganese: .47 mg
Total Fat: .37 g	Vitamin A: 87.00 IU
Saturated Fat: .08 g	Vitamin E: 0.00 mg
Monosaturated Fat: .02 g	Thiamin: .06 mg
Polyunsaturated: .15 g	Riboflavin: .04 mg
Cholesterol: 0.00 mg	Niacin: .28 mg
Carbohydrates: 14.84 g	Pantothenic Acid: .07 mg
Fiber: 1.44 g	Vitamin B6: .09 mg
Calcium: 18.62 mg	Folate: 9.83 ug
Phosphorous: 16.16 mg	Vitamin B12: 0.00 ug
Iron: .27 mg	Vitamin C: 29.80 mg
Sodium: 2.11 mg	Selenium: .12 ug
Sugar: 12.62 mg	

Tomato Broccoli Juice

1 cup any type of grapes - washed

3 large tomatoes, quartered - leave seeds

½ cup fresh broccoli

Directions: Place ingredients in jar and secure the lid. Press the **Whole Juice** button.

Nutritional Information

Yield: 4 cups
Serving Size: 1 cup

Amount per serving

Calories: 24	Magnesium: 8 mg
6% from Fat,	Zinc: 0 mg
13% from Protein	Copper: 0 mg
81% from Carb	Manganese: 0 mg
Protein: 1 g	Vitamin A: 237 mg
Total Fat: 0 g	Vitamin E: 0 mg
Saturated Fat: 0 g	Thiamin: 0 mg
Monosaturated Fat: 0 g	Riboflavin: 0 mg
Cholesterol: 0 mg	Niacin: 0 mg
Carbohydrates: 6 g	Pantothenic Acid: 0 mg
Fiber: 1 g	Vitamin B6: 0 mg
Sugar: 5 g	Folate: 15 ug
Calcium: 16 mg	Vitamin B12: 0 ug
Iron: 0 mg	Vitamin C: 13 mg
Sodium: 37 mg	Selenium: 1 ug
Cholesterol: 0 mg	
Potassium: 137 mg	

Tomato Carrot Juice

¼ cup water

1 medium orange - peeled and halved

1 carrot - cut into 3-inch pieces

½ cup broccoli

½ cup Ice

Directions: Place ingredients in jar and secure the lid. Press the **Whole Juice** button.

Nutritional Information

Yield: 3 ½ cups
Serving Size: 1 cup

Amount per serving

Calories: 27	Magnesium: 8 mg
3% from Fat	Zinc: 0 mg
13% from Protein	Copper: 0 mg
84% from Carb	Manganese: 0 mg
Protein: 1 g	Vitamin A: 304 mg
Total Fat: 0 g	Vitamin E: 0 mg
Saturated Fat: 0 g	Thiamin: 0 mg
Monosaturated Fat: 0 g	Riboflavin: 0 mg
Cholesterol: 0 mg	Niacin: 0 mg
Carbohydrates: 6 g	Pantothenic Acid: 0 mg
Fiber: 2 g	Vitamin B6: 0 mg
Calcium: 30 mg	Folate: 27 ug
Phosphorous: 16 mg	Vitamin B12: 0 ug
Iron: 0 mg	Vitamin C: 35 mg
Sodium: 5 mg	Selenium: 1 ug
Sugar: 5 mg	
Potassium: 125 mg	

Creamy Cucumber Juice

½ cup low-fat plain yogurt

3 cups green grapes - with or without seeds

½ cup cucumber - with or without peel, chopped

1 stalk celery cut into 3-inch pieces

Optional, 1 oz. wheat grass

½ cup ice

Directions: Place ingredients in jar and secure the lid. Press the **Whole Juice** button.

Chilled Broccoli Juice

3 cups washed green grapes

½ cup broccoli

¼ medium avocado, peeled

1 cup sweet peas, frozen or fresh

½ cup ice

Directions: Place ingredients in jar and secure the lid. Press the **Whole Juice** button.

Nutritional Information

Yield: 3 ½ cups
Serving Size: 1 cup

Amount per serving

Calories: 67	Magnesium: 10 mg
9% from Fat	Zinc: 0 mg
12% from Protein	Copper: 0 mg
79% from Carb	Manganese: 1 mg
Protein: 2 g	Vitamin A: 98 IU
Total Fat: 1 g	Vitamin E: 4 mg
Saturated Fat: 0 g	Thiamin: 0 mg
Monosaturated Fat: 0 g	Riboflavin: 0 mg
Cholesterol: 2 mg	Niacin: 0 mg
Carbohydrates: 14g	Pantothenic Acid: 0 mg
Fiber: 1 g	Vitamin B6: 0 mg
Calcium: 68 mg	Folate: 7 ug
Phosphorous: 54 mg	Vitamin B12: 0 ug
Iron: 0 mg	Vitamin C: 3 mg
Sodium: 23 mg	Selenium: 1 ug
Sugar: 14 mg	
Potassium: 223 mg	

Nutritional Information

Yield: 3 cups
Serving Size: 1 cup

Amount per serving

Calories: 123	Magnesium: 29 mg
23% from Fat	Zinc: 0 mg
10% from Protein	Copper: 0 mg
67% from Carb	Manganese: 1 mg
Protein: 3 g	Vitamin A: 966 IU
Total Fat: 3 g	Vitamin E: 0 mg
Saturated Fat: 1 g	Thiamin: 0 mg
Monosaturated Fat: 2 g	Riboflavin: 0 mg
Cholesterol: 0 mg	Niacin: 1 mg
Carbohydrates: 22 g	Pantothenic Acid: 1 mg
Fiber: 4 g	Vitamin B6: 0 mg
Calcium: 52 mg	Folate: 48 ug
Phosphorous: 62 mg	Vitamin B12: 0 ug
Iron: 2 mg	Vitamin C: 46 mg
Sodium: 12 mg	Selenium: 1 ug
Sugar: 17 mg	
Potassium: 456 mg	

Green Giant Vegetable Juice

¼ cup water

3 cups green grapes - with or without seeds

½ cup fresh cucumber

½ cup frozen or fresh sweet peas

1 stalk celery - cut into approximately 3-inch pieces

½ cup broccoli

Directions: Place ingredients in jar and secure the lid. Press the **Whole Juice** button.

Nutritional Information

Yield: 3 cups
Serving Size: 1 cup

Amount per serving

Calories: 202	Magnesium: 34 mg
58% from Fat,	Zinc: 1 mg
6% from Protein	Copper: 0 mg
36% from Carb	Manganese: 1 mg
Protein: 3 g	Vitamin A: 397 IU
Total Fat: 14 g	Vitamin E: 0 mg
Saturated Fat: 1 g	Thiamin: 0 mg
Monosaturated Fat: 8 g	Riboflavin: 0 mg
Cholesterol: 0 mg	Niacin: 1 mg
Carbohydrates: 20 g	Pantothenic Acid: 0 mg
Fiber: 3 g	Vitamin B6: 0 mg
Calcium: 42 mg	Folate: 25 ug
Phosphorous: 75 mg	Vitamin B12: 0 ug
Iron: 1 mg	Vitamin C: 19 mg
Sodium: 9 mg	Selenium: 2 ug
Sugar: 16 mg	
Potassium: 328 mg	

Veggie Cocktail

½ cup plain nonfat yogurt

½ cup peeled cucumber

¼ cup fresh broccoli

¾ cup frozen peas

⅛ tsp garlic powder

¼ cup ice cubes

Directions: Place ingredients in jar and secure the lid. Press the **Whole Juice** button.

Nutritional Information

Yield: 2 cups
Serving Size: 1 cup

Amount per serving

Calories: 95	Magnesium: 30 mg
3% from Fat	Zinc: 1 mg
17% from Protein	Copper: 0 mg
80% from Carb	Manganese: 0 mg
Protein: 4 g	Vitamin A: 539 IU
Total Fat: 0 g	Vitamin E: 0 mg
Saturated Fat: 0 g	Thiamin: 0 mg
Monosaturated Fat: 0 g	Riboflavin: 0 mg
Cholesterol: 0 mg	Niacin: 1 mg
Carbohydrates: 19 g	Pantothenic Acid: 0 mg
Fiber: 5 g	Vitamin B6: 0 mg
Calcium: 29 mg	Folate: 52 ug
Phosphorous: 85 mg	Vitamin B12: 0 ug
Iron: 1 mg	Vitamin C: 21 mg
Sodium: 281 mg	Selenium: 1 ug
Sugar: 1 mg	
Potassium: 409 mg	

Red Vegetable Juice

1 cup apple juice

½ cucumber - peeled

1 stalk celery - cut into 3-inch pieces

1 ½ cup carrots - chopped

¼ radish 1 apple - cored and cut into eighths

½ Tbsp dried parsley

¼ cup ice

Directions: Place ingredients in jar and secure the lid. Press the **Whole Juice** button.

Carrot Ginger Cider

1 cup apple juice

1 large carrot - halved

¼ tsp fresh ginger root - peeled

1 sprig parsley

½ cup frozen cider cubes

Directions: Place ingredients in jar and secure the lid. Press the **Whole Juice** button.

Nutritional Information

Yield: 3 ½ cups
Serving Size: 1 cup

Amount per serving

Calories: 49	Magnesium: 8 mg
3% from Fat	Zinc: 0 mg
4% from Protein	Copper: 0 mg
93% from Carb	Manganese: 0 mg
Protein: 1 g	Vitamin A: 5,794 IU
Total Fat: 0 g	Vitamin E: 0 mg
Saturated Fat: 0 g	Thiamin: 0 mg
Monosaturated Fat: 0 g	Riboflavin: 0 mg
Cholesterol: 0 mg	Niacin: 1 mg
Carbohydrates: 12 g	Pantothenic Acid: 0 mg
Fiber: 2 g	Vitamin B6: 0 mg
Calcium: 23 mg	Folate: 10 ug
Phosphorous: 22 mg	Vitamin B12: 0 ug
Iron: 1 mg	Vitamin C: 4 mg
Sodium: 36 mg	Selenium: 0 ug
Sugar: 9 mg	
Potassium: 235 mg	

Nutritional Information

Yield: 2 cups
Serving Size: 1 cup

Amount per serving

Calories: 33	Magnesium: 9 mg
5% from Fat	Zinc: 0 mg
10% from Protein	Copper: 0 mg
86% from Carb	Manganese: 0 mg
Protein: 1 g	Vitamin A: 2380 IU
Total Fat: 0 g	Vitamin E: 0 mg
Saturated Fat: 0 g	Thiamin: 0 mg
Monosaturated Fat: 0 g	Riboflavin: 0 mg
Cholesterol: 0 mg	Niacin: 0 mg
Carbohydrates: 8 g	Pantothenic Acid: 0 mg
Fiber: 2 g	Vitamin B6: 0 mg
Calcium: 10 mg	Folate: 2 ug
Phosphorous: 16 mg	Vitamin B12: 0 ug
Iron: 0 mg	Vitamin C: 4 mg
Sodium: 4 mg	Selenium: 0 ug
Sugar: 6 mg	
Potassium: 233 mg	

Carrot Milk

1 cup skim milk

2 large carrots - cut in half

¼ cup ice cubes

Directions: Place ingredients in jar in order listed above. Place carrots standing in jar. Press **Whole Juice** button.

Nutritional Information

Yield: 2 cups
Serving Size: 1cup

Amount per serving

Calories: 58	Magnesium: 21 mg
5% from Fat	Zinc: 1 mg
36% from Protein	Copper: 0 mg
59% from Carb	Manganese: 0 mg
Protein: 5 g	Vitamin A: 2318 mg
Total Fat: 0 g	Vitamin E: 75 mg
Saturated Fat: 0 g	Thiamin: 0 mg
Monosaturated Fat: 0 g	Riboflavin: 0 mg
Cholesterol: 2 mg	Niacin: 0 mg
Carbohydrates: 8 g	Pantothenic Acid: 1 mg
Fiber: 0 g	Vitamin B6: 0 mg
Calcium: 181 mg	Folate: 12 ug
Phosphorous: 142 mg	Vitamin B12: 1 ug
Iron: 0 mg	Vitamin C: 3 mg
Sodium: 84 mg	Selenium: 3 ug
Sugar: 1 mg	
Potassium: 259 mg	

Carrot Juice Plus

1 cup water

1 ½ cup carrots - chopped

2 tsps fresh lemon juice or lemonade concentrate

1 cup ice cubes

Directions: Place ingredients in jar and secure the lid. Press the **Whole Juice** button.

Nutritional Information

Yield: 2 ½ cups
Serving Size: 1 cup

Amount per serving

Calories: 32.66	Magnesium: 15.44 mg
5.57% from Fat,	Zinc: .24 mg
12.70% from Protein	Copper: .06 mg
81.70% from Carb	Manganese: .11 mg
Protein: 1.14 g	Vitamin A: .97 IU
Total Fat: .22 g	Vitamin E: 0 mg
Saturated Fat: 0 g	Thiamin: .03 mg
Monosaturated Fat: 0 g	Riboflavin: .04 mg
Cholesterol: 0 mg	Niacin: .50 mg
Carbohydrates: 7.30 g	Pantothenic Acid: .24 mg
Fiber: .02 g	Vitamin B6: .12 mg
Calcium: 32.95 mg	Folate: 4.15 ug
Phosphorous: 77.03 mg	Vitamin B12: 0 ug
Iron: .50 mg	Vitamin C: 6.52 mg
Sodium: 347.68 mg	Selenium: .47 ug
Sugar: .12 mg	
Potassium: 207.42 mg	

Fresh Vegetable Juice

¼ cup water

3 large tomatoes - quartered

¼ medium onion

1 stalk celery - cut into approximately 3-inch pieces

1 small carrot - cut into approximately 3-inch pieces

¼ cup ice

Directions: Place ingredients in blender in order as listed above. Secure lid and press the **Whole Juice** button.

Zesty Tomato Juice

3 large tomatoes - quartered

¼ lemon - peeled

1 cup cucumbers

½ cup frozen sweet peas

Directions: Place ingredient in order as listed above. Secure lid and press the **Whole Juice** button.

Nutritional Information

Yield: 3 cups
Serving Size: 1 cup

Amount per serving

Calories: 72.12	Potassium: 734.04 mg
7.03% from Fat	Magnesium: 36.43 mg
14.10% from Protein	Zinc: .59 mg
78.90% from Carb	Copper: .17 mg
Protein: 2.86 g	Manganese: .36 mg
Total Fat: .63 g	Vitamin A: 5506.48 mg
Saturated Fat: .14 g	Vitamin E: 0.00 mg
Monosaturated Fat: .13 g	Thiamin: .12 mg
Polyunsaturated: .38 g	Riboflavin: .09 mg
Cholesterol: 0.00 mg	Niacin: 1.86 mg
Carbohydrates: 15.97 g	Pantothenic Acid: .45 mg
Fiber: 4.33 g	Vitamin B6: .29 mg
Calcium: 53.52 mg	Folate: 40.67 ug
Phosphorous: 119.58 mg	Vitamin B12: 0.00 ug
Iron: 1.00 mg	Vitamin C: 31.49 mg
Sodium: 84.11 mg	Selenium: .41 ug
Sugar: 7.65 mg	

Nutritional Information

Yield: 4 cups
Serving Size: 1 cup

Amount per serving

Calories: 71.38	Potassium: 656.10 mg
7.55% from Fat	Magnesium: 39.67 mg
19.90% from Protein	Zinc: .70 mg
72.60% from Carb	Copper: .21 mg
Protein: 3.92 g	Manganese: .45 mg
Total Fat: .66 g	Vitamin A: 407.29 IU
Saturated Fat: .14 g	Vitamin E: 0 mg
Monosaturated Fat: .12 g	Thiamin: .17 mg
Polyunsaturated: .37 g	Riboflavin: .08 mg
Cholesterol: .00 mg	Niacin: 1.85 mg
Carbohydrates: 14.32 mg	Pantothenic Acid: .35 mg
Fiber: 4.2 g	Vitamin B6: .24 mg
Calcium: 36.05 mg	Folate: 54.66 ug
Phosphorous: 9.079 mg	Vitamin B12: 0 ug
Iron: 1.27 mg	Vitamin C: 35.64 mg
Sodium: 39.46 mg	Selenium: .57 ug
Sugar: 7.88 mg	

Tomato Treat

½ cup boiling water

1 cup tomatoes

½ Tbsp lemon juice

½ Chicken bouillon cube

Dash salt

Dash dry mustard

Directions: Place ingredients in order as listed above. Secure the lid and the press the **Whole Juice** button.

Note: For a cold cocktail, use ¾ cup ice at the end of the recipe

Nutritional Information

Yield: 1 ½ cups
Serving Size: 1 cup

Amount per serving

Calories: 16.87	Potassium: 185.56 mg
10.90% from Fat	Magnesium: 9.18 mg
17.80% from Protein	Zinc: .14 mg
71.30% from Carb	Copper: .05 mg
Protein: .86 g	Manganese: .09 mg
Total Fat: .23 g	Vitamin A: 621.42 IU
Saturated Fat: .05 g	Vitamin E: 0.00 mg
Monosaturated Fat: .06 g	Thiamin: .03 mg
Polyunsaturated: .12 g	Riboflavin: .02 mg
Cholesterol: .16 mg	Niacin: .50 mg
Carbohydrates: 3.46 g	Pantothenic Acid: .08 mg
Fiber: .91 g	Vitamin B6: .06 mg
Calcium: 10.45 mg	Folate: 11.94 ug
Phosphorous: 20.52 mg	Vitamin B12: 0.00 ug
Iron: .24 mg	Vitamin C: 10.43 mg
Sodium: 439.89 mg	Selenium: .34 ug
Sugar: 2.05 mg	

Vegetable Jubilee

⅓ cup water

5.5 ounce can V8™ Juice

¼ cup celery with leaves - cut into 3-inch pieces

¼ cup sweet green bell pepper

¼ cup sweet red bell pepper

⅓ cup broccoli

1 small sprig cilantro

½ clove garlic - peeled

¼ tsp celery salt

Dash salt

½ cup ice cubes

Directions: Place ingredients in order as listed above. Secure the lid and the press the **Whole Juice** button.

Nutritional Information

Yield: 2 cups
Serving Size: 1 cup

Amount per serving

Calories: 36.97	Potassium: 355.01 mg
6.13% from Fat,	Magnesium: 19.44 mg
17.30% from Protein	Zinc: .33 mg
76.60% from Carb	Copper: .13 mg
Protein: 1.86 g	Manganese: .26 mg
Total Fat: .29 g	Vitamin A: 962.40 IU
Saturated Fat: .05 g	Vitamin E: 0.01 mg
Monosaturated Fat: .03 g	Thiamin: .08 mg
Polyunsaturated: .11 g	Riboflavin: .08 mg
Cholesterol: 0.00mg	Niacin: .1.03 mg
Carbohydrates: 8.25 g	Pantothenic Acid: .36 mg
Fiber: 2.20 g	Vitamin B6: .26 mg
Calcium: 47.90 mg	Folate: 26.85 ug
Phosphorous: 43.55 mg	Vitamin B12: 0.00 ug
Iron: .80 mg	Vitamin C: 76.56 mg
Sodium: 468.76 mg	Selenium: 1.60 ug
Sugar: 4.04 mg	

Spicy Spinach and Celery

¼ cup cold water

5 spinach leaves

½ celery stock

4 sprigs parsley

2 small carrots or 1 large carrot

¼ apple - seeded

½ cup ice

Directions: Place ingredients in order as listed above. Secure the lid and the press the **Whole Juice** button.

Tomato Zing

1 cup boiling water

2 Roma tomatoes - quartered

½ cup carrots - chopped

1 stalk celery with leaves

¼ cup sweet red bell pepper

1 tsp dried basil

Directions: Place ingredients in order as listed above. Secure the lid and the press the **Whole Juice** button.

Note: This recipe may be turned into a Soup. Follow the above directions and press the Soup button. Optionally, add corn, peas, tortilla chips, cooked chicken, etc. to blender jar. Press the Pulse button four or five times, or until added ingredients are blended in soup to desired consistency.

Nutritional Information

Yield: 1 cup
Serving Size: 1 cup

Amount per serving

Calories: 73.30	Potassium: 614.54 mg
6.51% from Fat,	Magnesium: 52.01 mg
14.30% from Protein	Zinc: .61 mg
79.20% from Carb	Copper: .14 mg
Protein: 2.93 g	Manganese: .48 mg
Total Fat: .59 g	Vitamin A: 3641.38 IU
Saturated Fat: .05 g	Vitamin E: 0.00 mg
Monosaturated Fat: .04 g	Thiamin: .09 mg
Polyunsaturated: .11 g	Riboflavin: .15 mg
Cholesterol: 0.00 mg	Niacin: 1.13 mg
Carbohydrates: 16.21 g	Pantothenic Acid: .48 mg
Fiber: 2.30 g	Vitamin B6: .26 mg
Calcium: 98.23 mg	Folate: 89.59 ug
Phosphorous: 134.39 mg	Vitamin B12: 0.00 ug
Iron: 2.06 mg	Vitamin C: 26.66 mg
Sodium: 520.56 mg	Selenium: 1.09 ug
Sugar: 4.17 mg	

Nutritional Information

Yield: 2 cups
Serving Size: 1 cup

Amount per serving

Calories: 33.29	Potassium: 364.09 mg
7.95% from Fat	Magnesium: 18.66 mg
15.10% from Protein	Zinc: .29 mg
76.90% from Carb	Copper: 1.08 mg
Protein: 1.44 g	Manganese: .18 mg
Total Fat: .34 g	Vitamin A: 1341.49 IU
Saturated Fat: .06 g	Vitamin E: 0.00 mg
Monosaturated Fat: .05 g	Thiamin: .06 mg
Polyunsaturated: .16 g	Riboflavin: .06 mg
Cholesterol: 0.00 mg	Niacin: .90 mg
Carbohydrates: 7.30 g	Pantothenic Acid: .28 mg
Fiber: 1.77 g	Vitamin B6: .18 mg
Calcium: 31.24 mg	Folate: 26.87 ug
Phosphorous: 56.04 mg	Vitamin B12: 0.00 ug
Iron: .51 mg	Vitamin C: 47.28 mg
Sodium: 147.61 mg	Selenium: .30 ug
Sugar: 3.33 mg	

Garden Fresh Mix

1 cup fresh tomatoes - quartered

½ cup Romaine lettuce

¼ cup sliced carrots

1 Tbsp onion

1 sprig Parsley

¼ cup sweet red pepper*

⅛ tsp Tabasco sauce

½ tsp Worcerstershire sauce

⅛ tsp salt

1 cup ice cubes

Directions: Place ingredients in order as listed above. Secure the lid and the press the **Whole Juice** button.

*May use green bell pepper instead

Celery Blend

1 cup apple juice*

1 Tbsp lemon juice

½ cup celery with leaves - chopped

1 cup ice cubes

Directions: Place ingredients in order as listed above. Secure the lid and the press the **Whole Juice** button.

*See Apple Juice Recipe

Nutritional Information

Yield: 2 ½ cups
Serving Size: 1 cup

Amount per serving

Calories: 20.67	Potassium: 219.76 mg
7.77% from Fat	Magnesium: 10.52 mg
14.60% from Protein	Zinc: .18 mg
77.70% from Carb	Copper: .04 mg
Protein: .86 g	Manganese: .11 mg
Total Fat: .20 g	Vitamin A: 2737.79 IU
Saturated Fat: .04 g	Vitamin E: 0.00 mg
Monosaturated Fat: .03 g	Thiamin: .04 mg
Polyunsaturated: .12 g	Riboflavin: .04 mg
Cholesterol: 0.00 mg	Niacin: .57 mg
Carbohydrates: 4.59 g	Pantothenic Acid: .14 mg
Fiber: 1.45 g	Vitamin B6: .10 mg
Calcium: 14.98 mg	Folate: 26.94 ug
Phosphorous: 24.24 mg	Vitamin B12: 0.00 ug
Iron: .45 mg	Vitamin C: 36.15 mg
Sodium: 119.29 mg	Selenium: .08ug
Sugar: 2.58 mg	

Nutritional Information

Yield: 2 cups
Serving Size: 1 cup

Amount per serving

Calories: 64.08	Potassium: 233.34 mg
2.83% from Fat	Magnesium: 7.63 mg
1.87% from Protein	Zinc: .08 mg
95.30% from Carb	Copper: .04 mg
Protein: .31 g	Manganese: .17 mg
Total Fat: .21 g	Vitamin A: 137.08 IU
Saturated Fat: .04 g	Vitamin E: 0.00 mg
Monosaturated Fat: .02 g	Thiamin: .04 mg
Polyunsaturated: .07 g	Riboflavin: .04 mg
Cholesterol: 0.00 mg	Niacin: .24 mg
Carbohydrates: 15.87 g	Pantothenic Acid: .16 mg
Fiber: .63g	Vitamin B6: .06 mg
Calcium: 21.52 mg	Folate: 11.56 ug
Phosphorous: 16.57 mg	Vitamin B12: 0.00 ug
Iron: .53 mg	Vitamin C: 3.94 mg
Sodium: 29.32 mg	Selenium: .25 ug
Sugar: 14.25 mg	

Mega Fruit Mix

1 cup plain yogurt

1 mango - peeled, cored, and sliced

½ banana – peeled

½ cup baby carrots

1 Tbsp sugar

½ cup ice

Directions: Place ingredients in jar in order as listed and secure the lid. Press the **Whole Juice** button.

Orange Radish Cocktail

½ cup orange juice

½ orange - peeled and quartered

¼ cup radishes - cut in half

½ Tbsp sugar

½ cup ice cubes

Directions: Place ingredients in jar in order as listed and secure the lid. Press the **Whole Juice** button.

Nutritional Information

Yields: 3 cups
Serving Size: ½ cup

Amount per serving

Calories: 73.20	Potassium: 206.70 mg
17.20% from Fat	Magnesium: 13.27 mg
9.50% from Protein	Zinc: .31 mg
73.30% from Carb	Copper: .07 mg
Protein: 1.85 g	Manganese: .07 mg
Total Fat: 1.49 g	Vitamin A: 2918.66 IU
Saturated Fat: .90 g	Vitamin E: 11.02 mg
Monosaturated Fat: .40 g	Thiamin: .04 mg
Polyunsaturated: .08 g	Riboflavin: .09 mg
Cholesterol: 5.31 mg	Niacin: .42 mg
Carbohydrates: 14.28 g	Pantothenic Acid: .33 mg
Fiber: 1.29 g	Vitamin B6: .13 mg
Calcium: 59.55 mg	Folate: 16.43 ug
Phosphorous: 50.63 mg	Vitamin B12: .15 ug
Iron: .27 mg	Vitamin C: 12.44 mg
Sodium: 34.34 mg	Selenium: 1.41 ug
Sugar: 11.54 mg	

Nutritional Information

Yields: 2 cups
Serving Size: ½ cup

Amount per serving

Calories: 32.39	Potassium: 82.00 mg
2.41% from Fat	Magnesium: 4.15 mg
3.50% from Protein	Zinc: .03 mg
94.10% from Carb	Copper: .02 mg
Protein: .30 g	Manganese: .01 mg
Total Fat: .09 g	Vitamin A: 87.28 IU
Saturated Fat: .01 g	Vitamin E: 0.00 mg
Monosaturated Fat: .02 g	Thiamin: .04 mg
Polyunsaturated: .02 g	Riboflavin: .03 mg
Cholesterol: 0.00 mg	Niacin: .36 mg
Carbohydrates: 8.03 g	Pantothenic Acid: .07 mg
Fiber: .19 g	Vitamin B6: .05 mg
Calcium: 16.47 mg	Folate: 7.41 ug
Phosphorous: 10.15 mg	Vitamin B12: 0.00 ug
Iron: .08 mg	Vitamin C: 18.81 mg
Sodium: 3.39 mg	Selenium: .08 ug
Sugar: 4.55 mg	

Cucumber Apple Juice

½ cup apple juice

1 small cucumber - peeled and sliced

½ apple - cored and quartered

½ cup ice cubes

Directions: Place ingredients in jar in order as listed and secure the lid. Press the **Whole Juice** button.

Cran Beet Juice

1 cup cranberry juice cocktail - chilled

1 small radish - quartered

½ cup strawberries

1 Tbsp sugar

1 cup ice

Directions: Place ingredients in jar in order a listed and secure the lid. Press the **Whole Juice** button. Place juice in refrigerator and allow it to sit for at least 5 minutes.

Nutritional Information

Yields: 2 ½ cups
Serving Size: ½ cup

Amount per serving

Calories: 26.41	Potassium: 130.13 mg
3.30% from Fat	Magnesium: 9.53 mg
6.31% from Protein	Zinc: .14 mg
90.40% from Carb	Copper: .03 mg
Protein: .46 g	Manganese: .07 mg
Total Fat: .11 g	Vitamin A: 68.07 IU
Saturated Fat: .03 g	Vitamin E: 0.00 mg
Monosaturated Fat: 0.00 g	Thiamin: .02 mg
Polyunsaturated: .04 g	Riboflavin: .03 mg
Cholesterol: 0.00 mg	Niacin: .08 mg
Carbohydrates: 6.58 g	Pantothenic Acid: .18 mg
Fiber: .49 g	Vitamin B6: .04 mg
Calcium: 11.71 mg	Folate: 4.21 ug
Phosphorous: 17.53 mg	Vitamin B12: 0.00 ug
Iron: .24 mg	Vitamin C: 2.34 mg
Sodium: 2.88 mg	Selenium: .20 ug
Sugar: 4.91 mg	

Nutritional Information

Yields: 2 cups
Serving Size: ½ cup

Amount per serving

Calories: 56.59	Potassium: 54.94 mg
0.50% from Fat	Magnesium: 4.51 mg
0.91% from Protein	Zinc: .07 mg
98.60% from Carb	Copper: .02 mg
Protein: .13 g	Manganese: .11 mg
Total Fat: .03 g	Vitamin A: 18.84 IU
Saturated Fat: 0.00 g	Vitamin E: 0.00 mg
Monosaturated Fat: 0.00 g	Thiamin: .01 mg
Polyunsaturated: .02 g	Riboflavin: .02 mg
Cholesterol: 0.00 mg	Niacin: .14 mg
Carbohydrates: 14.50 g	Pantothenic Acid: .12 mg
Fiber: .68 g	Vitamin B6: .02 mg
Calcium: 8.14 mg	Folate: 5.26 ug
Phosphorous: 4.67 mg	Vitamin B12: 0.00 ug
Iron: .27 mg	Vitamin C: 17.90 mg
Sodium: 3.31 mg	Selenium: .23 ug
Sugar: 4.45 mg	

Carrot Peach Juice

2 oranges - peeled and halved

1 medium carrot – cut into 3-inch pieces

1 peach – pitted and peeled

1 Tbsp sugar

Optional, ½ cup ice

Directions: Place ingredients in jar in order as listed and secure the lid. Press the **Whole Juice** button.

Nutritional Information

Yields: 3 cups
Serving Size: ½ cup

Amount per serving

Calories: 35.63	Potassium: 148.51 mg
2.36% from Fat,	Magnesium: 7.54 mg
7.08% from Protein	Zinc: .07 mg
90.60% from Carb	Copper: .03 mg
Protein: .69 g	Manganese: .03 mg
Total Fat: .10 g	Vitamin A: 1429.18 IU
Saturated Fat: .01 g	Vitamin E: 0.00 mg
Monosaturated Fat: .02 g	Thiamin: .06 mg
Polyunsaturated: .03 g	Riboflavin: .03 mg
Cholesterol: 0.00 mg	Niacin: .29 mg
Carbohydrates: 8.85 g	Pantothenic Acid: .19 mg
Fiber: 1.84 g	Vitamin B6: .05 mg
Calcium: 28.13 mg	Folate: 20.50 ug
Phosphorous: 12.60 mg	Vitamin B12: 0.00 ug
Iron: .10 mg	Vitamin C: 35.69 mg
Sodium: 7.52 mg	Selenium: .33 ug
Sugar: 6.79 mg	

BREAKFAST

Breakfast Table of Contents

BATTERS

For most batter recipes, press the **Batters** button. For all batter recipes, any kind of flour may be substituted. For example: if the recipe calls for 1 cup flour, you may use 1 cup whole wheat flour, or ½ cup whole wheat flour and ½ cup allpurpose flour. You may mill wheat into flour to make homemade flour for your **Batters**. When recipe indicates butter as an ingredient, you may use margarine instead if necessary, and vice versa.

Baked French Toast

6 slices whole wheat bread - cut into three strips

Directions: Preheat oven to 350°F. Place bread on bottom of 8 x 8" square baking dish.

4 eggs

1 ½ cups milk

2 Tbsp sugar

¼ tsp salt

1 tsp vanilla

Directions: Place ingredients in blender jar. Secure lid and press the **Batters** button. Pour mixture over bread.

1 Tbsp margarine - melted

1 tsp cinnamon

3 Tbsp sugar

Pour margarine over bread. Combine sugar and cinnamon and sprinkle over top of bread. Bake 45-50 minutes.

Nutritional Information

Yields: 18 slices of French toast
Serving Size: 1 piece

Amount per serving

Calories: 63.02	Potassium: 62.95 mg
27.90% from Fat,	Magnesium: 7.36 mg
17.00% from Protein	Zinc: .28 mg
55.00% from Carb	Copper: .03 mg
Protein: 2.67 g	Manganese: .11 mg
Total Fat: 1.95 g	Vitamin A: 117.10 IU
Saturated Fat: .52 g	Vitamin E: 31.91 mg
Monosaturated Fat: .81 g	Thiamin: .05 mg
Polyunsaturated: .41 g	Riboflavin: .11 mg
Cholesterol: 41.30 mg	Niacin: .37 mg
Carbohydrates: 8.66 g	Pantothenic Acid: .25 mg
Fiber: .43 g	Vitamin B6: .03 mg
Calcium: 41.26 mg	Folate: 13.19
Phosphorous: 51.86 mg	Vitamin B12: .23 ug
Iron: .51 mg	Vitamin C: .04 mg
Sodium: 106.46 mg	Selenium: 6.29 ug
Sugar: 5.10 mg	

Pumpkin Muffins

2 large eggs

¼ cup vegetable oil

1 cup pumpkin cooked

¼ cup milk

¾ cup sugar

½ tsp salt

2 tsp baking soda

1 tsp allspice

1 tsp cinnamon

1 ¼ cups flour

Directions: Preheat oven to 350°F. Place ingredients in jar in order as listed and secure the lid. Press the **Batters** button. After cycle is completed, use a spatula to pull ingredients towards the blade. Secure the lid and Press the **Batters** button again. Pour into muffin cups, 1/3 full. Bake for 20-25 minutes at 350°F.

Nutritional Information

Yield: 12 muffins or 2 ½ cups batter
Serving Size: 1 muffin

Amount per serving

Calories: 158.11	Potassium: 138.14 mg
27.10% from Fat,	Magnesium: 27.65 mg
8.15% from Protein	Zinc: .59 mg
64.80% from Carb	Copper: .09 mg
Protein: 3.36 g	Manganese: .69 mg
Total Fat: 4.97 g	Vitamin A: 1032.18 IU
Saturated Fat: 3.68 g	Vitamin E: 3.13 mg
Monosaturated Fat: 1.16 g	Thiamin: .09 mg
Polyunsaturated: 2.81 g	Riboflavin: .09 mg
Cholesterol: .20 mg	Niacin: 1.21 mg
Carbohydrates: 26.74g	Pantothenic Acid: .25 mg
Fiber: .2.40 g	Vitamin B6: .07 mg
Calcium: 17.97 mg	Folate: 10.13 ug
Phosphorous: 73.39 mg	Vitamin B12: .03 ug
Iron: .82 mg	Vitamin C: 1.09 mg
Sodium: 321.42 mg	Selenium: 13.74 ug
Sugar: 12.91 mg	

Bran Muffins

2 eggs

Directions: Place eggs in jar and secure the lid. Press the Pulse button 2 to 3 times.

²/₃ cup milk

¼ cup olive oil

1 ¼ cups flour

½ cup soy flour

1 cup bran flake cereal

½ cup brown sugar

1 tsp baking powder

1 tsp baking soda

¾ tsp ground cinnamon

⅛ tsp ground cloves

Directions: Preheat oven to 400°F. Add ingredients and press the **Batters** button. Spoon batter into muffin cups so cups are 1/3 full. Bake for 15-20 minutes.

Blueberry Muffins

½ cup milk

1 egg

½ cube butter - softened

1 cup flour

¼ tsp salt

¾ cup sugar

1 tsp baking powder

Directions: Preheat oven to 375°F. Press the **Batters** button.

¼ cup fresh blueberries

Directions: Add blueberries and secure the lid. Press the Pulse button 4 to 5 times. Spoon into muffin cups 1/3 full. Bake for 25 minutes.

Nutritional Information

Yield: 12 muffins or 2 ½ cups
Serving Size: 1 muffin

Amount per serving

Calories: 150.79	Potassium: 226.10 mg
29.40% from Fat	Magnesium: 40.53 mg
11.10% from Protein	Zinc: .66 mg
59.40% from Carb	Copper: .29 mg
Protein: 4.43 g	Manganese: .84 mg
Total Fat: 5.21 g	Vitamin A: 210.89 IU
Saturated Fat: .78 g	Vitamin E: 8.34 mg
Monosaturated Fat: 3.46 g	Thiamin: .13 mg
Polyunsaturated: .69 g	Riboflavin: .13 mg
Cholesterol: .55 mg	Niacin: 1.62 mg
Carbohydrates: 23.63 mg	Pantothenic Acid: .31 mg
Fiber: .2.56 g	Vitamin B6: .15 mg
Calcium: 64.68 mg	Folate: 35.92 ug
Phosphorous: 113.43 mg	Vitamin B12: .28 ug
Iron: 1.67 mg	Vitamin C: 2.39 mg
Sodium: 196.54 mg	Selenium: 9.63 ug
Sugar: 9.60 mg	

Nutritional Information

Yield: 6 muffins or 2 cups
Serving Size: 1 muffin

Amount per serving

Calories: 260.95	Potassium: 135.13 mg
31.60% from Fat	Magnesium: 32.41 mg
7.47% from Protein	Zinc: .81 mg
60.90% from Carb	Copper: .08 mg
Protein: 5.05 g	Manganese: .76 mg
Total Fat: 9.49g	Vitamin A: 346.19 IU
Saturated Fat: 5.44 g	Vitamin E: 95.01 mg
Monosaturated Fat: 2.57 g	Thiamin: .11 mg
Polyunsaturated: .61 g	Riboflavin: .15 mg
Cholesterol: 69.21 mg	Niacin: 1.30 mg
Carbohydrates: 41.19 mg	Pantothenic Acid: .45 mg
Fiber: 2.44 g	Vitamin B6: .15 09mg
Calcium: 89.21 mg	Folate: 15.30 ug
Phosphorous: 130.52 mg	Vitamin B12: .23 ug
Iron: 1.01 mg	Vitamin C: .25 mg
Sodium: 260.93 mg	Selenium: 18.39 ug
Sugar: 25.39 mg	

Apple Cinnamon Muffins

2 eggs

2 cups biscuit baking mix

1 apple - peeled and quartered

½ cup sugar

⅔ cup milk

2 Tbsp vegetable oil

2 tsp cinnamon

Directions: Preheat oven to 400°F. Place ingredients in jar in order as listed and secure the lid. Press the **Batters** button. Pour batter into muffin cups, filling them 1/3 full. Bake at 400°F for 17 minutes.

Nutritional Information

Yield: 12 muffins or 3 cups batter
Serving Size: 1 muffin

Amount per serving

Calories: 149.46	Potassium: 76.30 mg
32.20% from Fat	Magnesium: 8.19 mg
7.18% from Protein	Zinc: .19 mg
60.70% from Carb	Copper: .04 mg
Protein: 2.71 g	Manganese: .13 mg
Total Fat: 5.39 g	Vitamin A: 34.18 IU
Saturated Fat: 1.15 g	Vitamin E: 8.72 mg
Monosaturated Fat: 2.23 g	Thiamin: .12 mg
Polyunsaturated: 1.73 g	Riboflavin: .14 mg
Cholesterol: .93 mg	Niacin: .90 mg
Carbohydrates: 22.88 mg	Pantothenic Acid: .24 mg
Fiber: .74 g	Vitamin B6: .03 mg
Calcium: 59.06 mg	Folate: 24.90 ug
Phosphorous: 128.56 mg	Vitamin B12: .14 ug
Iron: .69 mg	Vitamin C: .76 mg
Sodium: 259.71 mg	Selenium: 2.93 ug
Sugar: 11.73 mg	

Apple Cinnamon Pancake Batter

1 ¼ cups lowfat milk

1 ½ tsp olive oil

1 apple - cored and quartered (may leave peel on)

1 ½ tsp baking powder

½ tsp salt

2 Tbsp sugar

½ tsp cinnamon

½ tsp nutmeg

1 cup whole grain flour

Directions: Place ingredients in jar in order as listed and secure the lid. Press the **Batters** button.

Nutritional Information

Yield: 2 ½ cups or 16 pancakes
Serving Size: 1 pancake

Amount per serving

Calories: 49.11	Potassium: 72.92 mg
14.30% from Fat	Magnesium: 14.04 mg
14.00% from Protein	Zinc: .31 mg
71.70% from Carb	Copper: .03 mg
Protein: 1.81 g	Manganese: .30 mg
Total Fat: .83g	Vitamin A: 43.00 IU
Saturated Fat: .24 g	Vitamin E: 11.72 mg
Monosaturated Fat: .40 g	Thiamin: .04 mg
Polyunsaturated: .11 g	Riboflavin: .06 mg
Cholesterol: .77 mg	Niacin: .51 mg
Carbohydrates: 9.31 g	Pantothenic Acid: .15 mg
Fiber: 1.07 g	Vitamin B6: .04 mg
Calcium: 56.65 mg	Folate: 4.53 ug
Phosphorous: 57.81 mg	Vitamin B12: .08 ug
Iron: .39 mg	Vitamin C: .57 mg
Sodium: 130.96 mg	Selenium: 5.80 ug
Sugar: 2.43 mg	

Waffles

1 ¾ cup low-fat milk

3 eggs

¼ cup butter - softened

1 tsp salt

2 cups flour

2 tsp baking powder

Directions: Place ingredients in jar in order as listed and secure the lid. Press the **Batters** button.

Pancakes

1 ¼ cups milk

1 egg

2 Tbsp olive oil

½ tsp salt

2 Tbsp sugar*

1 cup flour

2 tsp baking powder

Directions: Place ingredients in jar in order as listed and secure the lid. Press the **Batters** button. Pour approximately ¼ cup batter onto hot griddle.

*May substitute brown sugar

Nutritional Information

Yield: 3 ½ cups or 10 waffles
Serving Size: 1 waffle

Amount per serving

Calories: 148.11	Potassium: 192.62 mg
32.30% from Fat,	Magnesium: 41.48 mg
15.80% from Protein	Zinc: .91 mg
51.90% from Carb	Copper: .10 mg
Protein: 6.12 g	Manganese: .91 mg
Total Fat: 5.57 g	Vitamin A: 231.37 IU
Saturated Fat: 3.31 g	Vitamin E: 64.34 mg
Monosaturated Fat: 1.39 g	Thiamin: .13 mg
Polyunsaturated: .38 g	Riboflavin: .18 mg
Cholesterol: 13.92 mg	Niacin: 1.58 mg
Carbohydrates: 20.12 g	Pantothenic Acid: .43 mg
Fiber: 2.93 g	Vitamin B6: .10 mg
Calcium: 125.56 mg	Folate: 13.71 ug
Phosphorous: 153.85 mg	Vitamin B12: .20 ug
Iron: 1.07 mg	Vitamin C: .52 mg
Sodium: 408.79 mg	Selenium: 20.11ug
Sugar: .17 mg	

Nutritional Information

Yield: 12 pancakes
Serving Size: 1 pancake

Amount per serving

Calories: 79.01	Potassium: 90.43 mg
33.20% from Fat	Magnesium: 18.39 mg
13.30% from Protein	Zinc: .44 mg
53.50% from Carb	Copper: .04 mg
Protein: 2.73 g	Manganese: 38 mg
Total Fat: 3.04 g	Vitamin A: 69.52 IU
Saturated Fat: .61 g	Vitamin E: 20.39 mg
Monosaturated Fat: 1.89 g	Thiamin: .06 mg
Polyunsaturated: .35 g	Riboflavin: .09 mg
Cholesterol: 13.04 mg	Niacin: .66 mg
Carbohydrates: 11.02 g	Pantothenic Acid: .24 mg
Fiber: 1.22 g	Vitamin B6: .05 mg
Calcium: 86.36 mg	Folate: 7.18 ug
Phosphorous: 84.71 mg	Vitamin B12: .14 ug
Iron: .54 mg	Vitamin C: .31 mg
Sodium: 198.45 mg	Selenium: 8.60 ug
Sugar: 2.17 mg	

Buttermilk Pancakes

1 ¼ cups buttermilk

1 egg

2 Tbsp olive oil

½ tsp salt

1 tsp sugar

1 ¼ cups flour

1 tsp baking soda

Directions: Place ingredients in jar in order as listed and secure the lid. Press the **Batters** button. Pour approximately ¼ cup batter onto hot griddle.

Crepes

1 cup evaporated milk

4 medium eggs or egg substitute equivalent

1 Tbsp Sugar

1 cup flour

Directions: Place ingredients in jar in order as listed and secure the lid. Press the **Batters** button. Pour approximately 3 Tbsp of crepe batter onto an 8 or 9inch buttered frying pan. Lift the frying pay up slightly above the stove and tilt pan so that batter spreads out into a circle. Crepe is done when set on top and lightly browned on bottom.

Nutritional Information

Yield: 12 pancakes
Serving Size: 1 pancake

Amount per serving

Calories: 78.22	Potassium: 92.78 mg
33.30% from Fat,	Magnesium: 20.34 mg
14.30% from Protein	Zinc: .50 mg
52.40% from Carb	Copper: .1005 mg
Protein: 2.91 g	Manganese: .48 mg
Total Fat: 3.01 g	Vitamin A: 24.36 IU
Saturated Fat: .58 g	Vitamin E: 6.55 mg
Monosaturated Fat: 1.87 g	Thiamin: .07 mg
Polyunsaturated: .37 g	Riboflavin: .08 mg
Cholesterol: 13.03 mg	Niacin: .81 mg
Carbohydrates: 10.68 g	Pantothenic Acid: .24 mg
Fiber: 1.52 g	Vitamin B6: .05 mg
Calcium: 35.36 mg	Folate: 8.02 ug
Phosphorous: 70.84 mg	Vitamin B12: .09 ug
Iron: .55 mg	Vitamin C: .26 mg
Sodium: 234.12 mg	Selenium: 10.22 ug
Sugar: 1.66 mg	

Nutritional Information

Yield: 10 to 12 crepes or 2 cups batter
Serving Size: 1 crepe

Amount per serving

Calories: 71.89	Potassium: 122.30 mg
21.80% from Fat,	Magnesium: 20.06 mg
21.60% from Protein	Zinc: .46 mg
56.60% from Carb	Copper: .04 mg
Protein: 4.01g	Manganese: .38 mg
Total Fat: 1.79 g	Vitamin A: 84.27 IU
Saturated Fat: 1.00 g	Vitamin E: 23.10 mg
Monosaturated Fat: .51 g	Thiamin: .06 mg
Polyunsaturated: .13 g	Riboflavin: .14 mg
Cholesterol: 6.09 mg	Niacin: .69 mg
Carbohydrates: 10.50 g	Pantothenic Acid: .26 mg
Fiber: 1.22 g	Vitamin B6: .05 mg
Calcium: 59.00 mg	Folate: 6.53 ug
Phosphorous: 78.90 mg	Vitamin B12: .04 ug
Iron: 1.44 mg	Vitamin C: .40 mg
Sodium: 41.24 mg	Selenium: 9.79 ug
Sugar: 1.17 mg	

Chocolate Chip Pancakes

1 1/3 cup flour

2 Tbsp sugar

1/4 tsp cinnamon

1 Tbsp baking powder

1/4 tsp salt

2 large eggs

1 cup milk

4 Tbsp butter - melted

1/2 tsp vanilla

Directions: Place ingredients in jar in order as listed and secure the lid. Press the **Batters** button.

Add:

1/3 cup chocolate chips

Directions: Tap the Pulse button approximately 5 times to combine chocolate chips into batter.

Blueberry Corn Pancakes

1 cup milk

1/2 cup water

1 cup flour

1/2 cup ground cornmeal

1 tsp baking powder

1/2 tsp baking soda

1/4 tsp salt

Directions: Place ingredients in jar in order as listed and secure the lid. Press the **Batters** button.

Add:

1/2 cup fresh or frozen blueberries*

Directions: Press the Pulse button approximately 5 times.

Nutritional Information

Yield: 16 pancakes or 4 cups batter
Serving Size: 1 pancake

Amount per serving

Calories: 94.64	Potassium: 89.46 mg
39.50% from Fat	Magnesium: 19.27 mg
11.20% from Protein	Zinc: .44 mg
49.40% from Carb	Copper: .06 mg
Protein: 2.73 g	Manganese: .40 mg
Total Fat: 4.29 g	Vitamin A: 126.94 IU
Saturated Fat: 2.47 g	Vitamin E: 34.86 mg
Monosaturated Fat: 1.28 g	Thiamin: .06 mg
Polyunsaturated: .22 g	Riboflavin: .08 mg
Cholesterol: 9.05 mg	Niacin: .67 mg
Carbohydrates: 12.08 g	Pantothenic Acid: .19 mg
Fiber: 1.36 g	Vitamin B6: .04 mg
Calcium: 84.23 mg	Folate: 6.03 ug
Phosphorous: 79.35 mg	Vitamin B12: .10 ug
Iron: .59 mg	Vitamin C: .19 mg
Sodium: 278.35 mg	Selenium: 8.49 ug
Sugar: 3.47 mg	

Nutritional Information

Yield: 8 pancakes or 2 cups batter
Serving Size: 1 pancake

Amount per serving

Calories: 102.42	Potassium: 135.43 mg
7.16% from Fat	Magnesium: 29.86 mg
15.20% from Protein	Zinc: .65 mg
77.60% from Carb	Copper: .07 mg
Protein: 4.04 g	Manganese: .59 mg
Total Fat: .84 g	Vitamin A: 86.69 IU
Saturated Fat: .30 g	Vitamin E: 18.76 mg
Monosaturated Fat: .18 g	Thiamin: .15 mg
Polyunsaturated: .22 g	Riboflavin: .13 mg
Cholesterol: 1.23 mg	Niacin: 1.47 mg
Carbohydrates: 20.62 g	Pantothenic Acid: .30 mg
Fiber: 2.73 g	Vitamin B6: .09 mg
Calcium: 84.10 mg	Folate: 29.22 ug
Phosphorous: 106.94 mg	Vitamin B12: .13 ug
Iron: 1.04 mg	Vitamin C: .61 mg
Sodium: 232.53 mg	Selenium: 12.06 ug
Sugar: .94 mg	

Banana Chocolate Chip Muffins

1 egg

1 large ripe banana - peeled and cut in half

3 Tbsp butter

½ cup buttermilk

½ tsp vanilla extract

Directions: Preheat oven to 350° F. Place ingredients in blender and secure lid. Press the Pulse Button and hold the button for 5 seconds.

⅓ cup sugar

1 cup flour

1 tsp baking soda

¼ tsp salt

Add ingredients to mixture in blender. Press the **Batters** button.

⅓ cups chocolate chips*

Add chocolate chips to batter, and press the Pulse button 3 to 5 times, until chocolate chips are mixed in with batter. Pour batter into muffin cups. Bake for 20 - 22 minutes

* May leave chocolate chips out if desired

Nutritional Information

Yields: 12 muffins
Serving Size: 1 muffin

Amount per serving

Calories: 133.42	Potassium: 95.55 mg
34.00% from Fat,	Magnesium: 10.32 mg
7.32% from Protein	Zinc: .28 mg
58.70% from Carb	Copper: .05 mg
Protein: 2.46 g	Manganese: .13 mg
Total Fat: 5.08 g	Vitamin A: 135.36 IU
Saturated Fat: 2.74 g	Vitamin E: 34.15 mg
Monosaturated Fat: 1.64 g	Thiamin: .10 mg
Polyunsaturated: .30 g	Riboflavin: .11 mg
Cholesterol: 26.63 mg	Niacin: .73 mg
Carbohydrates: 19.72 g	Pantothenic Acid: .20 mg
Fiber: .76 g	Vitamin B6: .06 mg
Calcium: 26.07 mg	Folate: 24.69 ug
Phosphorous: 41.63 mg	Vitamin B12: .11 mg
Iron: .71 mg	Vitamin C: 1.19 mg
Sodium: 301.89 mg	Selenium: 5.45 ug
Sugar: 10.10 mg	

SYRUPS

To blend syrups, add ingredients and press the **Syrups** button. For the fruit syrups, it is recommended to use fresh fruit in order to obtain a sweet flavor; however, you may use frozen fruit that has been thawed. This may result in less flavorful syrup.

If you would like thick chunky syrup, add only half of the fruit the recipe calls for, and press the **Syrups** button. Then add the rest of the fruit, and press the Pulse button approximately 5 times, or until syrup has reached desired consistency.

If you plan on storing your freshly made fruit syrup for long periods of time, you may consider adding fruit preservative.

To make syrup hotter and thicker, press the **Syrups** button twice.

Creamy Cinnamon Syrup

½ cup light corn syrup

¼ cup water

½ cup sugar

½ tsp cinnamon

½ cup evaporated milk

Directions: Place ingredients in jar and secure the lid. Press the **Syrups** button. When the cycle has ended, press the **Syrups** button once again.

Nutritional Information

Yields: 1 ½ cup
Serving Size: 2 Tbsp

Amount per serving

Calories: 86.87	Potassium: 33.00 mg
7.94% from Fat,	Magnesium: 2.90 mg
3.13% from Protein	Zinc: .09 mg
88.90% from Carb	Copper: 0.00 mg
Protein: .72 g	Manganese: .03 mg
Total Fat: .81 g	Vitamin A: 41.95 IU
Saturated Fat: .48 g	Vitamin E: 11.55 mg
Monosaturated Fat: .25 g	Thiamin: .01 mg
Polyunsaturated: .03 g	Riboflavin: .04 mg
Cholesterol: 3.05 mg	Niacin: .02 mg
Carbohydrates: 20.41 g	Pantothenic Acid: .07 mg
Fiber: .05 g	Vitamin B6: .01 mg
Calcium: 29.16 mg	Folate: .87 ug
Phosphorous: 21.65 mg	Vitamin B12: 0.02 ug
Iron: .06 mg	Vitamin C: .23 mg
Sodium: 27.79 mg	Selenium: .39 ug
Sugar: 19.28 mg	

Strawberry Syrup

2 cups strawberries

½ cup sugar

Directions: Place ingredients in jar and secure the lid. Press the **Syrups** button.

Nutritional Information

Yields: 1 ¾ cups
Serving Size: 2 Tablespoons

Amount per serving

Calories: 34.81	Potassium: 33.37 mg
1.60% from Fat,	Magnesium: 2.82 mg
1.59% from Protein	Zinc: .03 mg
96.80% from Carb	Copper: 0.01 mg
Protein: .05 g	Manganese: .08 mg
Total Fat: .07 g	Vitamin A: 2.61 IU
Saturated Fat: 0.00 g	Vitamin E: 0.00 mg
Monosaturated Fat: .01 g	Thiamin: .01 mg
Polyunsaturated: .03 g	Riboflavin: .01 mg
Cholesterol: 0.00 mg	Niacin: .08 mg
Carbohydrates: 8.87 g	Pantothenic Acid: .03 mg
Fiber: .43 g	Vitamin B6: .01 mg
Calcium: 3.55 mg	Folate: 5.21 ug
Phosphorous: 5.21 mg	Vitamin B12: 0.00 ug
Iron: .09 mg	Vitamin C: 12.97 mg
Sodium: .22 mg	Selenium: .13 ug
Sugar: 8.21 mg	

Blueberry Syrup

2 cups blueberries

1 ½ cups water

1 ½ cup sugar

½ tsp lemon juice

Directions: Place ingredients in jar and secure the lid. Press the **Syrups** button.

Raspberry Syrup

3 cups raspberries

¾ cup sugar

1 tsp lemon juice

Directions: Place ingredients in jar and secure the lid. Press the **Syrups** button. Once cycle has finished press the **Syrups** button again.

Nutritional Information

Yields: 3 ¼ cups
Serving Size: 2 Tablespoons

Amount per serving

Calories: 47.42	Potassium: 8.30 mg
0.62% from Fat,	Magnesium: .75 mg
0.62% from Protein	Zinc: .02 mg
98.80% from Carb	Copper: 0.01 mg
Protein: .08 g	Manganese: .03 mg
Total Fat: .03 g	Vitamin A: 5.61 IU
Saturated Fat: 0.00 g	Vitamin E: 0.00 mg
Monosaturated Fat: 0.00 g	Thiamin: 0.00 mg
Polyunsaturated: .02 g	Riboflavin: .01 mg
Cholesterol: 0.00 mg	Niacin: .04 mg
Carbohydrates: 12.31 g	Pantothenic Acid: .01 mg
Fiber: .25 g	Vitamin B6: .01 mg
Calcium: .99 mg	Folate: .63 ug
Phosphorous: 1.25 mg	Vitamin B12: 0.00 ug
Iron: .03 mg	Vitamin C: 1.05 mg
Sodium: .36 mg	Selenium: .08 ug
Sugar: 11.82 mg	

Nutritional Information

Yields: 3 cups
Serving Size: 2 Tablespoons

Amount per serving

Calories: 32.43	Potassium: 23.60 mg
2.63% from Fat	Magnesium: 3.40 mg
2.16% from Protein	Zinc: .06 mg
95.20% from Carb	Copper: 0.01 mg
Protein: .19 g	Manganese: .10 mg
Total Fat: .10 g	Vitamin A: 5.11 IU
Saturated Fat: 0.00 g	Vitamin E: 0.00 mg
Monosaturated Fat: .01 g	Thiamin: 0.00 mg
Polyunsaturated: .06 g	Riboflavin: .01 mg
Cholesterol: 0.00 mg	Niacin: .09 mg
Carbohydrates: 8.15 g	Pantothenic Acid: .05 mg
Fiber: 1.00 g	Vitamin B6: .01 mg
Calcium: 3.92 mg	Folate: 3.26 ug
Phosphorous: 4.47 mg	Vitamin B12: 0.00 ug
Iron: .11 mg	Vitamin C: 4.13 mg
Sodium: .16 mg	Selenium: .07 ug
Sugar: 6.98 mg	

Apricot Syrup

3 cups apricots
¾ cup sugar
1 tsp lemon juice

Directions: Place ingredients in jar and secure the lid. Press the **Syrups** button. Once the cycle has finished, press the **Syrups** button again.

Nutritional Information

Yields: 3 cups
Serving Size: 2 Tablespoons

Amount per serving

Calories: 63.60	Potassium: 189.21 mg
1.08% from Fat,	Magnesium: 5.21 mg
3.20% from Protein	Zinc: .06 mg
95.70% from Carb	Copper: 0.06 mg
Protein: .55 g	Manganese: .04 mg
Total Fat: .08 g	Vitamin A: 585.69 IU
Saturated Fat: 0.00 g	Vitamin E: 0.00 mg
Monosaturated Fat: .01 g	Thiamin: 0.00 mg
Polyunsaturated: .01 g	Riboflavin: .01 mg
Cholesterol: 0.00 mg	Niacin: .42 mg
Carbohydrates: 16.50 g	Pantothenic Acid: .08 mg
Fiber: 1.19 g	Vitamin B6: .02 mg
Calcium: 9.02 mg	Folate: 1.65 ug
Phosphorous: 11.55 mg	Vitamin B12: 0.00 ug
Iron: .43 mg	Vitamin C: .26 mg
Sodium: 1.63 mg	Selenium: .40 ug
Sugar: 14.98 mg	

Black Cherry Syrup

3 cups black cherries - pitted
¾ cup sugar
2 tsp lemon juice

Directions: Place ingredients in jar and secure the lid. Press the **Syrups** button. Once the cycle has finished, press the **Syrups** button again.

Nutritional Information

Yields: 3 cups
Serving Size: 2 Tablespoons

Amount per serving

Calories: 33.65	Potassium: 32.86 mg
0.74% from Fat	Magnesium: 1.62 mg
1.75% from Protein	Zinc: .01 mg
97.50% from Carb	Copper: .01 mg
Protein: .16 g	Manganese: .01 mg
Total Fat: .03 g	Vitamin A: 9.40 IU
Saturated Fat: .01 g	Vitamin E: 0.00 mg
Monosaturated Fat: .01g	Thiamin: 0.00 mg
Polyunsaturated: .01 g	Riboflavin: .01 mg
Cholesterol: 0.00 mg	Niacin: .02mg
Carbohydrates: 8.66 g	Pantothenic Acid: .03 mg
Fiber: .31 g	Vitamin B6: .01 mg
Calcium: 1.98 mg	Folate: .61 ug
Phosphorous: 3.08 mg	Vitamin B12: 0.00 ug
Iron: .05 mg	Vitamin C: 1.12 mg
Sodium: 0.00 mg	Selenium: .04 ug
Sugar: 8.17 mg	

Peach Syrup

3 cups peaches - peeled and pitted

¾ cup sugar

1 tsp lemon juice

Directions: Place ingredients in jar and secure the lid. Press the **Syrups** button. Once the cycle has finished, press the **Syrups** button again.

Nutritional Information

Serving Size: 2 Tablespoons

Amount per serving

Calories: 28.05	Potassium: 34.94 mg
1.38% from Fat	Magnesium: 1.65 mg
2.24% from Protein,	Zinc: .03 mg
96.40% from Carb	Copper: 0.01 mg
Protein: .717 g	Manganese: .01 mg
Total Fat: .05 g	Vitamin A: 59.41 IU
Saturated Fat: 0.00 g	Vitamin E: 0.00 mg
Monosaturated Fat: .01 g	Thiamin: 0.00 mg
Polyunsaturated: .02 g	Riboflavin: .01 mg
Cholesterol: 0.00 mg	Niacin: .15 mg
Carbohydrates: 7.15 g	Pantothenic Acid: .03 mg
Fiber: .27 g	Vitamin B6: 0.00 mg
Calcium: 1.16 mg	Folate: .75 ug
Phosphorous: 3.65 mg	Vitamin B12: 0.00 ug
Iron: .05 mg	Vitamin C: 1.29 mg
Sodium: 0.00 mg	Selenium: .05 ug
Sugar: 6.93 mg	

BREADS

Breads Table of Contents

BREAD BATTERS

Any type of flour may be substituted when recipe calls for flour, i.e., whole wheat, rye (See Flour Conversion Chart under Bread Dough Introduction)

Any type of sweetner may be substituted when recipe calls for sugar. If using honey, use 1/3 the amount of sugar the recipe asks for. For example: if the recipe asks for 1 cup sugar, use 1/3 cup honey.

All bread batter recipes can be adapted for muffins. Fill muffin cups 1/3 full and bake for same amount as bread.

You can also use your blender to mill wheat (or any other nutritious grains) into flour for use in bread batters.

Pumpkin/Squash Bread

1 cup milk

⅓ cup light olive oil

2 large eggs - omit yolks

1 cup cooked pumpkin*

½ tsp salt

1 tsp cinnamon

½ tsp ground cloves

¼ tsp nutmeg

2 tsps baking powder

⅓ cup sugar

1 cup flour

Directions: Preheat the oven to 350° F. Place ingredients in jar in order as listed above and secure the lid. Press **Speed Up** button until the blender reaches speed 6. Allow the blender to run for 30 seconds or until the batter is well mixed. Press any lower row button to stop. Pour into a sprayed 4 ½ x 8 ½ inch loaf pan. Bake for 40 minutes, or until golden.

*May substitute cooked squash

Nutritional Information

Yields: 1 loaf or 16 muffins
Serving Size: 1 slice/1 muffin

Amount per serving

Calories: 122.99	Potassium: 101.22 mg
45.80% from Fat,	Magnesium: 27.23 mg
7.71% from Protein	Zinc: .59mg
46.50% from Carb	Copper: .08 mg
Protein: 3.42 g	Manganese: .67 mg
Total Fat: 5.23 g	Vitamin A: 32.22 IU
Saturated Fat: .81 g	Vitamin E: 9.38 mg
Monosaturated Fat: 3.51g	Thiamin: .09 mg
Polyunsaturated: .67 g	Riboflavin: .08 mg
Cholesterol: 0.62 mg	Niacin: .78 mg
Carbohydrates: 16.63 g	Pantothenic Acid: .24 mg
Fiber: 1.89 g	Vitamin B6: .05 mg
Calcium: 62.50 mg	Folate: 8.77 ug
Phosphorous: 94.71 mg	Vitamin B12: 0.07 ug
Iron: .77 mg	Vitamin C: .18 mg
Sodium: 151.27 mg	Selenium: 9.20 ug
Sugar: 4.27 mg	

Pineapple Bread

¾ cup milk*

⅓ cup light olive oil

2 large eggs - omit yolks

1 cup fresh pineapple

½ tsp salt

2 ½ tsps baking powder

⅓ cup sugar

2 ½ cups flour

Directions: Preheat the oven to 350° F. Place ingredients in blender jar in order as listed and secure the lid. Press the **Speed Up** button until the blender reaches speed 6. Allow the blender to run for 30 seconds, or until the batter is well mixed. Pour into a sprayed 4 ½ x 8 ½ inch loaf pan. Bake for 40 minutes or until golden.

*May substitute juice from canned pineapple or 1 cup canned pineapple with juice drained.

Nutritional Information

Yields: 1 loaf or 16 muffins.
Serving Size: 1 slice/1 muffin

Amount per serving

Calories: 132.53	Potassium: 114.93 mg
32.50% from Fat,	Magnesium: 29.54 mg
10.20% from Protein	Zinc: .61 mg
57.40% from Carb	Copper: .08mg
Protein: 3.53 g	Manganese: .83 mg
Total Fat: 5.00 g	Vitamin A: 30.52 IU
Saturated Fat: .75 g	Vitamin E: 7.03 mg
Monosaturated Fat: 3.41 g	Thiamin: .10 mg
Polyunsaturated: .61 g	Riboflavin: .08 mg
Cholesterol: 0.46 mg	Niacin: 1.26 mg
Carbohydrates: 19.90 g	Pantothenic Acid: .26 mg
Fiber: 2.42 g	Vitamin B6: .08 mg
Calcium: 64.67 mg	Folate: 10.56 ug
Phosphorous: 94.82 mg	Vitamin B12: 0.05 ug
Iron: .87 mg	Vitamin C: 3.65 mg
Sodium: 164.66 mg	Selenium: 14.42 ug
Sugar: 5.20 mg	

Oat Bread

1 cup milk

⅓ cup light olive oil

2 large eggs - omit yolks

½ tsp salt

2 tsps baking powder

⅓ cup sugar

½ cup quick cooking oats

1 ½ cups flour

Directions: Preheat the oven to 350° F. Place ingredients in blender jar in order as listed and secure the lid. Press the **Speed Up** button until the blender reaches speed 6. Allow the blender to run for 30 seconds, or until the batter is well mixed. Pour into a sprayed 4 ½ x 8 ½ inch loaf pan. Bake for 40 minutes or until golden.

Nutritional Information

Yields: 1 loaf or 16 muffins
Serving Size: 1 slice/1 muffin

Amount per serving

Calories: 132.53	Potassium: 114.93 mg
37.00% from Fat,	Magnesium: 29.54 mg
10.80% from Protein	Zinc: .61 mg
52.30% from Carb	Copper: .08mg
Protein: 3.53 g	Manganese: .83 mg
Total Fat: 5.00 g	Vitamin A: 30.52 IU
Saturated Fat: .75 g	Vitamin E: 7.03 mg
Monosaturated Fat: 3.41 g	Thiamin: .10 mg
Polyunsaturated: .61 g	Riboflavin: .08 mg
Cholesterol: 0.46 mg	Niacin: 1.26 mg
Carbohydrates: 19.90 g	Pantothenic Acid: .26 mg
Fiber: 2.42 g	Vitamin B6: .08 mg
Calcium: 64.67 mg	Folate: 10.56 ug
Phosphorous: 94.82 mg	Vitamin B12: 0.05 ug
Iron: .87 mg	Vitamin C: 3.65 mg
Sodium: 164.66 mg	Selenium: 14.42 ug
Sugar: 5.20 mg	

Lemon Bread

1 cup orange juice

1 Tbsp lemon zest

1 lemon rind

⅓ cup light olive oil

2 large eggs omit yolks

½ tsp salt

2 tsps baking powder

¾ cup sugar

2 cups flour

Directions: Preheat the oven to 350° F. Place ingredients in blender jar in order as listed and secure the lid. Press the **Speed Up** button until the blender reaches speed 6. Allow the blender to run for 30 seconds, or until the batter is well mixed. Pour into a sprayed 4 ½ x 8 ½ inch loaf pan. Bake for 40 minutes or until golden.

Nutritional Information

Yields: 1 loaf or 16 muffins
Serving Size: 1 slice/1 muffin

Amount per serving

Calories: 137.75	Potassium: 103.09 mg
30.20% from Fat,	Magnesium: 23.37 mg
7.43% from Protein	Zinc: 45 mg
62.40% from Carb	Copper: .007mg
Protein: 2.68 g	Manganese: .58 mg
Total Fat: 4.84 g	Vitamin A: 14.47 IU
Saturated Fat: .66 g	Vitamin E: 0.00 mg
Monosaturated Fat: 3.37 g	Thiamin: .09 mg
Polyunsaturated: .58 g	Riboflavin: .06 mg
Cholesterol: 0.00 mg	Niacin: 1.01 mg
Carbohydrates: 22.49 g	Pantothenic Acid: .20 mg
Fiber: 2.00 g	Vitamin B6: .06 mg
Calcium: 42.37 mg	Folate: 10.02 ug
Phosphorous: 67.46 mg	Vitamin B12: 0.00 ug
Iron: .73 mg	Vitamin C: 7.53 mg
Sodium: 142.70 mg	Selenium: 11.53 ug
Sugar: 9.64 mg	

Apple Pear Bread

1 cup milk

⅓ cup light olive oil

2 large eggs - omit yolks

1 medium apple - cored and quartered

1 medium pear - cored and quartered

½ tsp salt

1 tsp cinnamon

½ tsp ground cloves

¼ tsp nutmeg

2 tsps baking powder

⅓ cup sugar

1 ½ cups flour

Directions: Preheat the oven to 350° F. Place ingredients in blender jar in order as listed and secure the lid. Press the **Speed Up** button until the display reads speed 6. Allow the blender to run for 30 seconds, or until the batter is well mixed. Pour into a sprayed 4 ½ x 8 ½ inch loaf pan. Bake for 40 minutes or until golden.

Nutritional Information

Yields: 1 loaf or 16 muffins
Serving Size: 1 slice/1 muffin

Amount per serving

Calories: 116.23	Potassium: 104.64 mg
36.60% from Fat	Magnesium: 20.16 mg
8.81% from Protein	Zinc: .42 mg
54.60% from Carb	Copper: .06 mg
Protein: 2.68 g	Manganese: .48 mg
Total Fat: 4.95 g	Vitamin A: 39.07 IU
Saturated Fat: .77 g	Vitamin E: 9.38 mg
Monosaturated Fat: 3.41 g	Thiamin: .06 mg
Polyunsaturated: .56 g	Riboflavin: .08 mg
Cholesterol: 0.62 mg	Niacin: .77 mg
Carbohydrates: 16.62 g	Pantothenic Acid: .19 mg
Fiber: 1.99 g	Vitamin B6: .05 mg
Calcium: 63.70 mg	Folate: 7.09 ug
Phosphorous: 71.77 mg	Vitamin B12: 0.07 ug
Iron: .63 mg	Vitamin C: 1.15 mg
Sodium: 151.52 mg	Selenium: 9.22 ug
Sugar: 6.38 mg	

Banana Bread

2 large eggs - omit yolks

½ cup light olive oil

½ tsp vanilla

2 bananas* - peeled and broken in half

1 tsp cinnamon

⅛ tsp nutmeg

½ tsp baking soda

¼ tsp baking powder

¾ cup sugar

1 ½ cups flour

Optional, add ½ cup nuts of choice

Directions: Preheat the oven to 325° F. Place ingredients in blender jar in order as listed and secure the lid. Press the Speed button until the display reads Speed 6. Allow the blender to run for 30 seconds, or until the batter is well mixed. Pour into a sprayed 4 ½ x 8 ½ inch loaf pan. Bake for 60 minutes or until golden.

*May add more or less banana for desired flavor

Nutritional Information

Yields: 1 loaf or 16 muffins
Serving Size: 1 slice/ 1 muffin

Amount per serving

Calories: 175.83	Potassium: 136.14 mg
45.40% from Fat	Magnesium: 27.60 mg
7.26% from Protein	Zinc: .50 mg
47.30% from Carb	Copper: .11 mg
Protein: 3.33 g	Manganese: .58 mg
Total Fat: 9.27 g	Vitamin A: 10.43 IU
Saturated Fat: 1.28 g	Vitamin E: 0.00 mg
Monosaturated Fat: 6.13 g	Thiamin: .08 mg
Polyunsaturated: 1.48 g	Riboflavin: .06 mg
Cholesterol: 0.00 mg	Niacin: 1.37 mg
Carbohydrates: 21.75 g	Pantothenic Acid: .25 mg
Fiber: 2.21 g	Vitamin B6: .11 mg
Calcium: 15.24 mg	Folate: 18.93 ug
Phosphorous: 61.51 mg	Vitamin B12: 0.00 ug
Iron: .79 mg	Vitamin C: 1.26 mg
Sodium: 129.34 mg	
Sugar: 11.44 mg	

Zucchini Bread

1 cup minced zucchini*

2 large eggs - omit yolks

½ cup light olive oil

½ tsp vanilla

½ tsp salt

1 ½ tsp cinnamon

¼ tsp nutmeg

½ tsp baking soda

¼ tsp baking powder

¼ cup nut

¾ cup sugar

1 ½ cups flour

Directions: Preheat the oven to 350° F. Place ingredients in blender jar in order as listed and secure the lid. Press the Speed button until the display reads Speed 6. Allow the blender to run for 30 seconds, or until the batter is well mixed. Pour into a sprayed 4 ½ x 8 ½ inch loaf pan. Bake for 40 minutes or until golden.

*May mince zucchini in blender before mixing bread batter. Place one medium zucchini in blender jar and Press the Speed button until blender reaches Speed 3. Allow the blender to run for approximately 15 seconds, or until zucchini is completely minced. When the display reads 15 seconds, press any lower row button to stop. Add remaining ingredients to blender jar.

Nutritional Information

Yields: 1 loaf or 16 muffins
Serving Size: 1 slice/ 1 muffin

Amount per serving

Calories: 151.90	Potassium: 90.42 mg
36.40% from Fat	Magnesium: 21.36 mg
9.09% from Protein	Zinc: .43 mg
54.50% from Carb	Copper: .07 mg
Protein: 2.69 g	Manganese: .52 mg
Total Fat: 8.12 g	Vitamin A: 17.14 IU
Saturated Fat: 1.11 g	Vitamin E: 0.00 mg
Monosaturated Fat: 5.57 g	Thiamin: .07 mg
Polyunsaturated: 1.12 g	Riboflavin: .06 mg
Cholesterol: 0.00 mg	Niacin: 1.04 mg
Carbohydrates: 18.49 g	Pantothenic Acid: .17 mg
Fiber: 1.77 g	Vitamin B6: .06 mg
Calcium: 14.46 mg	Folate: 1.04 ug
Phosphorous: 52.86 mg	Vitamin B12: 0.17 ug
Iron: .71 mg	Vitamin C: 1.38 mg
Sodium: 55.90 mg	Selenium: 9.03 ug
Sugar: 9.17 mg	

Whole Wheat Banana Nut Quick Bread

1 egg

¼ cup butter

⅓ cup milk

1 tsp lemon extract

2 bananas - peeled and broken in half

Directions: Preheat oven to 350° F. Place ingredients in blender jar and secure the lid. Press the Pulse button and hold for 10 seconds or until ingredients are well mixed.

2 tsps baking powder

1 tsp salt

⅔ cup sugar

1 ⅔ cups whole wheat flour

Directions: Place ingredients in separate bowl and mix well. Add flour mixture to wet mixture and secure the lid. Press the Pulse button 5 to 7 times. Remove the lid and scrape ingredients off the side of the jar with a rubber spatula. Repeat this process 2 to 3 times until the ingredients have been mixed.
Bake for 60 minutes.

Nutritional Information

Yields: 1 loaf or 16 muffins.
Serving Size: 1 slice/ 1 muffin

Amount per serving

Calories: 157.80	Potassium: 159.93 mg
36.40% from Fat	Magnesium: 34.23 mg
9.09% from Protein	Zinc: .63mg
54.50% from Carb	Copper: .14 mg
Protein: 3.79 g	Manganese: .73 mg
Total Fat: 6.75 g	Vitamin A: 135.25 IU
Saturated Fat: 2.22 g	Vitamin E: 32.47 mg
Monosaturated Fat: 1.76 g	Thiamin: .07 mg
Polyunsaturated: 2.12 g	Riboflavin: .07 mg
Cholesterol: 20.97 mg	Niacin: .95 mg
Carbohydrates: 22.76 g	Pantothenic Acid: .34 mg
Fiber: 2.37 g	Vitamin B6: .15 mg
Calcium: 52.19 mg	Folate: 12.78 ug
Phosphorous: 99.24 mg	Vitamin B12: 0.07 ug
Iron: .82 mg	Vitamin C: 1.86 mg
Sodium: 238.56 mg	Selenium: 11.11 ug
Sugar: 10.83 mg	

Cinnamon Raisin Bread

1 cup milk

2 large eggs - omit yolks

½ cup light olive oil

½ tsp vanilla

½ tsp salt

1 cup raisins

1 ½ tsp cinnamon

¼ tsp nutmeg

½ tsp baking soda

¼ tsp baking powder

½ cup sugar

1 ½ cups flour

Optional: add ¼ cup nuts of choice

Directions: Preheat the oven to 325° F. Place ingredients in blender jar in order as listed and secure the lid. Press the **Speed Up** button until the blender reaches speed 6. Allow the blender to run for 30 seconds, or until the batter is well mixed. Pour into a sprayed 4 ½ x 8 ½ inch loaf pan. Bake for 60 minutes or until golden.

Nutritional Information

Yields: 1 loaf or 16 muffins
Serving Size: 1 slice/ 1 muffin

Amount per serving

Calories: 163.75	Potassium: 158.90 mg
37.80% from Fat	Magnesium: 21.97 mg
6.83% from Protein	Zinc: .43mg
55.30% from Carb	Copper: .08 mg
Protein: 2.93 g	Manganese: .50 mg
Total Fat: 7.21 g	Vitamin A: 32.86 IU
Saturated Fat: 1.07 g	Vitamin E: 9.38 mg
Monosaturated Fat: 5.07 g	Thiamin: .07 mg
Polyunsaturated: .77 g	Riboflavin: .09 mg
Cholesterol: .62 mg	Niacin: .82 mg
Carbohydrates: 23.73 g	Pantothenic Acid: .19 mg
Fiber: 1.88 g	Vitamin B6: .06 mg
Calcium: 38.20 mg	Folate: 6.64 ug
Phosphorous: 68.82 mg	Vitamin B12: 0.07 ug
Iron: .78 mg	Vitamin C: .48 mg
Sodium: 138.45mg	Selenium: 9.28 ug
Sugar: 12.51 mg	

Cornbread

1 cup milk

⅓ cup light olive oil

2 large eggs - omit yolks

½ tsp salt

2 tsps baking powder

⅓ cup sugar

1 ¼ cup cornmeal

½ cup flour

Directions: Preheat the oven to 350° F. Place ingredients in blender jar in order as listed and secure the lid. Press the **Speed Up** button until the display reads speed 6. Allow the blender to run for 30 seconds, or until the batter is well mixed. Pour into a sprayed 4 ½ x 8 ½ inch loaf pan. Bake for 40 minutes or until golden.

Nutritional Information

Yields: 1 loaf or 16 muffins
Serving Size: 1 slice/ 1 muffin

Amount per serving

Calories: 157.80	Potassium: 159.93 mg
36.40% from Fat	Magnesium: 34.23 mg
9.09% from Protein	Zinc: .63mg
54.50% from Carb	Copper: .14 mg
Protein: 3.79 g	Manganese: .73 mg
Total Fat: 6.75 g	Vitamin A: 135.25 IU
Saturated Fat: 2.22 g	Vitamin E: 32.47 mg
Monosaturated Fat: 1.76 g	Thiamin: .07 mg
Polyunsaturated: 2.12 g	Riboflavin: .07 mg
Cholesterol: 20.97 mg	Niacin: .95 mg
Carbohydrates: 22.76 g	Pantothenic Acid: .34 mg
Fiber: 2.37 g	Vitamin B6: .15 mg
Calcium: 52.19 mg	Folate: 12.78ug
Phosphorous: 99.24 mg	Vitamin B12: 0.07 ug
Iron: .82 mg	Vitamin C: 1.86 mg
Sodium: 238.56 mg	Selenium. 11.11 ug
Sugar: 10.83 mg	

BREAD DOUGH

All Bread Dough Recipes are based on the basic Whole Wheat Bread Recipe. For various bread dough recipes, you will need to follow the Whole Wheat Bread Recipe, and add ingredients, which the specific recipe calls for. For example, if you are making Seed Bread, you will follow the Whole Wheat Bread Recipe, and add ingredients according to the instructions under the Seed Bread recipe. All additional ingredients must be added immediately after the yeast mixture is added to flour. Each Bread Dough Recipe will direct you to follow the Whole Wheat Bread Recipe, then list the changes you must make to the original recipe.

Bread Dough Tips:

Provided are tips for bread, in case you come across problems in baking.

Uneven Tops: Waves or bulges in the crust result when the dough mass in not molded properly in the bread pan.

Cracks on One Side: Poor heat circulation in the oven, particularly when you are baking more than one loaf at a time. To avoid this problem position the bread pan(s), allowing for large spaces in between pans.

Dough Overhangs on Pan: This happens when the dough rises too high. Reduce the amount of time the bread dough is allowed to rise. You may also reduce the amount of dough in pan.

Thick Crust: The dough most likely had risen too long. Reduce the amount of time the bread dough is allowed to rise.

Hollow Space under the Bread Crust: This occurs when large air bubbles are left in the dough when it is shaped. Stop the dough from rising too high and/or drying out.

Thick Walls: The gluten was underdeveloped. Blend the dough longer and lengthen the rising time.

Deep Cracks: Dough was under blended or too much flour was added. Blend the bread dough longer and/or add less flour.

Crumbly Bread: This difficulty usually occurs when too much flour is added to the recipe and/or the dough was allowed to rise too high. Add less flour and/or reduce the time allowed for the bread to rise.

The following is a chart that will allow you to substitute nutritious whole grain flours for allpurpose flour in almost any recipe.

1 cup allpurpose flour	1 cup finely ground general purpose whole wheat flour
1 cup allpurpose flour	3/4 cup coarsely or "stone" ground whole wheat flour
1 cup allpurpose flour	7/8 cup whole wheat flour
1 cup allpurpose flour	1/8 cup sunflower seed meal
1 cup allpurpose flour	3/4 cup rolled oats
1 cup allpurpose flour	1/4 cup whole wheat flour
1 cup allpurpose flour	7/8 cup whole wheat pastry flour
1 cup allpurpose flour	1/2 cup barley flour
1 cup allpurpose flour	3/4 cup buckwheat flour
1 cup allpurpose flour	1 cup corn flour
1 cup allpurpose flour	1 cup finely ground cornmeal
1 cup allpurpose flour	3/4 cup coarsely ground cornmeal
1 cup allpurpose flour	1 1/3 cup rolled oatmeal
1 cup allpurpose flour	1 cup rye flour
1 cup allpurpose flour	3/4 cup rice flour
1 cup allpurpose flour	1 cup rye meal

Whole Wheat Bread

1 ⅓ cups warm water

1 Tbsp active dry yeast

1 Tbsp molasses*

Directions: Preheat oven to 350° F. Add ingredients in a separate container. Stir well and allow the ingredients to sit at least 3 minutes.

*May use honey instead, in same amount

2 cups whole grain wheat*

½ tsp salt

Directions: Make sure jar is completely dry. Place ingredients in jar and secure the lid. Press the **Speed Up** button and hold down until the display reads speed 9. Allow the blender to run a complete cycle. The blender will stop on its own after 50 seconds.

*Note: If you have Whole Wheat flour, you may skip this step. Simply add 2 ½ cups flour to the jar.

Add yeast mixture to flour and secure the lid.

Note: If you are adding anything to bread (i.e., nuts, flavorings, fruit, etc.), place added ingredients immediately after placing yeast mixture in jar. Press the Pulse button approximately 20 times (hold the Pulse button down for 12 seconds each time). Remove the lid and with a rubber spatula, scrape dough off the bottom and corners of the jar. Place lid back on the jar and press the Pulse button 20 times again (holding the Pulse button down 2 to 3 seconds each time). If necessary, repeat this process one more time. The dough is done mixing when it forms a ball on top of the blade and the blade spins freely. Place bread dough in a sprayed 4 ½ x 8 ½ inch bread pan. Use a rubber spatula to grab dough stuck in the corners and around the blade of the jar.

Note: If bread is sticky, add a little bit of flour to bread before placing into pan. Also place flour on spatula and hands.

Form bread in pan so that the four corners are lower than the center and the bread dough has a mound appearance. Allow the dough to rise for 10 minutes. Bake 35 to 40 minutes.

Nutritional Information

Yields: 1 loaf
Serving Size: 1 slice of bread

Amount per serving

Calories: 69.59	Potassium: 110.23 mg
4.67% from Fat,	Magnesium: 30.00mg
15.40% from Protein	Zinc: .60 mg
80.00% from Carb	Copper: .08 mg
Protein: 2.86 g	Manganese: .74 mg
Total Fat: .39 g	Vitamin A: 1.69 IU
Saturated Fat: .07 g	Vitamin E: 0.00 mg
Monosaturated Fat: .06 g	Thiamin: .10 mg
Polyunsaturated: .15 g	Riboflavin: .08 mg
Cholesterol: 0.00 mg	Niacin: 1.50 mg
Carbohydrates: 14.88 g	Pantothenic Acid: .28 mg
Fiber: 2.44 g	Vitamin B6: .08 mg
Calcium: 10.00 mg	Folate: 25.80 ug
Phosphorous: 74.96 mg	Vitamin B12: 0.00 ug
Iron: .91 mg	Vitamin C: 0.00 mg
Sodium: 75.88 mg	Selenium: 13.67 ug
Sugar: .81 mg	

Pizza Dough

Follow the Whole Wheat Bread recipe.

Changes:

Instead of using whole wheat flour, use 2½ cups allpurpose flour. After bread dough has been mixed and formed into a ball, instead of molding into a bread pan, mold dough onto a pizza pan.

Raisin Bread

Follow the Whole Wheat Bread recipe

Changes:

Add ¾ cup raisins immediately after the yeast mixture has been added to flour.

Nutritional Information

Yields: 1 pizza crust (12 slices)
Serving Size: 1 slice of pizza

Amount per serving

Calories: 92.79	Potassium146.98 mg
4.67% from Fat,	Magnesium: 40.00 mg
15.40% from Protein	Zinc: .80 mg
80.00% from Carb	Copper: .11 mg
Protein: 3.81 g	Manganese: .98 mg
Total Fat: .52 g	Vitamin A: 2.25 IU
Saturated Fat: .04 g	Vitamin E: 0.00 mg
Monosaturated Fat: .08 g	Thiamin: .14 mg
Polyunsaturated: .20 g	Riboflavin: .11 mg
Cholesterol: 0.00 mg	Niacin: 2.01 mg
Carbohydrates: 19.84 g	Pantothenic Acid: .38 mg
Fiber: 3.26 g	Vitamin B6: .11 mg
Calcium: 13.33 mg	Folate: 34.40 ug
Phosphorous: 99.94 mg	Vitamin B12: 0.00 ug
Iron: 1.22 mg	Vitamin C: 0.00 mg
Sodium: 101.17 mg	Selenium: 18.23 ug
Sugar: 1.08 mg	

Nutritional Information

Yields: 1 loaf
Serving Size: 1 slice of bread

Amount per serving

Calories: 92.72	Potassium: 168.16 mg
3.79% from Fat,	Magnesium: 32.470mg
12.40% from Protein	Zinc: .62 mg
83.90% from Carb	Copper: .11 mg
Protein: 3.09 g	Manganese: .76 mg
Total Fat: .42 g	Vitamin A: 1.69 IU
Saturated Fat: .07 g	Vitamin E: 0.00 mg
Monosaturated Fat: .07 g	Thiamin: .10 mg
Polyunsaturated: .15 g	Riboflavin: .09 mg
Cholesterol: 0.00 mg	Niacin: 1.56 mg
Carbohydrates: 21.00 g	Pantothenic Acid: .29 mg
Fiber: 2.73 g	Vitamin B6: .10 mg
Calcium: 13.86 mg	Folate: 26.19 ug
Phosphorous: 82.77 mg	Vitamin B12: 0.00 ug
Iron: 1.06 mg	Vitamin C: 0.18mg
Sodium: 76.73 mg	Selenium: 13.72 ug
Sugar: 5.39 mg	

Onion Cheese Bread

Follow the Whole Wheat Bread Recipe

Changes:

¾ cup minced onion

1 tsp garlic powder

1 cup sharp cheddar cheese - shredded

Add ingredients immediately after the yeast mixture has been added to flour.

Nutritional Information

Yields: 1 loaf
Serving Size: 1 slice

Amount per serving

Calories: 106.57	Potassium: 131.05mg
4.67% from Fat,	Magnesium: 33.16 mg
15.40% from Protein	Zinc: .87 mg
80.00% from Carb	Copper: .09 mg
Protein: 5.01 g	Manganese: .75 mg
Total Fat: 3.13 g	Vitamin A: 84.50 IU
Saturated Fat: 1.81 g	Vitamin E: 21.28 mg
Monosaturated Fat: .84 g	Thiamin: .11 mg
Polyunsaturated: .23 g	Riboflavin: .11 mg
Cholesterol: 8.66 mg	Niacin: 1.52 mg
Carbohydrates: 15.87 g	Pantothenic Acid: .33 mg
Fiber: 2.57 g	Vitamin B6: .11 mg
Calcium: 71.27 mg	Folate: 28.71 ug
Phosphorous: 119.95 mg	Vitamin B12: 0.07 ug
Iron: .99 mg	Vitamin C: 0.51 mg
Sodium: 127.38 mg	Selenium: 14.92 ug
Sugar: 1.21 mg	

Dill Weed Bread

Follow the Whole Wheat Bread Recipe

Changes:

1¾ tsp dill weed

¼ tsp white pepper

½ tsp garlic powder

Add above ingredients immediately after the yeast mixture has been added to flour.

Nutritional Information

Yields: 1 loaf
Serving Size: 1 slice

Amount per serving

Calories: 70.28	Potassium: 114.96 mg
4.67% from Fat,	Magnesium: 30.59 mg
15.40% from Protein	Zinc: .61 mg
80.00% from Carb	Copper: .08 mg
Protein: 2.90g	Manganese: .74 mg
Total Fat: .39 g	Vitamin A: 8.30 IU
Saturated Fat: .07 g	Vitamin E: 0.00 mg
Monosaturated Fat: .06 g	Thiamin: .10 mg
Polyunsaturated: .15 g	Riboflavin: .08 mg
Cholesterol: 0.00 mg	Niacin: 1.51 mg
Carbohydrates: 15.03 g	Pantothenic Acid: .28 mg
Fiber: 2.48 g	Vitamin B6: .09 mg
Calcium: 12.18 mg	Folate: 25.81 ug
Phosphorous: 76.00 mg	Vitamin B12: 0.00 ug
Iron: .98mg	Vitamin C: 0.08 mg
Sodium: 76.14 mg	Selenium: 13.71 ug
Sugar: .83 mg	

Pumpernickel Bread

Follow the Whole Wheat Bread Recipe

Changes:

Instead of using 2 ½ cups whole wheat flour,
add 1 ¾ cup whole wheat flour and ¾ cup rye flour.
Add: 2 tsp cocoa powder* immediately after yeast mixture
has been added to flour.

*May substitute coffee powder

Nut Bread

Follow the Whole Wheat Bread Recipe

Changes:

Add ¾ cup desired nuts immediately after yeast mixture
has been added to flour.

Nutritional Information

Yields: 1 loaf
Serving Size: 1 slice

Amount per serving

Calories: 67.96	Potassium: 107.12 mg
4.93% from Fat,	Magnesium: 26.94 mg
14.30% from Protein	Zinc: .55 mg
80.80% from Carb	Copper: .08 mg
Protein: 2.58g	Manganese: .79 mg
Total Fat: .40 g	Vitamin A: 1.18 IU
Saturated Fat: .07 g	Vitamin E: 0.00 mg
Monosaturated Fat: .07 g	Thiamin: .09 mg
Polyunsaturated: .14 g	Riboflavin: .08 mg
Cholesterol: 0.00 mg	Niacin: 1.23g
Carbohydrates: 14.62 g	Pantothenic Acid: .25mg
Fiber: 2.53 g	Vitamin B6: .08mg
Calcium: 9.52 mg	Folate: 24.31
Phosphorous: 67.04 mg	Vitamin B12: 0.00 ug
Iron: .83 mg	Vitamin C: 0.00mg
Sodium: 75.78 mg	Selenium: 11.43
Sugar: .84 mg	

Nutritional Information

Yields: 1 loaf
Serving Size: 1 slice

Amount per serving

Calories: 108.40	Potassium: 158.48 mg
29.10% from Fat,	Magnesium: 41.49 mg
15.90% from Protein	Zinc: .83 mg
55.00% from Carb	Copper: .16 mg
Protein: 4.62 g	Manganese: .87 mg
Total Fat: 3.76 g	Vitamin A: 1.69 IU
Saturated Fat: .53 g	Vitamin E: 0.00 mg
Monosaturated Fat: 1.73 g	Thiamin: .15 mg
Polyunsaturated: 1.21 g	Riboflavin: .09 mg
Cholesterol: 0.00 mg	Niacin: 2.33 g
Carbohydrates: 15.98 g	Pantothenic Acid: .41 mg
Fiber: 3.03 g	Vitamin B6: .11 mg
Calcium: 16.29 mg	Folate: 42.22 ug
Phosphorous: 100.69 mg	Vitamin B12: 0.00 ug
Iron: 1.23 mg	Vitamin C: 0.00 mg
Sodium: 77.11 mg	Selenium: 14.16
Sugar: 1.08 mg	

Seed Bread

Follow the Whole Wheat Bread Recipe

Changes:

Add ¾ cup desired seed immediately after yeast mixture has been added to flour.

Nutritional Information

Yields: 1 loaf
Serving Size: 1 slice

Amount per serving

Calories: 108.27	Potassium: 141.82 mg
29.10% from Fat	Magnesium: 53.69 mg
14.00% from Protein	Zinc: 1.12 mg
56.90% from Carb	Copper: .36 mg
Protein: 4.05 g	Manganese: .90 mg
Total Fat: 3.74 g	Vitamin A: 2.30 IU
Saturated Fat: .53 g	Vitamin E: 0.00 mg
Monosaturated Fat: 1.33 g	Thiamin: .16 mg
Polyunsaturated: 1.62 g	Riboflavin: .10 mg
Cholesterol: 0.00 mg	Niacin: 1.81 mg
Carbohydrates: 16.46 g	Pantothenic Acid: .29 mg
Fiber: 3.24 g	Vitamin B6: .14 mg
Calcium: 75.81 mg	Folate: 32.35 ug
Phosphorous: 117.42 mg	Vitamin B12: 0.00 ug
Iron: 1.90 mg	Vitamin C: 0.00 mg
Sodium: 76.62 mg	Selenium: 14.06 ug
Sugar: .83 mg	

SOUPS

To blend a soup, press the Soups button. Any whole vegetable juice may be turned into a soup by simply pressing the **Soups** button after juice has been blended.

To heat soup, simply press the **Soups** button.
If water/milk added is hot, press the **Soups** button *once*
If water/milk added is warm, press the **Soups** button *twice*
If water/milk added is cold, press the **Soups** button *three times.*

Make sure liquid is the last ingredient added to the jar before blending.
If you would like the soup to be hotter, press the **Soups** button *again and allow the blender to run a complete cycle. If the soup appears to be finished in the middle of the Soups cycle, you may press any lower row button to stop at any point during the cycle. To make a chunky soup, you may add desired ingredient(s): baked potatoes, tortilla chips, cooked vegetables, cooked meat after the soup has been blended. Add the ingredients, secure the lid, and press the Pulse button 3 to 4 times until ingredients are blended to desired consitency. When cooking soup, liquid may jump through the hole in the steam cap. You may cover the steam cap with a paper towel.*

To make any soup a vegetarian recipe, substitute any chicken or beef bouillon with vegetable bouillon.

Soups Table of Contents

Shrimp Bisque

3 Tbsp butter

1 small rib celery

¼ small onion

1 small carrot – peeled and cut in half

⅛ tsp marjoram

⅛ tsp nutmeg

1 Tbsp lemon juice

2 cups chicken stock

Directions: Place above ingredients into blender jar in order as listed and secure the lid. Press the Pulse button for 3 to 6 seconds.

1 cup shrimp, cooked

1 cup milk

Pour soup from jar into pot and add shrimp. Cook for 15 minutes. Add milk and serve.

Nutritional Information

Yield: 4 cups
Serving Size: ½ cup

Amount per serving

Calories: 79.53	Potassium: 220.47 mg
57.90% from Fat,	Magnesium: 9.72 mg
24.20% from Protein	Zinc: .33 mg
18.00% from Carb	Copper: .08 mg
Protein: 4.85 g	Manganese: .15 mg
Total Fat: 5.16 g	Vitamin A: 1199.62 IU
Saturated Fat: 3.01 g	Vitamin E: 56.41 mg
Monosaturated Fat: 1.45 g	Thiamin: .03 mg
Polyunsaturated: .34 g	Riboflavin: .10 mg
Cholesterol: 18.38 mg	Niacin: 1.63 mg
Carbohydrates: 3.61 g	Pantothenic Acid: .19 mg
Fiber: .43 g	Vitamin B6: .05 mg
Calcium: 53.35 mg	Folate: 9.56 ug
Phosphorous: 84.31 mg	Vitamin B12: .30 ug
Iron: .42 mg	Vitamin C: 2.21
Sodium: 456.91 mg	Selenium: 3.66 ug
Sugar: 2.26 mg	

Cream Pea Surprise

½ cup sweet peas - steamed

½ cup potatoes - peeled and cooked

¼ cup nonfat sour cream

1 cup milk

1 tsp onion

¼ tsp chicken boullion

Directions: Place above ingredients into blender jar and secure the lid. Press the **Soups** button.

Nutritional Information

Yield: 2 cups
Serving Size: ½ cup

Amount per serving

Calories: 79.16	Potassium: 248.57 mg
36.30% from Fat,	Magnesium: 20.35 mg
18.30% from Protein	Zinc: .42 mg
45.40% from Carb	Copper: .06 mg
Protein: 3.67 g	Manganese: .06 mg
Total Fat: 3.23 g	Vitamin A: 435.09 IU
Saturated Fat: 1.99 g	Vitamin E: 62.38 mg
Monosaturated Fat: .92 g	Thiamin: .08 mg
Polyunsaturated: .15 g	Riboflavin: .15 mg
Cholesterol: 7.55 mg	Niacin: .45 mg
Carbohydrates: 9.11 g	Pantothenic Acid: .50 mg
Fiber: .92 g	Vitamin B6: .12 mg
Calcium: 105.26 mg	Folate: 12.55 ug
Phosphorous: 95.74 mg	Vitamin B12: .28 ug
Iron: .50 mg	Vitamin C: 12.91 mg
Sodium: 43.69 mg	Selenium: 1.87 ug
Sugar: 4.10 mg	

Tasty Taco Soup

2 cups hot water

1 Roma tomato - cut in half

1 rib celery - cut in half

1 carrot - cut in half

3 Tbsp popcorn kernels

1 Tbsp dry kidney beans

1 Tbsp taco seasoning

1 chicken boullion cube

1/8 tsp salt

1/8 tsp pepper

Directions: Place above ingredients into blender jar in order as listed and secure the lid. Press the **Soups** button.

Add: 2 cups tortilla chips*

Directions: Tap the Pulse button 3 times until chips are blended in soup.

*You may add corn, beans, cooked chicken, etc. to create a more chunky soup.

Nutritional Information

Yield: 4 cups
Serving Size: 1/2 cup

Amount per serving

Calories: 16.79	Potassium: 95.63 mg
8.43% from Fat.	Magnesium: 5.35 mg
14.10% from Protein	Zinc: .08 mg
77.50% from Carb	Copper: .03 mg
Protein: .56 g	Manganese: .05 mg
Total Fat: .15 g	Vitamin A: 1355.25 IU
Saturated Fat: .03 g	Vitamin E: 0.00 mg
Monosaturated Fat: .03 g	Thiamin: .02 mg
Polyunsaturated: .08 g	Riboflavin: .01 mg
Cholesterol: 0.00 mg	Niacin: .23 mg
Carbohydrates: 3.09 g	Pantothenic Acid: .06 mg
Fiber: .82 g	Vitamin B6: .03 mg
Calcium: 9.16 mg	Folate: 8.87 ug
Phosphorous: 11.73 mg	Vitamin B12: 0.00 ug
Iron: .14 mg	Vitamin C: 3.21 mg
Sodium: 189.19 mg	Selenium: .08 ug
Sugar: 1.00 mg	

Gazpacho

1 large tomato - quartered

1/2 cucumber - peeled and cut into 3inch pieces

1/2 small onion

1/2 green bell pepper - keep seeds

1 1/2 cups canned tomato juice

3 Tbsp red wine vinegar

2 Tbsp olive oil

Dash Tabasco sauce

1/8 tsp salt

1/8 tsp pepper

Directions: Place above ingredients into blender jar and secure the lid. Press the **Soups** button.

Nutritional Information

Yield: 4 cups
Serving Size: 1/2 cup

Amount per serving

Calories: 47.30	Potassium: 186.46 mg
60.90% from Fat	Magnesium: 10.44 mg
5.34% from Protein	Zinc: .13 mg
33.80% from Carb	Copper: .05 mg
Protein: .68 g	Manganese: .09 mg
Total Fat: 3.46 g	Vitamin A: 399.98 IU
Saturated Fat: .47 g	Vitamin E: 0.00 mg
Monosaturated Fat: 2.51 g	Thiamin: .04 mg
Polyunsaturated: .39 g	Riboflavin: .02 mg
Cholesterol: 0.00 mg	Niacin: .47mg
Carbohydrates: 4.32g	Pantothenic Acid: .16 mg
Fiber: .69 g	Vitamin B6: .10 mg
Calcium: 9.96 mg	Folate: 14.62 ug
Phosphorous: 17.92 mg	Vitamin B12: 0.00 ug
Iron: .36 mg	Vitamin C: 18.89 mg
Sodium: 161.53 mg	Selenium: .19 ug
Sugar: 3.05 mg	

Raw Vegetable Soup

2 cups hot water

½ carrot – place vertically in blender jar

½ rib celery – place vertically in blender jar

1 green scallion

1 chicken boullion cube

1 ½ Tbsp tomato paste

⅛ tsp salt

⅛ tsp pepper

Directions: Place above ingredients into blender jar and secure the lid. Press the **Soups** button.

Nutritional Information

Yield: 2 ½ cups
Serving Size: ½ cup

Amount per serving

Calories: 10.78	Potassium: 113.87 mg
4.97% from Fat,	Magnesium: 6.48 mg
16.10% from Protein	Zinc: .09 mg
79.00% from Carb	Copper: .04 mg
Protein: .50 g	Manganese: .05 mg
Total Fat: .07 g	Vitamin A: 972.78 IU
Saturated Fat: .01 g	Vitamin E: 0.00 mg
Monosaturated Fat: .01 g	Thiamin: .01 mg
Polyunsaturated: .03 g	Riboflavin: .02 mg
Cholesterol: 0.00 mg	Niacin: .29 mg
Carbohydrates: 2.47 g	Pantothenic Acid: .05 mg
Fiber: .77 g	Vitamin B6: .03 mg
Calcium: 15.48 mg	Folate: 10.39 ug
Phosphorous: 11.54 mg	Vitamin B12: 0.00 ug
Iron: .33 mg	Vitamin C: 3.71 mg
Sodium: 116.87 mg	Selenium: .36 ug
Sugar: 1.24 mg	

Creamy Potato Soup

1 ¾ cups milk

¼ cup sour cream

5 Tbsp butter - melted

3 Tbsp flour

⅔ cup cheddar cheese, shredded

1 green onion - cut in half

¼ tsp salt

¼ tsp pepper

Directions: Place above ingredients into blender jar and secure the lid. Press the **Soups** button twice.

3 slices cooked bacon - broken into 1inch pieces

1 medium potato - baked, peeled and cubed

Directions: Add ingredients and tap the Pulse button approximately 5 times.

Nutritional Information

Yields: 4 cups
Serving Size: ½ cup

Amount per serving

Calories: 201.42	Potassium: 268.63 mg
4.97% from Fat	Magnesium: 24.63 mg
16.10% from Protein	Zinc: .88 mg
79.00% from Carb	Copper: .09 mg
Protein: 7.11 g	Manganese: .16 mg
Total Fat: 13.83 g	Vitamin A: 498.61 IU
Saturated Fat: 8.33 g	Vitamin E: 133.41 mg
Monosaturated Fat: 3.93 g	Thiamin: .09 mg
Polyunsaturated: .61 g	Riboflavin: .17 mg
Cholesterol: 38.16 mg	Niacin: 1.08 mg
Carbohydrates: 12.79 g	Pantothenic Acid: .52 mg
Fiber: 1.04g	Vitamin B6: .16 mg
Calcium: 163.82 mg	Folate: 10.391 ug
Phosphorous: 161.37 mg	Vitamin B12: .37 ug
Iron: .39 mg	Vitamin C: 3.76 mg
Sodium: 296.90 mg	Selenium: 6.93 ug
Sugar: 3.12 mg	

Artichoke and Roasted Red Pepper Soup

1 ½ cup chicken stock

1 cup buttermilk

¼ small onion*

3 cloves garlic*

1 cup canned chickpeas - drained

1 cup canned artichokes - drained

¼ cup olive oil

⅛ tsp salt

⅛ tsp pepper

Directions: Place above ingredients into blender jar and secure the lid. Press the **Soups** button twice.
*Optional: Sautéed onions and roasted garlic greatly enhance flavor

1 cup chickpeas

1 cup artichokes

1 cup roasted red peppers - chopped

¼ cup fresh parsley

Add above ingredients to blender and press Pulse button approximately 5 times, until desired chunky consistency is reached.

Nutritional Information

Yield: 4 cups
Serving Size: ½ cup

Amount per serving

Calories: 296.92	Potassium: 736.44 mg
31.60% from Fat	Magnesium: 78.80 mg
18.80% from Protein	Zinc: 2.18 mg
49.60% from Carb	Copper: .51 mg
Protein: 14.43 g	Manganese: 1.37 mg
Total Fat: 10.82 g	Vitamin A: 852.09 IU
Saturated Fat: 1.60 g	Vitamin E: 2.14 mg
Monosaturated Fat: 5.98 g	Thiamin: .29 mg
Polyunsaturated: 2.26 g	Riboflavin: .26 mg
Cholesterol: 1.70 mg	Niacin: 2.44 mg
Carbohydrates: 38.16 g	Pantothenic Acid: 1.06 mg
Fiber: 11.15 g	Vitamin B6: .41 mg
Calcium: 107.38 mg	Folate: 338.88 ug
Phosphorous: 273.53 mg	Vitamin B12: .16 ug
Iron: 3.84 mg	Vitamin C: 43.15 mg
Sodium: 399.80 mg	Selenium: 6.15 ug
Sugar: 8.15 mg	

Spanish Soup

2 slices bread

Directions: Place above ingredients into blender jar and secure the lid. Press upper Pulse button and hold for 5 seconds, until bread turns into crumbs.

Add:

1 ¾ cup chicken broth

3 cloves garlic

10 almonds

1 tsp salt

⅛ tsp peppers

2 Tbsp olive oil

½ tsp vinegar

Directions: Place ingredients in jar in order as listed and secure the lid. Press the **Speed Up** button until blender reaches speed 7. Allow the blender to run for 30 seconds (watch timer on blender display) then press any lower row button to stop.

Add: 2 cups cantaloupe

Directions: Press Pulse button twice.

Nutritional Information

Yield: 3 cups
Serving Size: ½ cup

Amount per serving

Calories: 123.80	Potassium: 277.02 mg
51.90% from Fat,	Magnesium: 24.95 mg
12.30% from Protein	Zinc: .47 mg
35.80% from Carb	Copper: .14 mg
Protein: 3.95 g	Manganese: .39 mg
Total Fat: 7.43 g	Vitamin A: 1995.58 IU
Saturated Fat: .99 g	Vitamin E: 0.00 mg
Monosaturated Fat: 4.93 g	Thiamin: .08 mg
Polyunsaturated: 1.16 g	Riboflavin: .10 mg
Cholesterol: 0.00 mg	Niacin: 2.03 mg
Carbohydrates: 11.53 g	Pantothenic Acid: .16 mg
Fiber: 1.73 g	Vitamin B6: .12 mg
Calcium: 31.77 mg	Folate: 27.59 ug
Phosphorous: 70.64 mg	Vitamin B12: .08 ug
Iron: .88 mg	Vitamin C: 22.35 mg
Sodium: 677.49 mg	Selenium: 3.80 ug
Sugar: 5.94 mg	

Broccoli Cheese Soup

1 cup hot milk

⅛ cup cheddar cheese - shredded

1 cup broccoli – steamed*

¼ cup onion - steamed

1 tsp cornstarch

¼ tsp chicken boullion

Directions: Place above ingredients into blender jar and secure the lid. Press the **Soups** button.

*May substitute cauliflower

Nutritional Information

Yield 2 ¾ cups
Serving Size: ½ cup

Amount per serving

Calories: 63.98 (43.50% from Fat, 26.90% from Protein, 29.60% from Carb)	Magnesium: 14.33 mg
	Zinc: .58 mg
	Copper: .02 mg
Protein: 4.41 g	Manganese: .09 mg
Total Fat: 3.17 g	Vitamin A: 463.04 IU
Saturated Fat: 1.97 g	Vitamin E: 46.48 mg
Monosaturated Fat: .88 g	Thiamin: .04 mg
Polyunsaturated: .13 g	Riboflavin: .14 mg
Cholesterol: 10.18 mg	Niacin: .19 mg
Carbohydrates: 4.85 g	Pantothenic Acid: .27 mg
Fiber: .96 g	Vitamin B6: .07 mg
Calcium: 132.20 mg	Folate: 24.05 ug
Phosphorous: 101.73 mg	Vitamin B12: .24 ug
Iron: .32 mg	Vitamin C: 16.91 mg
Sodium: 81.37 mg	Selenium: 2.98ug
Sugar: .73 mg	
Potassium: 150.64 mg	

Bacon Cheddar Potato Soup

2 cups milk

1 medium potato - baked and cut in half

½ cup cheddar cheese - shredded

¼ cup onion - steamed

¼ tsp dill weed

¼ tsp rosemary

½ tsp salt

Directions: Place above ingredients into blender jar and secure the lid. Press the **Soups** button.

Note: If soup is not hot after first cycle, press the **Soups** button a second time.

Add:

3 slices bacon – crisped and broken into bits

1 baked potato - cut in half

Directions: Press the Pulse button approximately 5 times to blend in added ingredients.

Nutritional Information

Yield: 3 ½ cups
Serving Size: ½ cup

Amount per serving

Calories: 107.43	Potassium: 272.64 mg
32.10% from Fat	Magnesium: 21.76 mg
20.60% from Protein	Zinc: .70 mg
47.30% from Carb	Copper: .08 mg
Protein: 5.58 g	Manganese: .07 mg
Total Fat: 3.85 g	Vitamin A: 241.42 IU
Saturated Fat: 2.42 g	Vitamin E: 64.93 mg
Monosaturated Fat: 1.08 g	Thiamin: .08 mg
Polyunsaturated: .14 g	Riboflavin: .17 mg
Cholesterol: 12.70 mg	Niacin: .64 mg
Carbohydrates: 12.77 g	Pantothenic Acid: .50 mg
Fiber: .86 g	Vitamin B6: .16 mg
Calcium: 163.09 mg	Folate: 10.16 ug
Phosphorous: 137.15 mg	Vitamin B12: .34 ug
Iron: .26 mg	Vitamin C: 4.26 mg
Sodium: 265.76 mg	Selenium: 3.08 ug
Sugar: .66 mg	

Tomato Cheese Soup

1 large tomato - quartered

¼ cup onion

¼ cup sharp cheddar cheese - shredded

1 Tbsp tomato paste

1 ½ tsps vegetable boullion

1 cup hot water

Salt & pepper to taste

Directions: Place above ingredients into blender jar and secure the lid. Press **Soups** button.

Note: If soup is not hot after first cycle, you may need to press the **Soups** button twice.

Creamy Corn Soup

1 cup whole kernel corn - drained

1 medium carrot - peeled and cut in half

2 green onions

1 cup hot milk

¼ tsp dry mustard

¼ tsp paprika

1 chicken boullion cube

⅛ tsp white pepper

Directions: Place above ingredients into blender jar and secure the lid. Press the **Soups** button.

Nutritional Information

Yield: 3 ½ cups
Serving Size: ½ cup

Amount per serving

Calories: 27.20	Potassium: 87.12 mg
51.50% from Fat	Magnesium: 5.23 mg
21.40% from Protein	Zinc: .21 mg
27.10% from Carb	Copper: .02 mg
Protein: 1.52 g	Manganese: .04 mg
Total Fat: 1.62 g	Vitamin A: 260.34 IU
Saturated Fat: 1.01 g	Vitamin E: 12.16 mg
Monosaturated Fat: .46 g	Thiamin: .01 mg
Polyunsaturated: .08 g	Riboflavin: .03 mg
Cholesterol: 4.95 mg	Niacin: .21 mg
Carbohydrates: 1.92 g	Pantothenic Acid: .05 mg
Fiber: .44 g	Vitamin B6: .03 mg
Calcium: 38.27 mg	Folate: 5.42 ug
Phosphorous: 32.78 mg	Vitamin B12: .04 ug
Iron: .17 mg	Vitamin C: 3.58 mg
Sodium: 55.85 mg	Selenium: .82 ug
Sugar: 1.11 mg	

Nutritional Information

Yield: 2 ¾ cups
Serving Size: ½ cup

Amount per serving

Calories: 51.31	Potassium: 178.85 mg
11.40% from Fat,	Magnesium: 13.52 mg
18.80% from Protein	Zinc: .33 mg
69.80% from Carb	Copper: .02 mg
Protein: 2.62 g	Manganese: .06 mg
Total Fat: .71 g	Vitamin A: 1578.96 IU
Saturated Fat: .31 g	Vitamin E: 25.84 mg
Monosaturated Fat: .20 g	Thiamin: .05 mg
Polyunsaturated: .14 g	Riboflavin: .11 mg
Cholesterol: 1.78 mg	Niacin: .69 mg
Carbohydrates: 9.75 g	Pantothenic Acid: .27 mg
Fiber: 1.14 g	Vitamin B6: .09 mg
Calcium: 64.03 mg	Folate: 16.64 ug
Phosphorous: 70.17 mg	Vitamin B12: .17 ug
Iron: .23 mg	Vitamin C: 3.48 mg
Sodium: 38.27 mg	Selenium: 1.27 ug
Sugar: 1.58 mg	

French Onion Mushroom Soup

1 ½ medium onions peeled and quartered

3 cups beef broth

¼ cup canned mushrooms

Directions: Place above ingredients into blender jar and secure the lid. Press the Pulse button 5 to 10 times, until mushrooms and onions are chopped to desired consistency. Place in pot, and bring soup to a boil. Once it has reached a boil, turn heat to low and allow soup to simmer for 30 minutes.

3 slices French bread

1 ½ cups mozzarella cheese - shredded

Pour soup into bowls. Cover with bread and mozzarella cheese. Turn oven to low broil. Place soup bowls on pan or cookie sheet in oven for approximately 2 minutes, or until cheese has melted.

Nutritional Information

Yield: 4 cups
Serving Size: ½ cup

Amount per serving

Calories: 173.12	Potassium: 204.40 mg
37.50% from Fat,	Magnesium: 15.51 mg
36.60% from Protein	Zinc: 1.60 mg
25.90% from Carb	Copper: .23 mg
Protein: 15.68 g	Manganese: .37 mg
Total Fat: 7.16 g	Vitamin A: 205.00 IU
Saturated Fat: 4.38 g	Vitamin E: 52.73 mg
Monosaturated Fat: 2.07 g	Thiamin: .10 mg
Polyunsaturated: .30 g	Riboflavin: .20 mg
Cholesterol: 27.22 mg	Niacin: 1.25 mg
Carbohydrates: 11.12 g	Pantothenic Acid: .18 mg
Fiber: .71 g	Vitamin B6: .09 mg
Calcium: 353.10 mg	Folate: 28.13 ug
Phosphorous: 241.51 mg	Vitamin B12: .35 ug
Iron: .85 mg	Vitamin C: 2.16 mg
Sodium: 816.78 mg	Selenium: 12.15 ug
Sugar: 1.53 mg	

Tomato Tofu

1 medium onion - quartered and steamed

2 tsp soy oil

1 cup soy milk

10.5 oz. silken tofu

1 ½ large tomato - quartered

½ tsp salt

½ tsp minced garlic

½ tsp dried basil

½ tsp white pepper

Directions: Place above ingredients into blender jar and secure the lid. Press the **Soups** button.

Nutritional Information

Yield: 4 cups
Serving Size: ½ cup

Amount per serving

Calories: 44.98	Potassium: 135.17 mg
47.80% from Fat,	Magnesium: 15.01 mg
23.50% from Protein	Zinc: .32 mg
28.70% from Carb	Copper: .08 mg
Protein: 2.86 g	Manganese: .21 mg
Total Fat: 2.58 g	Vitamin A: 239.73 IU
Saturated Fat: .38 g	Vitamin E: 0.00 mg
Monosaturated Fat: .59 g	Thiamin: .04 mg
Polyunsaturated: .1.48 g	Riboflavin: .02 mg
Cholesterol: 0.00 mg	Niacin: .38mg
Carbohydrates: 3.49 g	Pantothenic Acid: .06 mg
Fiber: .68 g	Vitamin B6: .07 mg
Calcium: 49.18 mg	Folate: 23.60 ug
Phosphorous: 45.80 mg	Vitamin B12: 0.00 ug
Iron: .56 mg	Vitamin C: 4.71 mg
Sodium: 152.24 mg	Selenium: 3.42 ug
Sugar: 1.65 mg	

Bean Soup

1 ½ cups (12 oz.) chicken stock

1 cup canned black beans - drained

1 cup canned chickpeas - drained

¼ cup cooked onion

1 ½ cloves garlic

1 ½ Tbsp lime juice

½ jalapeño pepper - leave seeds

1 tsp cumin

2 tsp chili powder

Directions: Place above ingredients into blender jar and secure the lid. Press the **Soups** button.

Add:

6 oz. canned black beans - drained

7 oz. canned chickpeas - drained

¼ cup red pepper

¼ cup green pepper

¼ cup scallions - chopped

Directions: Press Pulse button 5 to10 times until all ingredients are blended.

Nutritional Information

Yield: 4 cups
Serving Size: ¼ cup

Amount per serving

Calories: 173.27	Potassium: 475.69 mg
13.10% from Fat.	Magnesium: 61.62 mg
23.30% from Protein	Zinc: 1.56 mg
63.60% from Carb	Copper: .38 mg
Protein: 10.40 g	Manganese: .94 mg
Total Fat: 2.59 g	Vitamin A: 280.35 IU
Saturated Fat: .36 g	Vitamin E: 0.00 mg
Monosaturated Fat: .64 g	Thiamin: .24 mg
Polyunsaturated: 1.07 g	Riboflavin: .11 mg
Cholesterol: .28 mg	Niacin: 1.39 mg
Carbohydrates: 28.39 g	Pantothenic Acid: .63 mg
Fiber: 8.65 g	Vitamin B6: .24 mg
Calcium: 50.22 mg	Folate: 232.40 ug
Phosphorous: 183.91 mg	Vitamin B12: .06 ug
Iron: 3.03 mg	Vitamin C: 10.98 mg
Sodium: 193.98 mg	Selenium: 3.79 ug
Sugar: 4.01 mg	

Tortilla Soup Variation

3 Roma tomatoes - halved

2 Tbsp taco seasoning

1 2"x2" cube of sharp cheddar cheese

1 small slice of jalapeño

3 sprigs cilantro

½ tsp garlic salt

1/3 large carrot

2 Tbsp onion

1 tsp chicken boullion

¼ tsp black pepper

2 cups hot water

Directions: Place above ingredients into blender jar and secure the lid. Press the **Soups** button.

Add:

½ cup tortilla chips*

Press the Pulse button approximately 3 times to blend in chips, to create a chunky soup.

* May also add any combination of chips, corn, or beans.

Nutritional Information

Yield: 4 cups
Serving Size: ¼ cup

Amount per serving

Calories: 26.35	Potassium: 110.19 mg
16.20% from Fat	Magnesium: 5.35 mg
15.60% from Protein	Zinc: .11 mg
68.10% from Carb	Copper: .03 mg
Protein: .94 g	Manganese: .05 mg
Total Fat: .43 g	Vitamin A: 1230.91 IU
Saturated Fat: .24 g	Vitamin E: 2.67mg
Monosaturated Fat: .12 g	Thiamin: .02 mg
Polyunsaturated: .07 g	Riboflavin: .01 mg
Cholesterol: 1.08 mg	Niacin: .27 mg
Carbohydrates: 4.08 g	Pantothenic Acid: .05 mg
Fiber: .89 g	Vitamin B6: .205 mg
Calcium: 13.56 mg	Folate: 7.45 ug
Phosphorous: 17.30 mg	Vitamin B12: .01 ug
Iron: .14 mg	Vitamin C: 5.65 mg
Sodium: 271.06 mg	Selenium: .23 ug
Sugar: 1.32 mg	

To blend Fondue, press the **Fondues** button. After blending fondue, place in a pot and continue to heat, according to directions. When blending fondues, ingredients may jump through the hole in the steam cap. You may place a paper towel over the steam cap to prevent any spilling.

Fondue Table of Contents

Vegan, Tofu, Dill, and Scallion Fondue

1 cup soy milk

1 cup silken tofu

8 oz. Vegan Rella cheese

1 Tbsp lemon juice

1 Tbsp cornstarch

2 scallions

2 Tbsp dill

1/8 tsp ground pepper

Directions: Place ingredients in blender jar in order as listed above and secure the lid. Press the **Fondues** button and allow the blender to run a complete cycle. After the cycle has ended, pour the fondue into a fondue pot and heat.

Nutritional Information

Yields: 3 ½ cups
Serving Size: ½ cup

Amount per serving

Calories: 166.79	Potassium: 193.94 mg
60.40% from Fat,	Magnesium: 23.78 mg
27.80% from Protein	Zinc: 1.35 mg
11.80% from Carb	Copper: .08 mg
Protein: 11.89 g	Manganese: .21 mg
Total Fat: 11.50 g	Vitamin A: 549.95 IU
Saturated Fat: 6.29 g	Vitamin E: 84.89 mg
Monosaturated Fat: 3.09 g	Thiamin: .09 mg
Polyunsaturated: 1.31 g	Riboflavin: .20 mg
Cholesterol: 30.13 mg	Niacin: .40 mg
Carbohydrates: 5.06 g	Pantothenic Acid: .09 mg
Fiber: 1.05 g	Vitamin B6: .08 mg
Calcium: 285.21 mg	Folate: 31.37 ug
Phosphorous: 201.79 mg	Vitamin B12: 0.09 ug
Iron: 1.46 mg	Vitamin C: 4.21 mg
Sodium: 234.86 mg	Selenium: 7.97 ug
Sugar: .63 mg	

Spinach and Artichoke Fondue

6 canned artichokes - drained and diced

3 oz. spinach

1 clove garlic - minced

2 Tbsp butter

Directions: Heat butter in sauté pan. Add ingredients to pan and sauté for 4 minutes on low heat.

¾ cup cooking wine

¾ cup water

2 tsps lemon juice

1 Tbsp cornstarch

1 tsp pepper

12 oz. Monterey Jack cheese - cubed

3 oz. grated Parmesan cheese

4 oz. Feta cheese - crumbled

Directions: Place ingredients in blender jar in order as listed above and secure the lid. Press the **Fondues** button and allow the blender to run a complete cycle. After the cycle has ended, pour the fondue into a fondue pot and heat. Add the spinach and artichoke mixture to the pot.

Nutritional Information

Yields: 4 cups
Serving Size: ½ cup

Amount per serving

Calories: 331.70	Potassium: 468.75 mg
58.80% from Fat	Magnesium: 87.32 mg
24.00% from Protein	Zinc: 2.65 mg
17.20% from Carb	Copper: .29 mg
Protein: 20.26 g	Manganese: .35 mg
Total Fat: 22.01 g	Vitamin A: 1829.24 IU
Saturated Fat: 13.93g	Vitamin E: 135.60 mg
Monosaturated Fat: 6.02 g	Thiamin: .11 mg
Polyunsaturated: .79 g	Riboflavin: .42 mg
Cholesterol: 67.44 mg	Niacin: 1.28 mg
Carbohydrates: 14.52 g	Pantothenic Acid: .60 mg
Fiber: 5.61 g	Vitamin B6: .24 mg
Calcium: 567.61 mg	Folate: 92.04 ug
Phosphorous: 410.91 mg	Vitamin B12: 0.84 ug
Iron: 2.03 mg	Vitamin C: 13.64 mg
Sodium: 808.32 mg	Selenium: 11.11 ug
Sugar: 1.35 mg	

Roasted Garlic and Leek Fondue

1 head garlic - separate into individual cloves

2 Tbsp olive oil

1 piece foil

Directions: Preheat oven to 350° F. Place garlic on tin foil and pour olive oil over. Wrap the garlic in the foil, place on a cookie sheet or pan and bake for 40 minutes.

2 leeks - white parts only, chopped

3 Tbsp olive oil

Directions: Place on sauce pan and sauté on low heat for 7 minutes.

¾ cup cooking wine

¾ cup water

2 tsps lemon juice

1 Tbsp cornstarch

¼ tsp nutmeg

1 tsp black pepper

Roasted garlic after it has baked for 40 minutes

8 oz. Gruyere cheese - cubed

8 oz. Emmental cheese - cubed

Directions: Place ingredients in jar in order as listed above and secure the lid. Press the **Fondues** button and allow the blender to run a complete cycle. After the cycle has ended, pour the fondue into a Fondue pot and heat. Add leeks to pot.

Nutritional Information

Yield: 4 cups
Serving Size: ½ cup

Amount per serving

Calories: 235.22	Potassium: 90.83 mg
71.50% from Fat,	Magnesium: 21.62 mg
16.90% from Protein	Zinc: 1.41mg
11.60% from Carb	Copper: .05 mg
Protein: 9.85 g	Manganese: .13 mg
Total Fat: 18.46 g	Vitamin A: 665.39 IU
Saturated Fat: 7.22 g	Vitamin E: 79.53 mg
Monosaturated Fat: 9.10 g	Thiamin: .03 mg
Polyunsaturated: 1.33 g	Riboflavin: .10 mg
Cholesterol: 33.33 mg	Niacin: .15 mg
Carbohydrates: 6.72 g	Pantothenic Acid: .20 mg
Fiber: .50 g	Vitamin B6: .08 mg
Calcium: 314.38 mg	Folate: 17.35 ug
Phosphorous: 205.30 mg	Vitamin B12: 0.82 ug
Iron: .76 mg	Vitamin C: 3.31 mg
Sodium: 230.53 mg	Selenium: 5.70 ug
Sugar: 1.54 mg	

Traditional Cheese Fondue

¾ cup dry white wine

¾ cup water

2 tsps lemon juice

1 Tbsp cornstarch

¼ tsp nutmeg

1 tsp black pepper

8 oz. Gruyere cheese - cubed into 1-inch squares

8 oz. Emmental cheese - cubed into 1-inch squares

Directions: Place ingredients into jar in order listed above and secure the lid. Press the **Fondues** button and allow the blender to run a complete cycle. After the cycle has ended, pour the fondue into a Fondue pot and heat.

Nutritional Information

Yields: 4 cups
Serving Size: ½ cup

Amount per serving

Calories: 137.34	Potassium: 50.43 mg
65.30% from Fat,	Magnesium: 15.36 mg
27.70% from Protein	Zinc: 1.39mg
7.04% from Carb	Copper: .02 mg
Protein: 9.51 g	Manganese: .02 mg
Total Fat: 9.96 g	Vitamin A: 294.48 IU
Saturated Fat: 6.08 g	Vitamin E: 79.53 mg
Monosaturated Fat: 2.86 g	Thiamin: .02 mg
Polyunsaturated: .45 g	Riboflavin: .10 mg
Cholesterol: 33.33 mg	Niacin: .06mg
Carbohydrates: 2.42 g	Pantothenic Acid: .16 mg
Fiber: .10 g	Vitamin B6: .03 mg
Calcium: 301.14 mg	Folate: 3.10 ug
Phosphorous: 197.47 mg	Vitamin B12: 0.82 ug
Iron: .23 mg	Vitamin C: .64 mg
Sodium: 89.32 mg	Selenium: 5.48 ug
Sugar: .57 mg	

Mexican Fondue

1 medium red onion - diced

1 jalapeno pepper - seeded and minced

1 clove garlic - minced

2 Tbsp butter

Directions: Place ingredients in sauce pan and sauté over medium heat.

14 oz. can diced tomatoes - drained

¾ cup beer

2 Tbsp lemon juice

2 tsps chili powder

½ tsp ground cumin

1 tsp dried oregano

1 Tbsp cornstarch

12 oz. sharp cheddar cheese - cubed

Directions: Place ingredients in jar in order as listed above and secure the lid. Press the **Fondues** button and allow the blender to run a complete cycle. After the cycle has ended, pour the fondue into a Fondue pot and heat. Add onion/jalapeno mixture to pot.

Nutritional Information

Yields: 4 cups
Serving Size: ½ cup

Amount per serving

Calories: 271.09	Potassium: 219.79 mg
66.70% from Fat	Magnesium: 21.78 mg
17.90% from Protein	Zinc: 1.49 mg
15.40% from Carb	Copper: .09 mg
Protein: 11.72 g	Manganese: .14 mg
Total Fat: 19.45 g	Vitamin A: 897.01 IU
Saturated Fat: 12.20 g	Vitamin E: 157.05 mg
Monosaturated Fat: 5.43 g	Thiamin: .06 mg
Polyunsaturated: .71 g	Riboflavin: .19 mg
Cholesterol: 60.50 mg	Niacin: .48 mg
Carbohydrates: 10.12 g	Pantothenic Acid: .33 mg
Fiber: 1.27 g	Vitamin B6: .15 mg
Calcium: 331.95 mg	Folate: 18.21 ug
Phosphorous: 245.41 mg	Vitamin B12: 0.37 ug
Iron: .82 mg	Vitamin C: 11.46 mg
Sodium: 412.41 mg	Selenium: 6.47 ug
Sugar: 4.27 mg	

Smoked Cheddar and Tomato Fondue

14 ounce can diced tomatoes - with liquid

¾ cup cooking wine

2 tsps lemon juice

1 Tbsp cornstarch

2 cups smoked cheddar cheese - grated

¼ tsp pepper

Directions: Place ingredients in jar in order as listed above and secure the lid. Press the **Fondues** button and allow the blender to run a complete cycle. After the cycle has ended, pour the fondue into a Fondue pot and heat.

Peanut Butter, Honey, and Chocolate Fondue

1 cup heavy cream - warmed

12 oz. milk chocolate - broken into 1-inch pieces

3 Tbsp honey

Directions: Place ingredients in jar and secure the lid. Press the **Fondues** button.

1 cup chunky peanut butter

Directions: Secure the lid. Press the Pulse button 5 times or until blended to desired consistency.

Note: If desiring a more chunky fondue, press the Pulse button less than 5 times. If desiring a more smooth fondue, you may need to press the Pulse button more than 5 times.

Nutritional Information

Yields: 3 ½ cups
Serving Size: ½ cup

Amount per serving

Calories: 184.08	Potassium: 203.52 mg
62.80% from Fat,	Magnesium: 19.45 mg
22.10% from Protein	Zinc: 1.29 mg
15.10% from Carb	Copper: .07 mg
Protein: 9.97 g	Manganese: .10 mg
Total Fat: 12.59 g	Vitamin A: 477.47 IU
Saturated Fat: 7.97 g	Vitamin E: 97.30 mg
Monosaturated Fat: 3.561g	Thiamin: .04 mg
Polyunsaturated: .39 g	Riboflavin: .16 mg
Cholesterol: 39.60 mg	Niacin: .44 mg
Carbohydrates: 6.82 g	Pantothenic Acid: .28 mg
Fiber: .81 g	Vitamin B6: .10 mg
Calcium: 289.06 mg	Folate: 12.92 ug
Phosphorous: 210.08 mg	Vitamin B12: 0.31 ug
Iron: .62 mg	Vitamin C: 9.27 mg
Sodium: 515.12 mg	Selenium: 5.61 ug
Sugar: 2.74 mg	

Nutritional Information

Yields: 3 cups
Serving Size: ½ cup

Amount per serving

Calories: 640.52	Potassium: 506.01 mg
62.40% from Fat	Magnesium: 134.05 mg
7.47% from Protein	Zinc: 2.12 mg
30.10% from Carb	Copper: .55 mg
Protein: 12.99 g	Manganese: 1.09 mg
Total Fat: 48.23 g	Vitamin A: 292.77 IU
Saturated Fat: 20.09 g	Vitamin E: 80.66 mg
Monosaturated Fat: 18.62 g	Thiamin: .07 mg
Polyunsaturated: 6.93 g	Riboflavin: .21 mg
Cholesterol: 27.29 mg	Niacin: 6.29 mg
Carbohydrates: 52.98g	Pantothenic Acid: .51 mg
Fiber: 5.98 g	Vitamin B6: .23 mg
Calcium: 44.82 mg	Folate: 42.27 ug
Phosphorous: 232.43 mg	Vitamin B12: .04 ug
Iron: 2.43 mg	Vitamin C: .17 mg
Sodium: 24.37 mg	Selenium: 5.00 ug
Sugar: 41.27 mg	

Margarita Fondue

¼ cup sun dried tomatoes

¾ cup hot water

Directions: Soak tomatoes in water for 20 minutes.

14 ounce can diced tomatoes with liquid

¾ cup hot water

2 tsps lemon juice

2 cloves garlic

1 Tbsp tomato paste

1 tsp dry oregano

1 tsp dry basil

1 Tbsp cornstarch

½ tsp red pepper flakes

12 oz. mozzarella cheese - cubed

6 oz. Parmesan cheese - grated

Directions: Remove sun dried tomatoes from water and place on paper towel. Pour the water that the tomatoes were soaking in into the blender. Place other ingredients in blender jar and secure the lid. Press the **Fondues** button. Pour the fondue into a fondue pot. Add the sun dried tomatoes and heat the fondue.

Nutritional Information

Yields: 4 cups
Serving Size: ½ cup

Amount per serving

Calories: 247.78	Potassium: 271.16 mg
58.30% from Fat,	Magnesium: 27.38 mg
29.40% from Protein	Zinc: 2.21 mg
12.30% from Carb	Copper: .14 mg
Protein: 18.37 g	Manganese: .16 mg
Total Fat: 16.20 g	Vitamin A: 603.73 IU
Saturated Fat: 9.36 g	Vitamin E: 9798.87 mg
Monosaturated Fat: 4.89 g	Thiamin: .06 mg
Polyunsaturated: .70 g	Riboflavin: .26 mg
Cholesterol: 52.31 mg	Niacin: .62 mg
Carbohydrates: 7.68 g	Pantothenic Acid: .26 mg
Fiber: 1.14 g	Vitamin B6: .12 mg
Calcium: 472.71 mg	Folate: 12.00 ug
Phosphorous: 326.26 mg	Vitamin B12: 1.45 ug
Iron: .88 mg	Vitamin C: 12.41 mg
Sodium: 725.96 mg	Selenium: 11.65 ug
Sugar: 2.78 mg	

SAUCES

Sauces Table of Contents

Cheesy Potatoes Sauce and Casserole

8 medium potatoes - peeled and quartered

¼ large onion

2-2½ cups water

Directions: Preheat oven to 350° F. Place 4 potatoes, onion, and enough water to cover the potatoes (approximately to the 4½ cups line) in the jar and secure the lid. Press the Pulse button for 3 to 5 seconds. Rinse and drain in colander. Place rest of potatoes in jar and repeat process. Rinse and drain in colander.

¼ cup margarine - melted

2 cups nonfat sour cream

10.5 oz. cream of chicken soup

1 cup cheddar cheese - shredded

1 cup mozzarella cheese – shredded*

1 tsp salt

1 tsp pepper

2 cups cornflakes

Directions: Place ingredients (except cornflakes) in jar and with a spatula, move cheese towards bottom of the jar. Secure the lid and press the **Dressings** button. Mix potatoes and sauce in a large bowl and place in a sprayed 9 x 13" baking dish. Sprinkle cornflakes over potatoes.
Bake uncovered at 350° F for 60 minutes.

*May substitute shredded Monterey Jack cheese

Nutritional Information

Yield: 12 cups
Serving Size: ¼ cup

Amount per serving

Calories: 101.03	Potassium: 190.12 mg
44.20% from Fat	Magnesium: 13.13 mg
12.40% from Protein	Zinc: .41 mg
43.40% from Carb	Copper: .09 mg
Protein: 3.17 g	Manganese: .09 mg
Total Fat: 5.03 g	Vitamin A: 167.59 IU
Saturated Fat: 2.60 g	Vitamin E: 41.20 mg
Monosaturated Fat: 1.65 g	Thiamin: .06 mg
Polyunsaturated: .51 g	Riboflavin: .05 mg
Cholesterol: 10.62 mg	Niacin: .71 mg
Carbohydrates: 11.10 g	Pantothenic Acid: .32 mg
Fiber: .92 g	Vitamin B6: .14 mg
Calcium: 74.09 mg	Folate: 6.67 ug
Phosphorous: 66.39 mg	Vitamin B12: 0.10 ug
Iron: .22 mg	Vitamin C: 3.91 mg
Sodium: 162.87 mg	Selenium: 1.82 ug
Sugar: .54 mg	

Strawberry Sauce

2 cups fresh strawberries

2 Tbsp sugar

½ Tbsp lemon juice

Directions: Place ingredients in jar in order as listed and press the **Dressings** button

Apple Pear Berry Sauce

2 apples - cored, peeled and cut into eighths

1 pear - cored, peeled and quartered

1 Tbsp sugar

2 Tbsp water

½ tsp lemon juice

Directions: Place ingredients in a saucepan, cover and cook 5 to 7 minutes. Allow the ingredients to cool, and then place in blender jar.

Add:

3 large strawberries fresh or frozen

Directions: Place all ingredients in jar and press the **Dressings** button.

Nutritional Information

Yield: 1 ¼ cups
Serving Size: ¼ cup

Amount per serving

Calories: 50.83	Potassium: 132.82 mg
1.58% from Fat,	Magnesium: 9.82 mg
2.79% from Protein	Zinc: .12 mg
95.60% from Carb	Copper: .04 mg
Protein: .39 g	Manganese: .26 mg
Total Fat: .10 g	Vitamin A: 40.07 IU
Saturated Fat: .01 g	Vitamin E: 0.00 mg
Monosaturated Fat: .01 g	Thiamin: .02 mg
Polyunsaturated: .05 g	Riboflavin: .03 mg
Cholesterol: 0.00 mg	Niacin: .41 mg
Carbohydrates: 13.24 g	Pantothenic Acid: .10 mg
Fiber: 1.86 g	Vitamin B6: .03 mg
Calcium: .33 mg	Folate: 15.23 ug
Phosphorous: 14.30 mg	Vitamin B12: 0.00 ug
Iron: 11.58 mg	Vitamin C: 37.12 mg
Sodium: .66 mg	Selenium: .65 ug
Sugar: 1.78 mg	

Nutritional Information

Yield: 3 cups
Serving Size: ½ cup

Amount per serving

Calories: 48.92	Potassium: 80.42 mg
1.63% from Fat	Magnesium: 4.22 mg
1.85% from Protein	Zinc: .06 mg
96.50% from Carb	Copper: .04 mg
Protein: .25 g	Manganese: .03 mg
Total Fat: .10 g	Vitamin A: 24.31 IU
Saturated Fat: .01 g	Vitamin E: 0.00 mg
Monosaturated Fat: .01 g	Thiamin: .01 mg
Polyunsaturated: .03 g	Riboflavin: .02 mg
Cholesterol: 0.00 mg	Niacin: .09 mg
Carbohydrates: 12.97 g	Pantothenic Acid: .05 mg
Fiber: 1.64 g	Vitamin B6: .03 mg
Calcium: 5.42 mg	Folate: 2.49 ug
Phosphorous: 8.55 mg	Vitamin B12: 0.00 ug
Iron: .09 mg	Vitamin C: 3.36 mg
Sodium: .45 mg	Selenium: .05 ug
Sugar: 9.83 mg	

Tartar Sauce

1 cup mayonnaise

1 Tbsp lemon juice

1 large dill pickle

3 pitted medium olives

1 hard boiled egg

½ onion

Directions: Place ingredients in jar in order as listed and secure the lid. Tap the Pulse button 10 to 15 times.

Hollandaise Sauce

8 egg yolks

4 Tbsp lemon juice

½ tsp Salt

¼ tsp parsley

1 cup melted butter

Directions: Place ingredients in jar in order as listed and secure the lid. Press the Pulse button for 3 to 6 seconds.

Nutritional Information

Yield: 2 cups
Serving Size: ¼ cup

Amount per serving

Calories: 208.98	Potassium: 41.09 mg
93.50% from Fat	Magnesium: 2.92 mg
1.41% from Protein	Zinc: .10 mg
5.13% from Carb	Copper: .02 mg
Protein: .75 g	Manganese: .01 mg
Total Fat: 21.99 g	Vitamin A: 122.96 IU
Saturated Fat: 3.38 g	Vitamin E: 25.57 mg
Monosaturated Fat: 5.64 g	Thiamin: .01 mg
Polyunsaturated: 11.80 g	Riboflavin: .02 mg
Cholesterol: 19.46 mg	Niacin: .02 mg
Carbohydrates: 2.72 g	Pantothenic Acid: .11 mg
Fiber: .34 g	Vitamin B6: .18 mg
Calcium: 10.88 mg	Folate: 4.97 ug
Phosphorous: 16.41 mg	Vitamin B12: .10 ug
Iron: .32 mg	Vitamin C: 1.64 mg
Sodium: 349.26 mg	Selenium: 1.18 ug
Sugar: 1.00 mg	

Nutritional Information

Yield: 1 ¾ cups
Serving Size: ¼ cup

Amount per serving

Calories: 295.80	Potassium: 39.55 mg
93.70% from Fat	Magnesium: 2.15 mg
4.41% from Protein	Zinc: .47 mg
1.93% from Carb	Copper: .02 mg
Protein: 3.32 g	Manganese: .01 mg
Total Fat: 31.34 g	Vitamin A: 1889.37 IU
Saturated Fat: 18.47 g	Vitamin E: 287.98mg
Monosaturated Fat: 9.04 g	Thiamin: .04 mg
Polyunsaturated: 1.78 g	Riboflavin: .11 mg
Cholesterol: 303.83 mg	Niacin: .03 mg
Carbohydrates: 1.46 g	Pantothenic Acid: .61 mg
Fiber: .04 g	Vitamin B6: .07 mg
Calcium: 33.03 mg	Folate: 29.87 ug
Phosphorous: 82.32 mg	Vitamin B12: .43 ug
Iron: .53 mg	Vitamin C: 4.07 mg
Sodium: 364.42 mg	Selenium: 10.96 ug
Sugar: .34 mg	

Good-for-You Gravy

1 ½ cups meat drippings

1 beef or chicken bouillon cubes

2 Tbsp cornstarch

⅛ tsp pepper

Directions: Place ingredients in jar in order as listed and secure the lid. Press the **Soups** button.

Note: If drippings are hot, press the **Soups** button once. if drippings are cold, press the **Soups** button twice.

Yogurt Herb Sauce

2 cups low-fat plain yogurt

½ cups low-fat mayonnaise

1 ¾ Tbsp tarragon vinegar

1 tsp thyme

1 tsp dry mustard

¾ tsp olive oil

1 ½ tsp soy sauce

1 clove garlic

Directions: Place ingredients in jar in order as listed and secure the lid. Press the **Dressings** button

Nutritional Information

Yield: 2 cups
Serving Size: ¼ cup

Amount per serving

Calories: 141.98	Potassium: 813.39 mg
7.65% from Fat	Magnesium: 92.42 mg
43.60% from Protein	Zinc: .95 mg
48.70% from Carb	Copper: .13 mg
Protein: 16.30 g	Manganese: .12 mg
Total Fat: 1.27 g	Vitamin A: 14.26 IU
Saturated Fat: .18 g	Vitamin E: 0.00 mg
Monosaturated Fat: .28 g	Thiamin: .30 mg
Polyunsaturated: .71 g	Riboflavin: .38 mg
Cholesterol: 0.00 mg	Niacin: 9.42 mg
Carbohydrates: 18.22 g	Pantothenic Acid: .64 mg
Fiber: 7.50 g	Vitamin B6: .57 mg
Calcium: 87.29 mg	Folate: 84.66 ug
Phosphorous: 273.49 mg	Vitamin B12: 2.57 ug
Iron: 5.14 mg	Vitamin C: .12 mg
Sodium: 8.46 mg	Selenium: 3.22 ug
Sugar: 0.00 mg	

Nutritional Information

Yield: 3 cups
Serving Size: ¼ cup

Amount per serving

Calories: 93.50	Potassium: 71.38 mg
82.20% from Fat	Magnesium: 6.11 mg
6.77% from Protein	Zinc: .27 mg
11.00% from Carb	Copper: .01 mg
Protein: 1.61g	Manganese: .02 mg
Total Fat: 8.66 g	Vitamin A: 73.89 IU
Saturated Fat: 1.97 g	Vitamin E: 18.36 mg
Monosaturated Fat: 2.25 g	Thiamin: .01 mg
Polyunsaturated: 3.97 g	Riboflavin: .06 mg
Cholesterol: 8.79 mg	Niacin: .07 mg
Carbohydrates: 2.62 g	Pantothenic Acid: .18 mg
Fiber: .07 g	Vitamin B6: .07 mg
Calcium: 54.43 mg	Folate: 4.10 ug
Phosphorous: 42.74 mg	Vitamin B12: .17 ug
Iron: .22 mg	Vitamin C: .36 mg
Sodium: 108.93 mg	Selenium: 1.11 ug
Sugar: 2.07 mg	

Chinese Hot Mustard

½ cup warm water

1⅓ Tbsp olive oil

¾ tsp sugar

½ cup dry mustard

Directions: Place ingredients in jar in order as listed and secure the lid. Press the Pulse button for 5 to 10 seconds or until well blended.

Cocktail Sauce

1 ¾ cups ketchup

2 Tbsp vinegar

¼ cup horseradish

2 drops Tabasco sauce

¼ cup lemon juice

1 Tbsp Worcestershire sauce

3 ribs celery - cut in 3-inch pieces

½ tsp salt

Directions: Place ingredients in jar in order as listed and secure the lid. Press the **Dressings** button.

Nutritional Information

Yield: 1 cup
Serving Size: ½ cup

Amount per serving

Calories: 74.92	Potassium: 56.47 mg
80.30% from Fat	Magnesium: .30 mg
9.05% from Protein	Zinc: .36 mg
10.70% from Carb	Copper: 0.00 mg
Protein: 1.72g	Manganese: 0.00 mg
Total Fat: 6.78 g	Vitamin A: 22.80 IU
Saturated Fat: .68 g	Vitamin E: 0.00 mg
Monosaturated Fat: 3.74 g	Thiamin: 0.00 mg
Polyunsaturated: .51 g	Riboflavin: 0.00 mg
Cholesterol: 0.00 mg	Niacin: .44 mg
Carbohydrates: 2.03 g	Pantothenic Acid: 0.00 mg
Fiber: .20 g	Vitamin B6: 0.00 mg
Calcium: 20.45 mg	Folate: 0.00 ug
Phosphorous: 0.00 mg	Vitamin B12: 0.00 ug
Iron: .59 mg	Vitamin C: 22.64mg
Sodium: 1.02 mg	Selenium: 0.00 ug
Sugar: .79 mg	

Nutritional Information

Yield: 3 cups
Serving Size: ½ cup

Amount per serving

Calories: 79.25	Potassium: 377.42 mg
5.10% from Fat	Magnesium: 19.92 mg
7.07% from Protein	Zinc: .30 mg
87.80% from Carb	Copper: .14 mg
Protein: 1.61g	Manganese: .12 mg
Total Fat: .52 g	Vitamin A: 748.51 IU
Saturated Fat: .08 g	Vitamin E: 0.00 mg
Monosaturated Fat: .08 g	Thiamin: .02 mg
Polyunsaturated: .22 g	Riboflavin: .35 mg
Cholesterol: 0.00 mg	Niacin: 1.16 mg
Carbohydrates: 20.02 g	Pantothenic Acid: .10 mg
Fiber: 1.60 g	Vitamin B6: .13 mg
Calcium: 26.92 mg	Folate: 24.72 ug
Phosphorous: 34.30 mg	Vitamin B12: 0.00 ug
Iron: .59 mg	Vitamin C: 22.86 mg
Sodium: 851.46 mg	Selenium: .61 ug
Sugar: 16.00 mg	

Chipotle Pepper Cream Sauce

6 oz. tofu

¾ Tbsp low-fat cream cheese

¼ tsp garlic salt

3 Tbsp Parmesan cheese

2 Tbsp Romano cheese

2 Tbsp butter

¼ tsp white pepper

½ canned chipotle pepper

Directions: Place ingredients in jar in order and secure the lid. Press the **Dressings** button.

Marinara Sauce

1 carrot

1 Tbsp olive oil

2 medium garlic cloves

¼ large onion

2 cups fresh tomatoes - quartered

½ tsp dried oregano

1 tsp crushed basil

¼ tsp black pepper

Directions: Place ingredients in jar in order as listed and secure the lid. Press the Pulse button for 10 to 15 seconds. Sauce should be chunky. Pour into saucepan, simmer over low heat.

Note: If not blending, half way through, remove jar and shake it so ingredients in jar move around. Place back on blender and continue pulsing.

Nutritional Information

Yield: 2 cups
Serving Size: ½ cup

Amount per serving

Calories: 67.10	Potassium: 45.27 mg
72.30% from Fat	Magnesium: 9.09 mg
21.30% from Protein	Zinc: .34 mg
6.31% from Carb	Copper: .05 mg
Protein: 3.68 g	Manganese: .10 mg
Total Fat: 5.54 g	Vitamin A: 157.90 IU
Saturated Fat: 3.10 g	Vitamin E: 32.28 mg
Monosaturated Fat: .1.46 g	Thiamin: .02 mg
Polyunsaturated: .61 g	Riboflavin: .04 mg
Cholesterol: 14.16mg	Niacin: .15 mg
Carbohydrates: 1.09 g	Pantothenic Acid: .04 mg
Fiber: .11 g	Vitamin B6: .03 mg
Calcium: 90.50 mg	Folate: 10.85 ug
Phosphorous: 68.27 mg	Vitamin B12: .11 ug
Iron: .36 mg	Vitamin C: 6.89 mg
Sodium: 104.88 mg	Selenium: 2.96 ug
Sugar: .37 mg	

Nutritional Information

Yield: 3 cups
Serving Size: ½ cup

Amount per serving

Calories: 49.77	Potassium: 264.72 mg
40.50% from Fat	Magnesium: 12.09 mg
6.73% from Protein	Zinc: .19 mg
52.80% from Carb	Copper: .10 mg
Protein: .91 g	Manganese: .20 mg
Total Fat: 2.44 g	Vitamin A: 1447.83 IU
Saturated Fat: .33 g	Vitamin E: 0.00 mg
Monosaturated Fat: .1.69 g	Thiamin: .06 mg
Polyunsaturated: .30 g	Riboflavin: .03 mg
Cholesterol: 0.00 mg	Niacin: .72 mg
Carbohydrates: 7.16 g	Pantothenic Acid: .23 mg
Fiber: 1.67g	Vitamin B6: .14 mg
Calcium: 32.89 mg	Folate: 11.33 ug
Phosphorous: 26.80 mg	Vitamin B12: 0.00 ug
Iron: .58 mg	Vitamin C: 14.08 mg
Sodium: 196.55 mg	Selenium: .66 ug
Sugar: 3.74 mg	

Tomato Sauce

6 Roma tomatoes - quartered

½ large onion

2 Tbsp tomato paste

1 clove garlic

½ tsp basil

½ tsp oregano

½ tsp lemon juice

½ tsp brown sugar

½ tsp salt

Directions: See Marinara Sauce recipe.

Spaghetti Sauce

3 cups tomatoes - peeled and quartered

½ medium onion - quartered

6 oz. canned tomato paste

1 clove garlic

1 tsp dried parsley

1 tsp dried oregano

½ tsp dried basil

¼ tsp black pepper

⅛ tsp salt

½ tsp sugar

1 bay leaf

Directions: Place ingredients in jar in order as listed and secure the lid. Press the **Dressings** button. Pour into saucepan and simmer for 30 minutes.

Nutritional Information

Yield: 3 ½ cups
Serving Size: ½ cup

Amount per serving

Calories: 29.16	Potassium: 253.31 mg
4.33% from Fat	Magnesium: 11.67 mg
11.00% from Protein	Zinc: .17 mg
84.70% from Carb	Copper: .10 mg
Protein: .91 g	Manganese: .16 mg
Total Fat: .16 g	Vitamin A: 207.24 IU
Saturated Fat: .03 g	Vitamin E: 0.00 mg
Monosaturated Fat: .02 g	Thiamin: .05 mg
Polyunsaturated: .07 g	Riboflavin: .03 mg
Cholesterol: 0.00 mg	Niacin: .67 mg
Carbohydrates: 7.03 g	Pantothenic Acid: .18 mg
Fiber: 1.44 g	Vitamin B6: .12 mg
Calcium: 26.31 mg	Folate: 10.07 ug
Phosphorous: 24.49 mg	Vitamin B12: 0.00 ug
Iron: .57 mg	Vitamin C: 12.98 mg
Sodium: 367.68 mg	Selenium: .73 ug
Sugar: 4.05 mg	

Nutritional Information

Yield: 3 ¾ cups
Serving Size: ½ cup

Amount per serving

Calories: 52.84	Potassium: 514.09 mg
4.72% from Fat,	Magnesium: 22.98 mg
13.00% from Protein	Zinc: .35 mg
82.30% from Carb	Copper: .20 mg
Protein: 1.99 g	Manganese: .28 mg
Total Fat: .32 g	Vitamin A: 568.17 IU
Saturated Fat: .06 g	Vitamin E: 0.00 mg
Monosaturated Fat: .05g	Thiamin: .08 mg
Polyunsaturated: .14 g	Riboflavin: .07 mg
Cholesterol: 0.00 mg	Niacin: 1.43 mg
Carbohydrates: 12.56 g	Pantothenic Acid: .27 mg
Fiber: 2.78 g	Vitamin B6: .20 mg
Calcium: 42.75 mg	Folate: 15.91 ug
Phosphorous: 47.48 mg	Vitamin B12: 0.00 ug
Iron: 1.37 mg	Vitamin C: 21.63 mg
Sodium: 445.54 mg	Selenium: 1.92 ug
Sugar: 7.38 mg	

Raw Applesauce

4 apples cored - leave peel on

¼ cup pineapple juice

1 tsp fresh fruit

¼ tsp cinnamon (optional)

4 Tbsp sugar

Directions: Place ingredients in jar in order as listed and secure the lid. Tap the Pulse button 3 to 5 times. Remove jar and shake it so that ingredients move around in jar. Place back on blender and tap the Pulse button 3 to 5 more times. Press the **Smoothie** button.

Low-fat Alfredo Sauce

1⅓ cup steaming skim milk*

1 small garlic clove

1 Tbsp flour

2 Tbsp fat free cream cheese

½ cup grated Parmesan cheese**

1 ½ Tbsp Molly McButter™, butter flavor

Directions: Place ingredients in jar in order as listed and secure the lid. Press the **Soups** button.

*May heat milk in blender by pressing the **Soups** button twice.
**May substitute Romano cheese

Nutritional Information

Yield: 2 ½ cups
Serving Size: ½ cup

Amount per serving

Calories: 95.78	Potassium: 111.04 mg
1.29% from Fat,	Magnesium: 5.89 mg
1.26% from Protein	Zinc: .07 mg
97.40% from Carb	Copper: .04 mg
Protein: .32 g	Manganese: .18 mg
Total Fat: .15 g	Vitamin A: 40.27 IU
Saturated Fat: .02 g	Vitamin E: 0.00 mg
Monosaturated Fat: .01 g	Thiamin: .03 mg
Polyunsaturated: .04 g	Riboflavin: .03 mg
Cholesterol: 0.00 mg	Niacin: .13 mg
Carbohydrates: 25.04 g	Pantothenic Acid: .09 mg
Fiber: 1.44 g	Vitamin B6: .05 mg
Calcium: 8.88 mg	Folate: 3.06 ug
Phosphorous: 12.45 mg	Vitamin B12: 0.00 ug
Iron: .16 mg	Vitamin C: 5.85 mg
Sodium: .17 mg	Selenium: .08 ug
Sugar: 22.16 mg	

Nutritional Information

Yield: 3 cups
Serving Size: ½ cup

Amount per serving

Calories: 98.19	Potassium: 122.46 mg
57.10% from Fat	Magnesium: 13.78 mg
24.00% from Protein	Zinc: .63 mg
18.90% from Carb	Copper: .03 mg
Protein: 5.93 g	Manganese: .06 mg
Total Fat: 6.26 g	Vitamin A: 268.19 IU
Saturated Fat: 3.88 g	Vitamin E: 75.31 mg
Monosaturated Fat: 1.72 g	Thiamin: .03 mg
Polyunsaturated: .25 g	Riboflavin: .15 mg
Cholesterol: 18.69 mg	Niacin: .15 mg
Carbohydrates: 4.65 g	Pantothenic Acid: .23 mg
Fiber: .20 g	Vitamin B6: .05 mg
Calcium: 169.59 mg	Folate: 5.07 ug
Phosphorous: 131.39 mg	Vitamin B12: .44 ug
Iron: .24 mg	Vitamin C: .63 mg
Sodium: 190.87 mg	Selenium: 3.96 ug
Sugar: 2.94 mg	

Sweet and Sour Sauce

½ cup soy sauce

¼ cup pineapple juice

¼ cup white vinegar

¼ cup brown sugar - firmly packed

⅛ tsp garlic powder

Directions: Place ingredients in jar in order as listed and secure the lid. Press the Pulse button for 5 to 10 seconds. Allow the sauce to sit for at least 5 minutes.

Sofrito

½ cup water

1 ½ large green bell pepper - quartered

1 ½ large red bell pepper - quartered

¼ cup minced garlic

¾ large onion

½ cup fresh cilantro

6 small sweet peppers, ajies dulce

¼ cup water

Directions: Press **Speed Up** button until blender reaches speed 10. Allow it to run a complete cycle.

Nutritional Information

Yield: 1 ½ cups
Serving Size: ¼ cup

Amount per serving

Calories: 53.05	Potassium: 86.07 mg
0.42% from Fat	Magnesium: 13.47 mg
8.21% from Protein	Zinc: .11 mg
91.40% from Carb	Copper: .07 mg
Protein: 1.14 g	Manganese: .22 mg
Total Fat: .03 g	Vitamin A: .52 IU
Saturated Fat: 0.00 g	Vitamin E: 0.00 mg
Monosaturated Fat: 0.00 g	Thiamin: .02 mg
Polyunsaturated: .01 g	Riboflavin: .03 mg
Cholesterol: 0.00 mg	Niacin: .75 mg
Carbohydrates: 12.71 g	Pantothenic Acid: .09 mg
Fiber: .20 g	Vitamin B6: .05 mg
Calcium: 13.22 mg	Folate: 5.89 ug
Phosphorous: 26.47 mg	Vitamin B12: 0.00 ug
Iron: .63 mg	Vitamin C: 1.13 mg
Sodium: 1218.23 mg	Selenium: .36 ug
Sugar: 11.11 mg	

Nutritional Information

Yield: 4 cups
Serving Size: ½ cup

Amount per serving

Calories: 20.95	Potassium: 123.42 mg
5.47% from Fat	Magnesium: 7.39 mg
13.40% from Protein	Zinc: .15 mg
81.20% from Carb	Copper: .04 mg
Protein: .79 g	Manganese: .14 mg
Total Fat: .14 g	Vitamin A: 1085.65 IU
Saturated Fat: .03 g	Vitamin E: .06 mg
Monosaturated Fat: .01 g	Thiamin: .04 mg
Polyunsaturated: .07 g	Riboflavin: .04 mg
Cholesterol: 0.00 mg	Niacin: .39 mg
Carbohydrates: 4.80 g	Pantothenic Acid: .15 mg
Fiber: 1.05 g	Vitamin B6: .18 mg
Calcium: 15.32 mg	Folate: 10.14 ug
Phosphorous: 20.27 mg	Vitamin B12: 0.00 ug
Iron: .29 mg	Vitamin C: 63.64 mg
Sodium: 3.75 mg	Selenium: .71 ug
Sugar: 1.93 mg	

Hot Sauce

30 oz. canned whole tomatoes - drained

1 onion - peeled and quartered

2 jalapenos - cut in half

1 sprig cilantro*

Directions: Place ingredients in jar in order as listed and secure the lid. Tap the Pulse button until sauce has reached desired consistency.

*May substitute 1/8 tsp dried cilantro

Mediterranean Sauce

15 oz. canned whole tomatoes

¼ cup roasted red pepper

6 oz. jar marinated artichoke hearts - drained

2 cloves garlic - cut in half

1 tsp cinnamon

1 small onion - quartered

1 tsp dried oregano

1 tsp dried basil

Directions: Place tomatoes in jar in order as listed and secure the lid. Press the Pulse button 3 to 5 times or until pureed. Add remaining ingredients to jar and press the Pulse button 3 to 5 times until the ingredients are coarsely chopped. Place in saucepan and heat to desired temperature.

Nutritional Information

Yield: 3 ½ cups
Serving Size: ½ cup

Amount per serving

Calories: 40.14	Potassium: 339.36 mg
4.63% from Fat	Magnesium: 15.90 mg
10.30% from Protein	Zinc: .23 mg
85.00% from Carb	Copper: .14 mg
Protein: 1.18 g	Manganese: .23 mg
Total Fat: .23 g	Vitamin A: 246.04 IU
Saturated Fat: .03 g	Vitamin E: 0.00 mg
Monosaturated Fat: .04 g	Thiamin: .08 mg
Polyunsaturated: .10 g	Riboflavin: .04 mg
Cholesterol: 0.00 mg	Niacin: .88 mg
Carbohydrates: 9.67 g	Pantothenic Acid: .30 mg
Fiber: 2.06 g	Vitamin B6: .19 mg
Calcium: 35.92 mg	Folate: 17.43 ug
Phosphorous: 33.96 mg	Vitamin B12: 0.00 ug
Iron: .62 mg	Vitamin C: 20.92 mg
Sodium: 264.29 mg	Selenium: .71 ug
Sugar: 5.40 mg	

Nutritional Information

Yield: 3 cups
Serving Size: ½ cup

Amount per serving

Calories: 45.81	Potassium: 339.53 mg
3.95% from Fat	Magnesium: 29.09 mg
14.20% from Protein	Zinc: .34 mg
81.90% from Carb	Copper: .16 mg
Protein: 1.88 g	Manganese: .32 mg
Total Fat: .23 g	Vitamin A: 338.07 IU
Saturated Fat: .04 g	Vitamin E: 0.00 mg
Monosaturated Fat: .03 g	Thiamin: .08 mg
Polyunsaturated: .10 g	Riboflavin: .05 mg
Cholesterol: 0.00 mg	Niacin: .89 mg
Carbohydrates: 10.83 g	Pantothenic Acid: .30 mg
Fiber: 3.29 g	Vitamin B6: .19 mg
Calcium: 48.10 mg	Folate: 32.27 ug
Phosphorous: 52.22 mg	Vitamin B12: 0.00 ug
Iron: 1.04 mg	Vitamin C: 27.61 mg
Sodium: 181.59 mg	Selenium: .74 ug
Sugar: 3.80 mg	

White Sauce

1 cup hot milk

2 Tbsp butter

2 Tbsp flour

½ tsp salt

Directions: Place ingredients in jar in order as listed and secure the lid. Place paper towel over the top of the lid and press the **Soups** button. Press the **Soups** button two more times to allow sauce to thicken.

Pesto Sauce

2 cups fresh basil leaves*

2 medium cloves of garlic - peeled and minced

⅛ cup lemon juice

1 cup slivered almonds

¾ cup olive oil

½ tsp oregano

¼ cup fresh parsley

½ cup grated Parmesan cheese

⅛ tsp salt

⅛ tsp pepper

Direction: Place ingredients in jar in order as listed and secure the lid. Press the **Dressings** button.

*May substitute cilantro

Nutritional Information

Yields: 1 ¼ cups
Serving Size: ½ cup

Amount per serving

Calories: 137.74	Potassium: 444.12 mg
31.40% from Fat	Magnesium: 30.66 mg
26.30% from Protein	Zinc: 1.07 mg
42.20% from Carb	Copper: .02 mg
Protein: 9.14 g	Manganese: .12 mg
Total Fat: 4.84 g	Vitamin A: 147.37 IU
Saturated Fat: 3.04 g	Vitamin E: 39.52 mg
Monosaturated Fat: 1.25 g	Thiamin: .11 mg
Polyunsaturated: .20 g	Riboflavin: .38 mg
Cholesterol: 17.00 mg	Niacin: .42 mg
Carbohydrates: 14.66 g	Pantothenic Acid: .89 mg
Fiber: .37 g	Vitamin B6: .10 mg
Calcium: 304.21 mg	Folate: 13.49 ug
Phosphorous: 244.06 mg	Vitamin B12: .98 ug
Iron: .20 mg	Vitamin C: 1.63 mg
Sodium: 397.02 mg	Selenium: 8.73 ug
Sugar: 12.49 mg	

Nutritional Information

Yields: 2 cups
Serving Size: ¼ cup

Amount per serving

Calories: 280.64	Potassium: 151.04 mg
87.20% from Fat	Magnesium: 41.07 mg
7.20% from Protein	Zinc: .74 mg
5.62% from Carb	Copper: .17 mg
Protein: 5.22 g	Manganese: .36 mg
Total Fat: 28.12 g	Vitamin A: 291.16 IU
Saturated Fat: 4.27 g	Vitamin E: 7.31 mg
Monosaturated Fat: 19.32 g	Thiamin: .04 mg
Polyunsaturated: 3.58 g	Riboflavin: .13 mg
Cholesterol: 5.50 mg	Niacin: .59 mg
Carbohydrates: 4.08 g	Pantothenic Acid: .08 mg
Fiber: 1.95 g	Vitamin B6: .06 mg
Calcium: 126.94 mg	Folate: 10.50ug
Phosphorous: 110.07 mg	Vitamin B12: .14 ug
Iron: 1.31 mg	Vitamin C: 5.35 mg
Sodium: 134.77 mg	Selenium: 1.63 ug
Sugar: .77 mg	

Stir Fry Sauce

¼ cup soy sauce

1 ½ cups water

2 Tbsp cornstarch

1 Tbsp sherry cooking wine*

1 tsp sugar

1 tsp chicken bouillon

⅛ tsp red pepper**

Directions: Place ingredients in jar in order as listed and secure the lid. Press the Pulse button for 3 to 6 seconds, or until completely blended.

*May substitute with water
**May substitute with white pepper

Pizza Sauce

1 cup tomato sauce

1 Tbsp olive oil

3 large tomatoes - quartered

½ small bell pepper

¼ medium onion - peeled

2-3 cloves garlic - peeled

½ tsp dried parsley

1 tsp dried basil

1 ½ tsps dried oregano

½ tsp salt

¼ tsp ground pepper

¼ cup grated parmesan

Directions: Place ingredients in jar in order as listed and secure the lid. Press the **Speed Up** button until blender reaches Speed 5. Allow the cycle to run for 50 seconds.

Nutritional Information

Yield: 2 cups
Serving Size: ½ cup

Amount per serving

Calories: 29.68	Potassium: 32.39 mg
0.52% from Fat	Magnesium: 6.83 mg
11.90% from Protein	Zinc: .06 mg
87.60% from Carb	Copper: .03 mg
Protein: .86 g	Manganese: .07 mg
Total Fat: .02 g	Vitamin A: 3.04 IU
Saturated Fat: 0.00 g	Vitamin E: 0.00 mg
Monosaturated Fat: 0.00 g	Thiamin: .01 mg
Polyunsaturated: .01 g	Riboflavin: .02 mg
Cholesterol: 0.00 mg	Niacin: .54 mg
Carbohydrates: 6.30 g	Pantothenic Acid: .05 mg
Fiber: .17 g	Vitamin B6: .03 mg
Calcium: 4.98 mg	Folate: 2.61 ug
Phosphorous: 18.69 mg	Vitamin B12: 0.00 ug
Iron: .36 mg	Vitamin C: .18 mg
Sodium: 943.97 mg	Selenium: .26 ug
Sugar: 1.38 mg	

Nutritional Information

Yield: 4 cups
Serving Size: ½ cup

Amount per serving

Calories: 71.17	Potassium: 388.79 mg
33.20% from Fat	Magnesium: 19.67 mg
13.80% from Protein	Zinc: .40 mg
53.00% from Carb	Copper: .16 mg
Protein: 2.67 g	Manganese: .26 mg
Total Fat: 2.87 g	Vitamin A: 345.38 IU
Saturated Fat: .81 g	Vitamin E: 3.66 mg
Monosaturated Fat: 1.55 g	Thiamin: .08 mg
Polyunsaturated: .33 g	Riboflavin: .07 mg
Cholesterol: 2.75 mg	Niacin: 1.05 mg
Carbohydrates: 10.28 g	Pantothenic Acid: .34 mg
Fiber: 2.21 g	Vitamin B6: .020 mg
Calcium: 75.03 mg	Folate: 15.49 ug
Phosphorous: 60.34 mg	Vitamin B12: .07 ug
Iron: .1.02 mg	Vitamin C: 25.44 mg
Sodium: 569.00 mg	Selenium: 1.45 ug
Sugar: 5.39 mg	

Buffalo Barbecue Sauce

²/₃ cup orange marmalade

1 cup ketchup

¼ cup cider vinegar

1 Tbsp soy sauce

¾ tsp celery seeds

½ tsp ground red pepper

Directions: Secure lid and press the **Sauces** button.

Nutritional Information

Yield: 2 cups
Serving Size: ½ cup

Amount per serving

Calories: 197.35	Potassium: 289.50 mg
2.74% from Fat	Magnesium: 22.58 mg
3.08% from Protein	Zinc: .28 mg
94.20% from Carb	Copper: .18 mg
Protein: 1.68 g	Manganese: .23 mg
Total Fat: .67 g	Vitamin A: 598.11 IU
Saturated Fat: .08 g	Vitamin E: 0.00 mg
Monosaturated Fat: .25 g	Thiamin: .02 mg
Polyunsaturated: 3.19 g	Riboflavin: .30 mg
Cholesterol: 0.00 mg	Niacin: 1.10 mg
Carbohydrates: 51.45 g	Pantothenic Acid: .05 mg
Fiber: 1.33 g	Vitamin B6: .12 mg
Calcium: 54.25mg	Folate: 14.65 ug
Phosphorous: 34.51 mg	Vitamin B12: 0.00 ug
Iron: 1.11 mg	Vitamin C: 12.78 mg
Sodium: 927.50 mg	Selenium: .70 ug
Sugar: 45.27 mg	

SALAD DRESSINGS

To blend salad dressings, press the
Dressings button. When using spices,
use either all fresh or all dry ingredients,
if possible. When recipe asks for milk
use any kind of desired milk: soy, nonfat,
whole, etc.

Salad Dressings Table of Contents

Tofu Ranch Salad Dressing

1 ¼ cups milk

10.5 oz. tofu

1 oz. packet ranch dressing mix

Directions: Place ingredients into blender jar and secure the lid. Press the **Dressings** button.

Caesar Salad Dressing

6 Tbsp olive oil

4 Tbsp egg substitute

2 cloves garlic

2 tsp red wine vinegar

2 Tbsp lemon juice

½ cup grated parmesan cheese

1 Tbsp bleu cheese

1 tsp salt

½ tsp dry mustard

¼ tsp pepper

Directions: Place ingredients into blender jar and secure the lid. Press the Pulse button for 5 to10 seconds.

Nutritional Information

Yield: 2 ½ cups
Serving Size: 2 Tablespoons

Amount per serving

Calories: 18.50	Potassium: 42.67 mg
33.60% from Fat,	Magnesium: 6.16 mg
32.30% from Protein	Zinc: .16 mg
34.10% from Carb	Copper: .02 mg
Protein: 1.51 g	Manganese: .06 mg
Total Fat: .70 g	Vitamin A: 32.38 IU
Saturated Fat: .17 g	Vitamin E: 8.88 mg
Monosaturated Fat: .16 g	Thiamin: .01 mg
Polyunsaturated: .32 g	Riboflavin: .03 mg
Cholesterol: .61 mg	Niacin: .09 mg
Carbohydrates: 1.60 g	Pantothenic Acid: .06 mg
Fiber: .03 g	Vitamin B6: .01 mg
Calcium: 36.12 mg	Folate: 7.31 ug
Phosphorous: 29.01 mg	Vitamin B12: .06 ug
Iron: .17 mg	Vitamin C: .18 mg
Sodium: 190.59 mg	Selenium: 1.68 ug
Sugar: .10 mg	

Nutritional Information

Yield: 1 cup
Serving Size: 1 Tablespoon

Amount per serving

Calories: 83.78	Potassium: 32.54 mg
79.80% from Fat,	Magnesium: 3.81 mg
16.40% from Protein	Zinc: .36 mg
3.77% from Carb	Copper: .02 mg
Protein: .3.47 g	Manganese: .02 mg
Total Fat: 7.51 g	Vitamin A: 61.21 IU
Saturated Fat: 2.10 g	Vitamin E: 9.99 mg
Monosaturated Fat: 4.44 g	Thiamin: .01 mg
Polyunsaturated: .66 g	Riboflavin: .05 mg
Cholesterol: 6.94 mg	Niacin: .04 mg
Carbohydrates: .80 g	Pantothenic Acid: .15 mg
Fiber: .03 g	Vitamin B6: .01 mg
Calcium: 87.07 mg	Folate: 2.04 ug
Phosphorous: 61.15 mg	Vitamin B12: .18 ug
Iron: .21 mg	Vitamin C: 2.76 mg
Sodium: 275.35 mg	Selenium: 2.44 ug
Sugar: .22 mg	

Red Wine Vinegar Dressing

3 cups olive oil

1 cup red wine vinegar

2 Tbsp sugar

¼ tsp dry mustard

1 ½ tsp salt

3 tsp garlic powder

¼ tsp pepper

¼ tsp cayenne pepper

Directions: Place ingredients into blender jar and secure the lid. Press the **Dressings** button.

Basic Vinaigrette

1 cup olive oil

½ cup red wine vinegar

1 tsp Dijon mustard

¼ tsp black pepper

Directions: Place ingredients into blender jar and secure the lid. Press the Pulse button for approximately 6 seconds.

Nutritional Information

Yield: 4 cups
Serving Size: 1 Tablespoon

Amount per serving

Calories: 92.03	Potassium: 5.53 mg
96.90% from Fat,	Magnesium: .92 mg
0.10% from Protein	Zinc: 0.00 mg
3.04% from Carb	Copper: 0.00 mg
Protein: .02 g	Manganese: .01 mg
Total Fat: 10.13 g	Vitamin A: 3.03 IU
Saturated Fat: 1.36 g	Vitamin E: .92 mg
Monosaturated Fat: 7.48 g	Thiamin: 0.00 mg
Polyunsaturated: 1.01 g	Riboflavin: 0.00 mg
Cholesterol: 0.00 mg	Niacin: 0.00 mg
Carbohydrates: .72 g	Pantothenic Acid: 0.00 mg
Fiber: .02 g	Vitamin B6: 0.00 mg
Calcium: .49 mg	Folate: .01 ug
Phosphorous: .91 mg	Vitamin B12: 0.00 ug
Iron: .09 mg	Vitamin C: .06 mg
Sodium: 55.64 mg	Selenium: .06 ug
Sugar: .65 mg	

Nutritional Information

Yield: 1 cup
Serving Size: 1 Tablespoon

Amount per serving

Calories: 120.62	Potassium: 8.29 mg
98.40% from Fat,	Magnesium: 1.79 mg
0.04% from Protein	Zinc: 0.00 mg
1.53% from Carb	Copper: 0.00 mg
Protein: .01 g	Manganese: .02 mg
Total Fat: 13.51 g	Vitamin A: 1.01 IU
Saturated Fat: 1.82 g	Vitamin E: 0.00 mg
Monosaturated Fat: 9.98 g	Thiamin: 0.00 mg
Polyunsaturated: 1.35 g	Riboflavin: 0.00 mg
Cholesterol: 0.00 mg	Niacin: 0.00 mg
Carbohydrates: .47 g	Pantothenic Acid: 0.00 mg
Fiber: .01 g	Vitamin B6: 0.00 mg
Calcium: .85 mg	Folate: .04 ug
Phosphorous: .98 mg	Vitamin B12: 0.00 ug
Iron: .14 mg	Vitamin C: .13 mg
Sodium: 4.13 mg	Selenium: .12 ug
Sugar: .45 mg	

Bleu Cheese Dressing

1 cup late plain yogurt

½ cup low-fat cottage cheese

¼ cup nonfat mayonnaise

¼ cup sour cream

Directions: Place ingredients into blender jar and secure the lid. Press **Dressings** button.

Add: 1 cup bleu cheese

Directions: Tap the Pulse button 3 to 5 times until blue cheese is blended into dressing.

Non-Dairy Dressing

1 Tbsp peanut butter

3 Tbsp balsamic vinegar

1 Tbsp lemon juice

1 ½ cups soft tofu

2 Tbsp sugar

1 Tbsp honey

2 small cloves garlic - cut in half

1 Tbsp Dijon mustard

Directions: Place ingredients into blender jar and secure the lid. Press the **Dressings** button.

Nutritional Information

Yield: 2 ½ cups
Serving Size: 2 Tablespoons

Amount per serving

Calories: 18.78	Potassium: 38.11 mg
34.90% from Fat,	Magnesium: 2.85 mg
30.40% from Protein	Zinc: .15 mg
34.70% from Carb	Copper: 0.00 mg
Protein: 1.43 g	Manganese: .0.00 mg
Total Fat: .73 g	Vitamin A: 20.57 IU
Saturated Fat: .42 g	Vitamin E: 5.57 mg
Monosaturated Fat: .24 g	Thiamin: .01 mg
Polyunsaturated: .03 g	Riboflavin: .04 mg
Cholesterol: 2.05 mg	Niacin: .02 mg
Carbohydrates: 1.63 g	Pantothenic Acid: .09 mg
Fiber: .06 g	Vitamin B6: .01 mg
Calcium: 29.06 mg	Folate: 2.33 ug
Phosphorous: 25.61 mg	Vitamin B12: .11 ug
Iron: .02 mg	Vitamin C: .14 mg
Sodium: 36.64 mg	Selenium: .91 ug
Sugar: 1.34 mg	

Nutritional Information

Yield: 2 cups
Serving Size: 2 Tablespoons

Amount per serving

Calories: 32.31	Potassium: 43.75 mg
35.70% from Fat,	Magnesium: 9.09 mg
21.00% from Protein	Zinc: .19 mg
43.30% from Carb	Copper: .05 mg
Protein: 1.85 g	Manganese: .13 mg
Total Fat: 1.39 g	Vitamin A: 3.10 IU
Saturated Fat: .22 g	Vitamin E: 0.00 mg
Monosaturated Fat: .45 g	Thiamin: .01 mg
Polyunsaturated: .63 g	Riboflavin: .01 mg
Cholesterol: 0.00 mg	Niacin: .27 mg
Carbohydrates: 3.80 g	Pantothenic Acid: .03 mg
Fiber: .16 g	Vitamin B6: .02 mg
Calcium: 28.29 mg	Folate: 11.40 ug
Phosphorous: 26.62 mg	Vitamin B12: 0.00 ug
Iron: .33 mg	Vitamin C: .69 mg
Sodium: 13.15 mg	Selenium: 2.60 ug
Sugar: 3.12 mg	

Raspberry Vinaigrette Dressing

½ cup olive oil

½ cup apple cider vinegar

1 tsp black pepper

1 tsp salt

1 Tbsp sugar

1 tsp ground oregano

3 Tbsp red raspberry preserves

Directions: Place ingredients into blender jar and secure the lid. Press the **Dressings** button.

Poppy Seed Dressing

1 cup cold water

1 cup apple cider vinegar

1 thin slice onion

¾ cup sugar

1 tsp dry mustard

1 tsp salt

2 Tbsp cornstarch

Directions: Place ingredients into blender jar and secure the lid. Press the **Dressings** button.

Add: **1 Tbsp poppy seeds**

Directions: Press the Pulse button 3 to 4 times. Pour into a separate container and microwave dressing for 2 minutes. Mix so the seeds are no longer sitting on top. Microwave again for 2 minutes.

Nutritional Information

Yield: 1 ½ cup
Serving Size: 1 Tablespoon

Amount per serving

Calories: 49.64	Potassium: 8.14 mg
79.60% from Fat	Magnesium: 1.35 mg
0.13% from Protein	Zinc: 0.00 mg
20.30% from Carb	Copper: .01 mg
Protein: .02 g	Manganese: .02 mg
Total Fat: 4.51 g	Vitamin A: 4.41 IU
Saturated Fat: .61 g	Vitamin E: 0.00 mg
Monosaturated Fat: 3.33 g	Thiamin: 0.00 mg
Polyunsaturated: .45 g	Riboflavin: .0.00 mg
Cholesterol: 0.00 mg	Niacin: 0.00 mg
Carbohydrates: 2.58g	Pantothenic Acid: 0.00 mg
Fiber: .05 g	Vitamin B6: 0.00 mg
Calcium: 1.59 mg	Folate: .42 ug
Phosphorous: 1.07 mg	Vitamin B12: 0.00 ug
Iron: .09 mg	Vitamin C: .56 mg
Sodium: 99.24 mg	Selenium: .06 ug
Sugar: 2.04 mg	

Nutritional Information

Yield: 1 ½ cups
Serving Size: 1 Tablespoon

Amount per serving

Calories: 29.59	Potassium: 6.66 mg
5.16% from Fat	Magnesium: 2.08 mg
1.05% from Protein	Zinc: .04 mg
93.80% from Carb	Copper: .01 mg
Protein: .08 g	Manganese: .03 mg
Total Fat: .18 g	Vitamin A: .16 IU
Saturated Fat: .02 g	Vitamin E: 0.00 mg
Monosaturated Fat: .02 g	Thiamin: 0.00 mg
Polyunsaturated: .11 g	Riboflavin: .0.00 mg
Cholesterol: 0.00 mg	Niacin: .01 mg
Carbohydrates: 7.21 g	Pantothenic Acid: 0.00 mg
Fiber: .05 g	Vitamin B6: 0.00 mg
Calcium: 6.01 mg	Folate: .24 ug
Phosphorous: 3.54 mg	Vitamin B12: 0.00 ug
Iron: .06 mg	Vitamin C: .02 mg
Sodium: 98.61 mg	Selenium: .07 ug
Sugar: 6.55 mg	

Dill Dressing

3 cups low-fat sour cream

2 Tbsp lemon juice

3 green onions - halved

¾ tsp salt

¾ tsp dried dill weed

¼ tsp freshly ground pepper

1 clove garlic – halved

Directions: Place ingredients into blender jar and secure the lid. Press the **Dressings** button.

Thousand Island Dressing

1 cup low-fat mayonnaise

1 cup low-fat plain yogurt

⅛ lemon - peeled*

½ cup chili sauce

2 Tbsp raw honey

¼ cup fresh parsley

¼ onion - peeled

3 Tbsp sweet pickle relish **

Directions: Place ingredients into blender jar and secure the lid. Press the **Dressings** button.

*May substitute 1 tsp lemon juice
**May substitute 1 medium dill pickle

Nutritional Information

Yield: 3 cups
Serving Size: 1 Tablespoon

Amount per serving

Calories: 31.18	Potassium: 23.40 mg
85.00% from Fat	Magnesium: 1.79 mg
5.90% from Protein	Zinc: .04 mg
9.11% from Carb	Copper: 0.00 mg
Protein: .47 g	Manganese: 0.00 mg
Total Fat: 3.01 g	Vitamin A: 98.30 IU
Saturated Fat: 1.88 g	Vitamin E: 25.01 mg
Monosaturated Fat: .87 g	Thiamin: .01 mg
Polyunsaturated: .11 g	Riboflavin: .02 mg
Cholesterol: 6.32 mg	Niacin: .01 mg
Carbohydrates: .73 g	Pantothenic Acid: .05 mg
Fiber: .02 g	Vitamin B6: 0.00 mg
Calcium: 17.42 mg	Folate: 1.92 ug
Phosphorous: 12.59 mg	Vitamin B12: .04 ug
Iron: .02 mg	Vitamin C: .56 mg
Sodium: 44.57 mg	Selenium: .33 ug
Sugar: .05 mg	

Nutritional Information

Yield: 3 cups
Serving Size: 2 Tablespoons

Amount per serving

Calories: 25.57	Potassium: 38.36 mg
11.60% from Fat,	Magnesium: 2.75 mg
10.80% from Protein	Zinc: .12mg
77.60% from Carb	Copper: .01 mg
Protein: .72 g	Manganese: .01 mg
Total Fat: .34 g	Vitamin A: 140.59 IU
Saturated Fat: .08 g	Vitamin E: .20 mg
Monosaturated Fat: .21 g	Thiamin: .01 mg
Polyunsaturated: .01 g	Riboflavin: .03 mg
Cholesterol: 1.16 mg	Niacin: .03 mg
Carbohydrates: 5.19 g	Pantothenic Acid: .07 mg
Fiber: .31 g	Vitamin B6: .01 mg
Calcium: 23.44 mg	Folate: 2.50 ug
Phosphorous: 17.65 mg	Vitamin B12: .06 ug
Iron: .10 mg	Vitamin C: 2.13 mg
Sodium: 142.14 mg	Selenium: .42 ug
Sugar: 3.79 mg	

Creamy Italian Dressing

½ cup low-fat mayonnaise

½ cup low-fat plain yogurt

2 Tbsp vinegar

2 Tbsp olive oil

¾ tsp garlic powder

¼ cup fresh parsley *

¼ cup fresh oregano **

¼ tsp freshly ground pepper

Directions: Place ingredients into blender jar and secure the lid. Press the **Dressings** button.

*May substitute 1 tsp dried parsley
**May substitute 1 tsp dried oregano

Parmesan Vinaigrette

½ cup parmesan cheese - shredded

1 cup vegetable oil

½ cup red wine vinegar

2 fresh green onions

¼ cup fresh basil*

¼ cup fresh parsley**

⅓ tsp salt

¼ tsp ground pepper

Optional, 1 tsp poppy seeds

Directions: Place ingredients into blender jar and secure the lid. Press the **Dressings** button. May stir in poppy seeds after blending.

*May substitute 1 tsp dried basil
**May substitute 1 tsp dried parsley

Nutritional Information

Yield: 1 ¼ cups
Serving Size: 2 Tablespoons

Amount per serving

Calories: 43.41	Potassium: 50.54 mg
62.30% from Fat	Magnesium: 4.40 mg
7.34% from Protein	Zinc: .15 mg
30.40% from Carb	Copper: .01 mg
Protein: .82 g	Manganese: .01 mg
Total Fat: 3.09 g	Vitamin A: 135.04 IU
Saturated Fat: .46 g	Vitamin E: .25 mg
Monosaturated Fat: 2.25 g	Thiamin: .01 mg
Polyunsaturated: .29 g	Riboflavin: .03 mg
Cholesterol: 1.40 mg	Niacin: .04 mg
Carbohydrates: 3.39 g	Pantothenic Acid: .08 mg
Fiber: .36 g	Vitamin B6: .02 mg
Calcium: .29 mg	Folate: 4.05 ug
Phosphorous: 21.85 mg	Vitamin B12: .07 ug
Iron: .19 mg	Vitamin C: 2.38 mg
Sodium: 111.32 mg	Selenium: .58 ug
Sugar: 2.48 mg	

Nutritional Information

Yield: 1 ½ cups
Serving Size: 1 Tablespoon

Amount per serving

Calories: 91.26	Potassium: 24.64 mg
93.40% from Fat	Magnesium: 3.79 mg
3.77% from Protein	Zinc: .11 mg
2.88% from Carb	Copper: .01 mg
Protein: .88 g	Manganese: .03 mg
Total Fat: 9.70 g	Vitamin A: 100.25 IU
Saturated Fat: 1.52 g	Vitamin E: 2.44 mg
Monosaturated Fat: 2.38 g	Thiamin: 0.00 mg
Polyunsaturated: .5.37 g	Riboflavin: .01 mg
Cholesterol: 1.83 mg	Niacin: .04 mg
Carbohydrates: .67 g	Pantothenic Acid: .01 mg
Fiber: .18 g	Vitamin B6: .01 mg
Calcium: 32.06 mg	Folate: 2.46 ug
Phosphorous: 17.92 mg	Vitamin B12: .05 ug
Iron: .24 mg	Vitamin C: 1.22 mg
Sodium: 65.21 mg	Selenium: .39 ug
Sugar: .34 mg	

French Dressing

1 ½ cup vegetable oil

½ cup apple cider vinegar

¾ cup ketchup

2 Tbsp honey

⅓ tsp garlic powder

⅓ tsp celery salt

¼ tsp onion powder

Directions: Place ingredients into blender jar and secure the lid. Press the **Dressings** button.

Restaurant Ranch Salad Dressing

1 cup buttermilk

1 cup mayonnaise

1 tsp garlic salt

1 tsp onion salt

1 Tbsp dried parsley flakes

Directions: Place ingredients into blender jar and secure the lid. Press the **Dressings** button.

Nutritional Information

Yield: 3 cups
Serving Size: 1 Tablespoon

Amount per serving

Calories: 66.92	Potassium: 17.61 mg
89.20% from Fat	Magnesium: 1.31 mg
0.43% from Protein	Zinc: .01 mg
10.40% from Carb	Copper: .01 mg
Protein: .08 g	Manganese: .01 mg
Total Fat: 6.83 g	Vitamin A: 34.99 IU
Saturated Fat: .87 g	Vitamin E: 0.00 mg
Monosaturated Fat: 1.65 g	Thiamin: 0.00 mg
Polyunsaturated: 4.01 g	Riboflavin: .02 mg
Cholesterol: 0.00 mg	Niacin: .06 mg
Carbohydrates: 1.79 g	Pantothenic Acid: 0.00 mg
Fiber: .05 g	Vitamin B6: .01 mg
Calcium: .95 mg	Folate: .60 ug
Phosphorous: 1.62 mg	Vitamin B12: 0.00 ug
Iron: .04 mg	Vitamin C: .58 mg
Sodium: 58.18 mg	Selenium: .03 ug
Sugar: 1.65 mg	

Nutritional Information

Yield: 2 ½ cups
Serving Size: 2 Tbsp

Amount per serving

Calories: 16.70	Potassium: 29.87 mg
23.90% from Fat	Magnesium: 1.99 mg
11.20% from Protein	Zinc: .07 mg
64.90% from Carb	Copper: 0.00 mg
Protein: .48 g	Manganese: .01 mg
Total Fat: .46 g	Vitamin A: 9.80 IU
Saturated Fat: .14 g	Vitamin E: .86 mg
Monosaturated Fat: .27 g	Thiamin: .01 mg
Polyunsaturated: .01 g	Riboflavin: .02 mg
Cholesterol: 1.64 mg	Niacin: .01 mg
Carbohydrates: 2.80 g	Pantothenic Acid: .03 mg
Fiber: .28 g	Vitamin B6: .01 mg
Calcium: 16.46 mg	Folate: .92 ug
Phosphorous: 12.75 mg	Vitamin B12: .03 ug
Iron: .09 mg	Vitamin C: .24 mg
Sodium: 114.12 mg	Selenium: .36 ug
Sugar: 1.98 mg	

Honey Mustard Dressing

1 ½ cup mayonnaise

⅓ cup honey

1 Tbsp vinegar

⅔ cup vegetable oil

½ tsp onion powder

2 tsp minced fresh parsley

2 Tbsp prepared mustard

Directions: Place ingredients into blender jar and secure the lid. Press the **Dressings** button.

Nutritional Information

Yield: 3 cups
Serving Size: 1 Tbsp

Amount per serving

Calories: 41.38	Potassium: 7.28 mg
69.00% from Fat,	Magnesium: .35 mg
0.61% from Protein	Zinc: .02 mg
30.40% from Carb	Copper: 0.00 mg
Protein: .07 g	Manganese: .01 mg
Total Fat: 3.28 g	Vitamin A: 2.31 IU
Saturated Fat: .43 g	Vitamin E: 0.00 mg
Monosaturated Fat: .88 g	Thiamin: 0.00 mg
Polyunsaturated: 1.78 g	Riboflavin: 0.00 mg
Cholesterol: .72 mg	Niacin: .01 mg
Carbohydrates: 3.25 g	Pantothenic Acid: 0.00 mg
Fiber: .17 g	Vitamin B6: 0.00 mg
Calcium: 1.39 mg	Folate: .12 ug
Phosphorous: .64 mg	Vitamin B12: 0.00 ug
Iron: .05 mg	Vitamin C: .05 mg
Sodium: 63.24 mg	Selenium: .05 ug
Sugar: 2.78 mg	

PUREED FOODS

Most pureé foods require only 2 ingredients. The first ingredient is the flavor: carrots, peas, pears, etc. If the ingredient is a vegetable, it must be steamed prior to blending.

The second ingredient is either water or baby formula. Where the recipe calls for water, a formula/water mixture may be substitued. Do not add the formula in powder form.

For most pureed foods, press the **Speed Up** button until blender reaches speed 4. Allow the blender to run for 15 seconds and then press any lower row button to stop.

Pureed Foods Table of Contents

Pureed Peas

1 ½ cup peas - steamed
3 Tbsp water

Directions: Add ingredients to jar and secure the lid. Press the **Speed Up** button until blender reaches Speed 4. Allow the blender to run for 15 seconds. When the display reads 15 seconds, press any lower row button to stop.

Nutritional Information

Yields: 1 cup
Serving Size: ½ cup

Amount per serving

Calories: 93.60	Potassium: 132.00 mg
3.03% from Fat	Magnesium: 26.62 mg
25.70% from Protein	Zinc: .80 mg
71.20% from Carb	Copper: .13 mg
Protein: 6.18 g	Manganese: .33
Total Fat: .32 g	Vitamin A: 2520.00 IU
Saturated Fat: .06 g	Vitamin E: 0.00 mg
Monosaturated Fat: .03 g	Thiamin: .34 mg
Polyunsaturated: .15 g	Riboflavin: .12 mg
Cholesterol: 0.00 g	Niacin: 1.78 mg
Carbohydrates: 17.11 g	Pantothenic Acid: .17 mg
Fiber: 6.60 g	Vitamin B6: .14 mg
Calcium: 29.24 mg	Folate: 70.80 ug
Phosphorous: 92.40 mg	Vitamin B12: 0.00 ug
Iron: 1.82 mg	Vitamin C: 11.88 mg
Sodium: 86.84 mg	Selenium: 1.20 ug
Sugar: 5.58 mg	

Pureed Carrots

3 cups carrots - peeled, cut into 3-inch pieces, and steamed
⅓ cup water

Directions: Add ingredients to jar and secure the lid. Press the **Speed Up** button until blender reaches Speed 4. Allow the blender to run for 15 seconds. When the display reads 15 seconds, press any lower row button to stop.

Nutritional Information

Yields: 2 cups
Serving Size: ½ cup

Amount per serving

Calories: 39.36	Potassium: 307.20 mg
4.89% from Fat	Magnesium: 11.72 mg
8.42% from Protein	Zinc: .23 mg
86.70% from Carb	Copper: .04 mg
Protein: .89 g	Manganese: .14 mg
Total Fat: .23 g	Vitamin A: 11554.60 IU
Saturated Fat: .03 g	Vitamin E: 0.00 mg
Monosaturated Fat: .01 g	Thiamin: .06 mg
Polyunsaturated: .10 g	Riboflavin: .06 mg
Cholesterol: 0.00 mg	Niacin: .94 mg
Carbohydrates: 9.20 g	Pantothenic Acid: .26 mg
Fiber: 2.88 g	Vitamin B6: .13 mg
Calcium: 32.08 mg	Folate: 18.24 ug
Phosphorous: 33.60 mg	Vitamin B12: 0.00 ug
Iron: .29 mg	Vitamin C: 5.66 mg
Sodium: 66.63 mg	Selenium: .10 ug
Sugar: 4.36 mg	

Pureed Squash

1 ¼ cups steamed summer squash

¼ cup water

Directions: Add ingredients to jar and secure the lid. Press the **Speed Up** button until speed 4 is reached. Allow the blender to run for 15 seconds. When the display reads 15 seconds, press any lower row button to stop.

Nutritional Information

Yields: 2 cups
Serving Size: ½ cup

Amount per serving

Calories: 11.25	Potassium: 95.63 mg
11.80% from Fat	Magnesium: 8.64 mg
15.40% from Protein	Zinc: .12 mg
72.80% from Carb	Copper: .04 mg
Protein: .51 g	Manganese: .91.69 IU
Total Fat: .17 g	Vitamin E: 0.00 mg
Saturated Fat: .04 g	Thiamin: .03 mg
Monosaturated Fat: .01 g	Riboflavin: .03 mg
Polyunsaturated: .07 g	Niacin: .20 mg
Cholesterol: 0.00 g	Pantothenic Acid: .08 mg
Carbohydrates: 2.42 g	Vitamin B6: .05 mg
Fiber: 1.79 g	Folate: 11.25 ug
Calcium: 12.77 mg	Vitamin B12: 0.00 ug
Phosphorous: 16.31 mg	Vitamin C: 3.09 mg
Iron: .21 mg	Selenium: .11 ug
Sodium: .40 mg	
Sugar: 1.06 mg	

Pureed Corn

1 cup corn, steamed

¼ cup water

Directions: Place above ingredients into blender jar and secure the lid. Press the **Speed Up** button until speed 4 is reached. Run for 15 seconds then press any lower row button to stop.

Nutritional Information

Yield: 2 cups
Serving Size: ½ cup

Amount per serving

Calories: 72.16	Potassium: 172.20 mg
6.78% from Fat,	Magnesium: 15.06 mg
11.80% from Protein	Zinc: .30 mg
81.40% from Carb	Copper: .03 mg
Protein: 2.48 g	Manganese: .10
Total Fat: .63 g	Vitamin A: 177.94 IU
Saturated Fat: .10 g	Vitamin E: 0.00 mg
Monosaturated Fat: .19 g	Thiamin: .07 mg
Polyunsaturated: .30 g	Riboflavin: .06 mg
Cholesterol: 0.00 mg	Niacin: 1.42 mg
Carbohydrates: 17.06 g	Pantothenic Acid: .23 mg
Fiber: 1.97 g	Vitamin B6: .15 mg
Calcium: 3.87 mg	Folate: 29.52 ug
Phosphorous: 56.58 mg	Vitamin B12: 0.00 ug
Iron: .34 mg	Vitamin C: 5.25 mg
Sodium: 3.05 mg	Selenium: .57 ug
Sugar: 2.76 mg	

Pureed Peaches

2 cups fresh peaches - peeled*

Directions: Place above ingredients into blender jar and secure the lid. Press the **Speed Up** button until speed 4 is reached. Run for 15 seconds then press any lower row button to stop.

*May substitute canned peaches

Pureed Chicken

½ cup water or formula (may use gravy)

1 ½ cups cooked and cubed chicken

Directions: Place above ingredients into blender jar and secure the lid. Press the **Speed Up** button until blender reaches speed 4. Run for 15 seconds then press any lower row button to stop. Use rubber spatula to move ingredients from corner and bottom of jar. Repeat process, until chicken is pureed to desired consistency.

Nutritional Information

Yield: 2 cups
Serving Size: ½ cup

Amount per serving

Calories: 33.15	Potassium: 161.50 mg
5.11% from Fat,	Magnesium: 7.65 mg
8.26% from Protein	Zinc: .14mg
86.60% from Carb	Copper: .06 mg
Protein: 2.77 g	Manganese: .05 mg
Total Fat: .21 g	Vitamin A: 277.10 IU
Saturated Fat: .02 g	Vitamin E: 0.00 mg
Monosaturated Fat: .06 g	Thiamin: .02 mg
Polyunsaturated: .07 g	Riboflavin: .03 mg
Cholesterol: 0.00 mg	Niacin: .69 mg
Carbohydrates: 8.11 g	Pantothenic Acid: .13 mg
Fiber: 1.27 g	Vitamin B6: .02 mg
Calcium: 5.10 mg	Folate: 3.40 ug
Phosphorous: 17.00 mg	Vitamin B12: 0.00 ug
Iron: .21 mg	Vitamin C: 5.61 mg
Sodium: 0.00 mg	Selenium: .09 ug
Sugar: 7.13 mg	

Nutritional Information

Yield: 2 cups
Serving Size: ½ cup

Amount per serving

Calories: 86.63	Potassium: 134.40 mg
20.60% from Fat	Magnesium: 15.52 mg
79.40% from Protein	Zinc: .52 mg
0.00% from Carb	Copper: .03 mg
Protein: 16.29 g	Manganese: .01 mg
Total Fat: 1.87 g	Vitamin A: 10.50 IU
Saturated Fat: .53 g	Vitamin E: 3.15 mg
Monosaturated Fat: .65 g	Thiamin: .04 mg
Polyunsaturated: .40 g	Riboflavin: .06 mg
Cholesterol: 44.63 mg	Niacin: 7.20 mg
Carbohydrates: 0.00 g	Pantothenic Acid: .51 mg
Fiber: 0.0 g	Vitamin B6: .31 mg
Calcium: 8.47 mg	Folate: 2.10 ug
Phosphorous: 119.50 mg	Vitamin B12: .18 ug
Iron: .55 mg	Vitamin C: 0.00 mg
Sodium: 39.44 mg	Selenium: 14.49 ug
Sugar: 0.00 mg	

Pureed Beef

2 cups beef - cooked and cubed

1 cup water or formula

Directions: Place above ingredients into blender jar and secure the lid. Press **Speed Up** button until speed 4 is reached. Run for 15 seconds then press any lower row button to stop. Use rubber spatula to move ingredients from corner and bottom of jar. Repeat process.

Nutritional Information

Yield: 3 cups
Serving Size: ¼ cup

Amount per serving

Calories: 98.66	Potassium: 122.85 mg
56.60% from Fat	Magnesium: 8.89 mg
43.40% from Protein	Zinc: 2.31 mg
0.00% from Carb	Copper: .04 mg
Protein: 10.38 g	Manganese: .01
Total Fat: 6.02 g	Vitamin A: 0.00 IU
Saturated Fat: 2.37 g	Vitamin E: 0.00 mg
Monosaturated Fat: 2.56 g	Thiamin: .03 mg
Polyunsaturated: .22 g	Riboflavin: .08 mg
Cholesterol: 32.51 mg	Niacin: 1.39 mg
Carbohydrates: 0.00 g	Pantothenic Acid: .14 mg
Fiber: 0.00 g	Vitamin B6: .12 mg
Calcium: 3.80 mg	Folate: 2.65 ug
Phosphorous: 80.14 mg	Vitamin B12: 0.95 ug
Iron: 1.04 mg	Vitamin C: 0.00 mg
Sodium: 24.21 mg	Selenium: 7.56 ug
Sugar: 0.00 mg	

Pureed Bananas

2 ripe bananas - cut in half

1 Tbsp water

Directions: Place above ingredients into blender jar and secure the lid. Press **Speed Up** button until speed 4 is reached. Run for 15 seconds then press any lower row button to stop.

Nutritional Information

Yield: 1 cup
Serving Size: ¼ cup

Amount per serving

Calories: 66.75	Potassium: 268.50 mg
3.00% from Fat	Magnesium: 20.29 mg
4.41% from Protein	Zinc: .11 mg
92.60% from Carb	Copper: .06 mg
Protein: .82 g	Manganese: .20
Total Fat: .25 g	Vitamin A: 48.00 IU
Saturated Fat: .08 g	Vitamin E: 0.00 mg
Monosaturated Fat: .02 g	Thiamin: .02 mg
Polyunsaturated: .05 g	Riboflavin: .05 mg
Cholesterol: 0.00 mg	Niacin: .50mg
Carbohydrates: 17.13 g	Pantothenic Acid: .25 mg
Fiber: 1.95 g	Vitamin B6: .28 mg
Calcium: 3.82 mg	Folate: 15.00 ug
Phosphorous: 16.50 mg	Vitamin B12: 0.00 ug
Iron: .19 mg	Vitamin C: 6.52 mg
Sodium: .82 mg	Selenium: .75 ug
Sugar: 9.17 mg	

Pureed Pears

2 cups pears - peeled, cored and steamed

Directions: Place above ingredients into blender jar and secure the lid. Press **Speed Up** button until speed 4 is reached. Run for 15 seconds then press any lower row button to stop.

Nutritional Information

Yield: ¾ cups
Serving Size: ¼ cup

Amount per serving

Calories: 63.80	Potassium: 130.90 mg
1.68% from Fat	Magnesium: 7.70 mg
2.36% from Protein	Zinc: .11 mg
96.00% from Carb	Copper: .09 mg
Protein: .42 g	Manganese: .05 mg
Total Fat: .13 g	Vitamin A: 25.30 IU
Saturated Fat: .01 g	Vitamin E: 0.00 mg
Monosaturated Fat: .03 g	Thiamin: .01 mg
Polyunsaturated: .03 g	Riboflavin: .03 mg
Cholesterol: 0.00 mg	Niacin: .17 mg
Carbohydrates: 17.01 g	Pantothenic Acid: .05 mg
Fiber: 3.41 g	Vitamin B6: .12 mg
Calcium: 9.90 mg	Folate: 7.70 ug
Phosphorous: 12.10 mg	Vitamin B12: 0.00 ug
Iron: .19 mg	Vitamin C: 4.62 mg
Sodium: 1.10 mg	Selenium: .11 ug
Sugar: 10.78 mg	

Pureed Sweet Potatoes

¾ cup large sweet potatoes - cooked, peeled and cubed
⅔ cup water or formula

Directions: Place above ingredients into blender jar and secure the lid. Press **Speed Up** button until speed 4 is reached. Run for 15 seconds then press any lower row button to stop.

Nutritional Information

Yield: 1 ½ cups
Serving Size: ½ cup

Amount per serving

Calories: 62.32	Potassium: 188.60 mg
1.62% from Fat,	Magnesium: 15.29 mg
7.06% from Protein	Zinc: .16 mg
91.30% from Carb	Copper: .06 mg
Protein: 1.12 g	Manganese: .22 mg
Total Fat: .11 g	Vitamin A: 12931.60 IU
Saturated Fat: .03 g	Vitamin E: 0.00 mg
Monosaturated Fat: 0.00 g	Thiamin: .05 mg
Polyunsaturated: .05 g	Riboflavin: .04 mg
Cholesterol: 0.00 mg	Niacin: .44 mg
Carbohydrates: 14.53 g	Pantothenic Acid: .48 mg
Fiber: 2.05 g	Vitamin B6: .14 mg
Calcium: 23.19 mg	Folate: 4.92 ug
Phosphorous: 26.24 mg	Vitamin B12: 0.00 ug
Iron: .59 mg	Vitamin C: 10.50 mg
Sodium: 23.19 mg	Selenium: .16 ug
Sugar: 4.71 mg	

Pureed Green Beans

1 cup green beans - steamed

2 Tbsp water or formula

Directions: Place above ingredients into blender jar and secure the lid. Press the **Speed Up** button until speed 4 is reached. Run for 15 seconds then press any lower row button to stop.

Nutritional Information

Yield: 1 cup
Serving Size: ½ cup

Amount per serving

Calories: 17.05	Potassium: 114.95 mg
2.93% from Fat,	Magnesium: 13.90 mg
19.70% from Protein	Zinc: .13 mg
77.40% from Carb	Copper: .04 mg
Protein: 1.00 g	Manganese: .12 mg
Total Fat: .07 g	Vitamin A: 379.50 IU
Saturated Fat: .01 g	Vitamin E: 0.00 mg
Monosaturated Fat: 0.00 g	Thiamin: .05 mg
Polyunsaturated: .03g	Riboflavin: .06 mg
Cholesterol: 0.00 mg	Niacin: .41 mg
Carbohydrates: 3.93 g	Pantothenic Acid: .05 mg
Fiber: 1.87 g	Vitamin B6: .04 mg
Calcium: 20.65 mg	Folate: 20.35 ug
Phosphorous: 20.90 mg	Vitamin B12: 0.00 ug
Iron: .57 mg	Vitamin C: 8.96 mg
Sodium: 3.60 mg	Selenium: .33 ug
Sugar: .77 mg	

Desserts Table of Contents

CAKES

To blend most cake batters, press the **Batters** button. See specific recipes for varying directions. Add raisins and desired nuts after mixing by pressing the Pulse button for 2 to 5 seconds if you do not want the items chopped or minced. In cake batters the baking powder starts to work as soon as liquid is added. If the batter is not used immediately, it may need to be blended again. Thin the batter, if needed, with a small amount of milk. Raisins and bananas are both high glycemic fruits. Such high glycemic fruits tend to spike the blood sugar shortly after eaten and require the body to produce or need insulin, especially when 2 or more highly glycemic fruits are eaten at a time. If you are a diabetic, it is recommended to avoid any recipe that contains 2 or more high glycemic fruits.

Coffee Cake

2 cups flour

1 Tbsp baking powder

1 tsp salt

1 cup brown sugar

Directions: Preheat oven to 350° F. Hold the Pulse button for 5 to 10 seconds, until dry ingredients are blended.

1 egg

1 cup lowfat milk

⅓ cup butter

Directions: Press the Pulse button 5 to 6 times or until blended. Pour into sprayed 9x13" baking pan. Add Crunchy Topping (See Crunchy Topping Recipe). Bake 35 minutes.

Crunchy Topping

¼ cup walnuts*

Directions: Place walnuts in blender jar and secure the lid. Press the Pulse button until the walnuts are chopped to desired consistency.

¼ cup brown sugar

2 Tbsp flour

1 Tbsp cinnamon

2 Tbsp margarine, melted

Directions: Knead together rest of ingredients in small bowl. Add nuts to mixture and blend together with hands. Sprinkle on top of cake.

* May use nut of choice instead

Nutritional Information

Yields: 1 cake/ 12 pieces
Serving Size: 1 piece

Amount per serving

Calories: 209.5	Potassium: 124.8 mg
25.30% from Fat,	Magnesium: 12.79 mg
6.48% from Protein	Zinc: .32 mg
68.20% from Carb	Copper: .09 mg
Protein: 3.42 g	Manganese: .20 mg
Total Fat: 5.92 g	Vitamin A: 227.17 IU
Saturated Fat: 3.46 g	Vitamin E: 62.16 IU
Monosaturated Fat: 1.6 g	Thiamin: .18 mg
Polyunsaturated: .38 g	Riboflavin: .16 mg
Cholesterol: 31.48 mg	Niacin: 1.27 mg
Carbohydrates: 35.99 g	Pantothenic Acid: .25 mg
Fiber: .56 g	Vitamin B6: .03 mg
Calcium: 49.13 mg	Folate: 41.47 ug
Phosphorous: 56.75 mg	Vitamin B12: .17 ug
Iron: 1.4 mg	Vitamin C: 1.41 mg
Sodium: 257.27 mg	Selenium: 9.30 ug
Sugar: 19.97 mg	

Nutritional Information

Yields: Topping for one 9x13" cake
Serving Size: 1 Tablespoon

Amount per serving

Calories: 67.79	Potassium: 41.63 mg
52.70% from Fat	Magnesium: 8.69 mg
5.44% from Protein	Zinc: .14 mg
41.90% from Carb	Copper: .06 mg
Protein: .97 g	Manganese: .26 mg
Total Fat: 4.15 g	Vitamin A: 104.03 IU
Saturated Fat: .54 g	Vitamin E: 21.66 IU
Monosaturated Fat: 1.51 g	Thiamin: .02 mg
Polyunsaturated: 1.81 g	Riboflavin: .01 mg
Cholesterol: 0.00 mg	Niacin: .12 mg
Carbohydrates: 7.42 g	Pantothenic Acid: .07 mg
Fiber: .62 g	Vitamin B6: .02 mg
Calcium: 16.01 mg	Folate: 4.11 ug
Phosphorous: 19.99 mg	Vitamin B12: 0.00 ug
Iron: .53 mg	Vitamin C: .25 mg
Sodium: 29.01 mg	Selenium: 1.13 ug
Sugar: 5.34 mg	

Creamy Cheesecake

2 (8 oz.) packages cream cheese

2 large eggs

1 cup sugar

½ tsp lemon juice

Directions: Preheat oven to 350°F. Place ingredients in blender jar and secure the lid. Press the **Batters** button. After blended, pour into graham cracker crust, filling a 9x13" baking pan. Bake for 40 minutes

Note: The longer you bake the cake, the thicker it will be. If you desire a cheesecake that is creamier then bake for only 30 to 35 minutes. However, if you prefer it to be thick, then bake for 45 minutes to an hour. After baked, place the cheesecake in the refrigerator for at least 30 minutes before serving.

Cheesecake

1 can (14 oz.) sweetened condensed milk

⅓ cup lemon juice

1 (8 oz.) package cream cheese - softened

1 tsp vanilla

1 graham cracker crust

10 oz. whipped cream

Directions: Place ingredients into blender jar and secure the lid. Press the **Batters** button. Pour into already baked and cooled pie crest. Chill 3 hours. Top with whipped cream.

Nutritional Information

Yield: 1 cake
Serving Size: 1 slice

Amount per serving

Calories: 234.48	Potassium: 110.00 mg
38.30% from Fat,	Magnesium: 5.54 mg
11.80% from Protein	Zinc: .43 mg
49.90% from Carb	Copper: .01 mg
Protein: 6.92 g	Manganese: 0.00 mg
Total Fat: 9.99 g	Vitamin A: 385.05 IU
Saturated Fat: 6.29 g	Vitamin E: 102.63 mg
Monosaturated Fat: 2.82 g	Thiamin: .01 mg
Polyunsaturated: .36 g	Riboflavin: .20 mg
Cholesterol: 31.75 mg	Niacin: .09 mg
Carbohydrates: 29.32g	Pantothenic Acid: .02 mg
Fiber: 0.00 g	Vitamin B6: .04 mg
Calcium: 64.42 mg	Folate: 10.58 ug
Phosphorous: 84.09 mg	Vitamin B12: .35 ug
Iron: .96 mg	Vitamin C: .15 mg
Sodium: 181.74 mg	Selenium: 4.09 ug
Sugar: 25.43 mg	

Nutritional Information

Yield: 1 cake
Serving Size: 1 slice

Amount per serving

Calories: 234.48	Potassium: 110.00 mg
38.30% from Fat,	Magnesium: 5.54 mg
11.80% from Protein	Zinc: .43 mg
49.90% from Carb	Copper: .01 mg
Protein: 6.92 g	Manganese: 0.00 mg
Total Fat: 9.99 g	Vitamin A: 385.05 IU
Saturated Fat: 6.29 g	Vitamin E: 102.63 mg
Monosaturated Fat: 2.82 g	Thiamin: .01 mg
Polyunsaturated: .36 g	Riboflavin: .20 mg
Cholesterol: 31.75 mg	Niacin: .09 mg
Carbohydrates: 29.32g	Pantothenic Acid: .02 mg
Fiber: 0.00 g	Vitamin B6: .04 mg
Calcium: 64.42 mg	Folate: 10.58 ug
Phosphorous: 84.09 mg	Vitamin B12: .35 ug
Iron: .96 mg	Vitamin C: .15 mg
Sodium: 181.74 mg	Selenium: 4.09 ug
Sugar: 25.43 mg	

Carrot Cake

2 ½ medium carrots, cut in half

Directions: Place above ingredients into blender jar and secure the lid. Be sure carrots are placed vertically in blender jar. Press the **Speed Up** button blender reaches speed 3. Allow the cycle to run for 50 seconds. Pour carrots into a separate bowl.

Note: If batter is not blended to desired consistency, remove jar after the cycle has finished and shake until the batter moves around in the jar. Place back on the motor base and tap the Pulse button 3 to 4 times.

1 medium apple – cored, cut into eighths
½ medium orange peeled

Directions: Place ingredients into blender jar and tap the Pulse button 30 to 40 times. After every 10 taps, remove container, shake, place back on blender and continue to tap pulse button.

½ cup water

¼ cup oil

1 tsp cinnamon

1 tsp salt

½ tsp allspice

1 tsp baking soda

¼ cup cornstarch

1 ¼ cups sugar

2 cups flour

Directions: Preheat oven 350°. Add above ingredients and carrot mixture into jar. Press the **Speed Up** button until blender reaches speed 7. Press any lower row button to stop halfway through the cycle (when the display reads 30 seconds). Pour into round 9x9" sprayed baking pan. Bake for 30 minutes.

Nutritional Information

Yield: 1 cake
Serving Size: 1 slice

Amount per serving

Calories: 209.68	Potassium: 99.38 mg
38.30% from Fat,	Magnesium: 28.62 mg
11.80% from Protein	Zinc: .60 mg
49.90% from Carb	Copper: .08 mg
Protein: 2.80 g	Manganese: .80 mg
Total Fat: 4.95 g	Vitamin A: 286.23 IU
Saturated Fat: .65 g	Vitamin E: 0.00 mg
Monosaturated Fat: 1.15 g	Thiamin: .09 mg
Polyunsaturated: 2.83 g	Riboflavin: .06 mg
Cholesterol: 0.00 mg	Niacin: 1.38 mg
Carbohydrates: 40.70 g	Pantothenic Acid: .22 mg
Fiber: 2.76 g	Vitamin B6: .08 mg
Calcium: 15.23 mg	Folate: 9.50 ug
Phosphorous: 73.21 mg	Vitamin B12: 0.00 ug
Iron: .89 mg	Vitamin C: 3.17 mg
Sodium: 304.46 mg	Selenium: 14.36 ug
Sugar: 23.17 mg	

Hawaiian Coffee Cake

¼ cup softened butter

½ cup crushed pineapple

1 large egg

Directions: Place ingredients in jar in order as listed and secure the lid. Press the Pulse button 2 to 3 times.

1 ½ cups flour

2 ½ tsps baking powder

½ tsp salt

½ cup sugar

Directions: Preheat oven to 400°F. Press the Pulse button 5 times. After pulsing, scrape sides of jar with a spatula. Hold down the Pulse button 5 to 10 seconds. Sprinkle topping on cake.

Hawaiian Coffee Cake Topping

2 Tbsp butter - melted

½ cup coconut - shredded

½ cup brown sugar

Directions: Combine in separate bowl and mix. Sprinkle on cake and bake for 25 minutes at 400°F.

Nutritional Information

Yield: 1 cake/8 pieces
Serving Size: 1 piece

Amount per serving

Calories: 293.95	Potassium: 186.67 mg
33.70% from Fat	Magnesium: 41.48 mg
5.83% from Protein	Zinc: .88 mg
60.50% from Carb	Copper: .16 mg
Protein: 4.46 g	Manganese: 1.18mg
Total Fat: 11.45 g	Vitamin A: 323.59 IU
Saturated Fat: 7.14 g	Vitamin E: 85.68 mg
Monosaturated Fat: 2.70 g	Thiamin: .12 mg
Polyunsaturated: .64 g	Riboflavin: .10 mg
Cholesterol: 58.92 mg	Niacin: 1.51 mg
Carbohydrates: 46.29 g	Pantothenic Acid: .42 mg
Fiber: 3.07 g	Vitamin B6: .11 mg
Calcium: 113.78 mg	Folate: 15.24 ug
Phosphorous: 134.78 mg	Vitamin B12: .11 ug
Iron: 1.54 mg	Vitamin C: 1.18 mg
Sodium: 390.05 mg	Selenium: 19.68 ug
Sugar: 29.17 mg	

Hawaiian Dessert

1 white or yellow cake mix

1 ¾ cups milk

1 (8 oz.) package cream cheese softened

1 (5 oz.) box instant vanilla pudding

1 (20 oz.) can crushed pineapple

12 oz. whipped cream

Directions: Prepare cake mix and bake according to directions. Let cool. Combine milk, cream cheese, instant vanilla pudding in blender jar and press the **Batters** button. When cake is cool, place pudding mixture over cake. Drain pineapple and spread over mixture. Spread whipped cream over pineapple.

Nutritional Information

Yield: 1 cake/ 16 pieces
Serving Size: 1 piece

Amount per serving

Calories: 384.99	Potassium: 378.49 mg
37.20% from Fat,	Magnesium: 30.18 mg
10.10% from Protein	Zinc: .92 mg
52.70% from Carb	Copper: .09 mg
Protein: 9.86 g	Manganese: .51 mg
Total Fat: 16.13 g	Vitamin A: 357.00 IU
Saturated Fat: 7.57 g	Vitamin E: 93.11 mg
Monosaturated Fat: 5.63 g	Thiamin: .20 mg
Polyunsaturated Fat: 2.06 g	Riboflavin: .42 mg
Cholesterol: 35.27 mg	Niacin: 1.11 mg
Carbohydrates: 51.33 g	Pantothenic Acid: .66 mg
Fiber: .73 g	Vitamin B6: 01.10 mg
Calcium: 273.98 mg	Folate: 32.80 ug
Phosphorous: 276.15 mg	Vitamin B12: .70 mg
Iron: 1.27 g	Vitamin C: 3.86 mg
Sodium: 428.70 mg	Selenium: 11.67 ug
Sugar: 37.44 mg	

ICE CREAM

To blend ice cream, press the **Ice Cream** button. To change an ice cream recipe into a low-fat/no fat recipe, substitute the cream with any of the following options: nondairy creamer, low-fat, skim, rice, or soy milk.

When the recipe calls for sugar, you may use any kind of desired sweetener: (i.e., Splenda™, honey) If you are using a liquid sweetener, such as honey, then use only 1/3 the amount that the recipe calls for.

These recipes assume that you will be using crecent-shaped ice cubes. If you are using different kinds of ice, you may need to adjust the amounts of ice used in each recipe.

Crushed Ice: increase amount of ice by ½ cup

Tray Ice: allow ice to sit out for 5 minutes before using

Wet(melted) ice: increase amount of ice by ½ cup

Your blender may begin to cavitate while attempting to make an ice cream. This means that ice is formed in the blender creating a pocket around the blade and causing it to spin freely. This occurs when too much ice is added to the recipe, or when the ingredients are too cold. If this occurs while making ice cream, remove 2 oz. ice and 1 ounce liquid.

If the recipe calls for non-fat dry powdered milk, you may use tofu instead, in the same amount. For frozen yogurt, substitute 1 cup of cream with 1 cup of yogurt (this may be plain or vanilla). Also reduce the amount of ice by 1 cup.

Key Lime Pie Ice Cream

1 cup vanilla coffee creamer

3 Tbsp powdered lemonade drink mix

4-5 vanilla wafers

3 cups ice

Directions: Place ingredients in jar in order listed, and secure the lid. Press the **Ice Cream** button.

Nutritional Information

Yields: 4 cups
Serving Size: ½ cup

Amount per serving	
Calories: 91.90	Potassium: 45.94 mg
60.90% from Fat,	Magnesium: 3.11 mg
3.99% from Protein	Zinc: .10 mg
35.10% from Carb	Copper: .01 mg
Protein: .94 g	Manganese: .01 mg
Total Fat: 6.38 g	Vitamin A: 196.83 IU
Saturated Fat: 3.75 g	Vitamin E: 53.40 mg
Monosaturated Fat: 2.01 g	Thiamin: .02 mg
Polyunsaturated: .29 g	Riboflavin: .05 mg
Cholesterol: 19.80 mg	Niacin: .11 mg
Carbohydrates: 8.28 g	Pantothenic Acid: .09 mg
Fiber: .06 g	Vitamin B6: .01 mg
Calcium: 41.91 mg	Folate: 2.55 ug
Phosphorous: 32.36 mg	Vitamin B12: .07 ug
Iron: .10 mg	Vitamin C: 1.83mg
Sodium: 22.36 mg	Selenium: .55 ug
Sugar: 5.09 mg	

Caramel Cashew Ice Cream

1 cup vanilla nondairy creamer

½ cup cashew butter

¼ cup caramel

3 cups ice

Directions: Place ingredients in blender jar in order listed and secure the lid. Press the **Ice Cream** button.

*You may make cashew butter in the blender. See the "Spreads" section for the recipe.

Hazelnut Coffee Ice Cream

1 cup hazelnut coffee creamer

⅓ cup chocolate syrup

3 cups ice

Directions: Place ingredients in jar in order as listed, and secure the lid. Press the **Ice Cream** button.

Nutritional Information

Yields: 3 cups
Serving Size: ½ cup

Amount per serving

Calories: 203.23	Potassium: 165.28 mg
77.10% from Fat,	Magnesium: 58.64 mg
9.06% from Protein	Zinc: 1.21 mg
13.80% from Carb	Copper: .47 mg
Protein: 4.83 g	Manganese: .17 mg
Total Fat: 18.26 g	Vitamin A: 262.40 IU
Saturated Fat: 6.89 g	Vitamin E: 71.20 mg
Monosaturated Fat: 8.44 g	Thiamin: .08 mg
Polyunsaturated: 2.07 g	Riboflavin: .05 mg
Cholesterol: 26.40 mg	Niacin: .36 mg
Carbohydrates: 7.35 g	Pantothenic Acid: .37 mg
Fiber: .43 g	Vitamin B6: .07 mg
Calcium: 47.57 mg	Folate: 15.31 ug
Phosphorous: 129.49 mg	Vitamin B12: .09 ug
Iron: 1.09 mg	Vitamin C: .32 mg
Sodium: 19.20 mg	Selenium: 2.69 ug
Sugar: .06 mg	

Nutritional Information

Yields: 3 cups
Serving Size: ½ cup

Amount per serving

Calories: 109.83	Potassium: 74.35mg
63.40% from Fat	Magnesium: 11.01 mg
4.73% from Protein	Zinc: .19 mg
31.90% from Carb	Copper: .06 mg
Protein: 1.32 g	Manganese: .04 mg
Total Fat: 7.85 g	Vitamin A: 262.51 IU
Saturated Fat: 4.87 g	Vitamin E: 71.20 mg
Monosaturated Fat: 2.26 g	Thiamin: .01 mg
Polyunsaturated: .29 g	Riboflavin: .06 mg
Cholesterol: 26.40 mg	Niacin: .06 mg
Carbohydrates: 8.89 g	Pantothenic Acid: .11 mg
Fiber: .30 g	Vitamin B6: .01 mg
Calcium: 40.00 mg	Folate: 1.03 ug
Phosphorous: 46.72 mg	Vitamin B12: .09 ug
Iron: .26 mg	Vitamin C: .34 mg
Sodium: 24.21 mg	Selenium: .46 ug
Sugar: 5.72 mg	

Cookies 'n Cream

¾ cup non dairy creamer

¾ cup sugar

8 to 10 chocolate sandwich cookies*

3 cups ice

Directions: Place ingredients in jar in order as listed, and secure the lid. Press the **Ice Cream** button.

Note: If you would like chunks of cookies in milkshake, add all the ingredients except the cookies, and push **Ice Cream** button. When the cycle has completed, add cookies and hold down the Pulse button for approximately 10 seconds, or until cookies are blended to desired consistency.

* May substitute any type of cookie

Peanut Butter Ice Cream

⅔ cup nondairy creamer

⅔ cup crunchy peanut butter

½ cup sugar

1 tsp vanilla

4 cups frozen non dairy creamer cubes*

Directions: Place ingredients in jar in order as listed, and secure the lid. Press the **Ice Cream** button.

*May substitute 3 cups ice

Nutritional Information

Yields: 4 cups
Serving Size: ½ cup

Amount per serving

Calories: 164.22	Potassium: 45.33 mg
34.10% from Fat,	Magnesium: 6.53 mg
2.55% from Protein	Zinc: .14 mg
63.30% from Carb	Copper: .04 mg
Protein: 1.08 g	Manganese: .05 mg
Total Fat: 6.40 g	Vitamin A: 147.80 IU
Saturated Fat: 3.07 g	Vitamin E: 40.05 mg
Monosaturated Fat: 2.11 g	Thiamin: .02 mg
Polyunsaturated: .89 g	Riboflavin: .05 mg
Cholesterol: 14.85 mg	Niacin: .22 mg
Carbohydrates: 26.75 g	Pantothenic Acid: .08 mg
Fiber: .32 g	Vitamin B6: .01 mg
Calcium: 24.39 mg	Folate: 5.55 ug
Phosphorous: 27.80 mg	Vitamin B12: .05 ug
Iron: .40 mg	Vitamin C: .18 mg
Sodium: 69.40 mg	Selenium: .75 ug
Sugar: 22.55 mg	

Nutritional Information

Yields: 4 cups
Serving Size: ½ cup

Amount per serving

Calories: 215.96	Potassium: 186.06 mg
58.00% from Fat	Magnesium: 36.05 mg
10.10% from Protein	Zinc: .65 mg
31.90% from Carb	Copper: .11 mg
Protein: 5.71 g	Manganese: .40 mg
Total Fat: 14.60 g	Vitamin A: 131.20 IU
Saturated Fat: 4.46 g	Vitamin E: 35.60 mg
Monosaturated Fat: 6.18g	Thiamin: .03 mg
Polyunsaturated: 3.19 g	Riboflavin: .06 mg
Cholesterol: 13.20 mg	Niacin: 2.96 mg
Carbohydrates: 18.04 g	Pantothenic Acid: .26 mg
Fiber: 1.42 g	Vitamin B6: .010 mg
Calcium: 28.20 mg	Folate: 20.18 ug
Phosphorous: 84.19 mg	Vitamin B12: .04 ug
Iron: .42 mg	Vitamin C: .16 mg
Sodium: 11.70 mg	Selenium: 1.81 ug
Sugar: 14.36 mg	

Blueberry Ice Cream

1 cup non dairy creamer

2 cups frozen blueberries

¾ cup sugar

½ tsp vanilla extract

¾ cup ice

Directions: Place ingredients in jar in order as listed, and secure the lid. Press the **Ice Cream** button.

Orange Sorbet

2 oranges - peeled and cut in half

2 Tbsp sugar

2 ½ cups ice

Directions: Place ingredients in jar in order as listed, and secure the lid. Press the **Ice Cream** button.

Nutritional Information

Yields: 4 cups
Serving Size: ½ cup

Amount per serving

Calories: 153.09	Potassium: 65.29 mg
33.50% from Fat	Magnesium: 4.91 mg
2.72% from Protein	Zinc: .14 mg
63.70% from Carb	Copper: .02 mg
Protein: 1.08 g	Manganese: .12 mg
Total Fat: 5.91 g	Vitamin A: 216.38 IU
Saturated Fat: 3.62 g	Vitamin E: 53.40 mg
Monosaturated Fat: 1.69 g	Thiamin: .02 mg
Polyunsaturated: .27 g	Riboflavin: .06 mg
Cholesterol: 19.80 mg	Niacin: .17 mg
Carbohydrates: 25.28 g	Pantothenic Acid: .13 mg
Fiber: .87 g	Vitamin B6: .03 mg
Calcium: 31.19 mg	Folate: 2.78 ug
Phosphorous: 28.37 mg	Vitamin B12: .07 ug
Iron: .12 mg	Vitamin C: 3.76 mg
Sodium: 12.39 mg	Selenium: .33 ug
Sugar: 22.57 mg	

Nutritional Information

Yields: 3 cups
Serving Size: ½ cup

Amount per serving

Calories: 45.08	Potassium: 110.10 mg
1.36% from Fat	Magnesium: 6.13 mg
4.75% from Protein	Zinc: .04 mg
93.90% from Carb	Copper: .03 mg
Protein: .58 g	Manganese: .02 mg
Total Fat: .07 g	Vitamin A: 138.00 IU
Saturated Fat: .01 g	Vitamin E: 0.00 mg
Monosaturated Fat: .01 g	Thiamin: .05 mg
Polyunsaturated: .02 g	Riboflavin: .03 mg
Cholesterol: 0.00 mg	Niacin: .17 mg
Carbohydrates: 8.59 g	Pantothenic Acid: .15 mg
Fiber: 1.47 g	Vitamin B6: .04 mg
Calcium: 24.58 mg	Folate: 18.40 ug
Phosphorous: 8.59 mg	Vitamin B12: 0.00 ug
Iron: 0.06 mg	Vitamin C: 32.63 mg
Sodium: 0.00 mg	Selenium: .33 ug
Sugar: 9.93 mg	

Peach Ice Cream

1 cup half and half

2 ½ cups frozen peaches

½ cup sugar

½ tsp vanilla flavoring

¼ tsp almond extract

½ cup ice

Directions: Place ingredients in jar in order listed, and secure the lid. Press the **Ice Cream** button.

Note: This ice cream recipe may be finished after just 15 seconds after pushing the **Ice Cream** button. If you notice that the ice cream looks complete, press any lower row button to stop.

Tropical Ice Cream

⅔ cup tropical juice concentrate

⅔ cup non-fat dry powdered milk*

½ banana peeled

½ cup pineapple

3 cups ice

Directions: Place ingredients in blender jar in order listed and secure the lid. Press the **Ice Cream** button.

*May use tofu instead, in same amount

Nutritional Information

Yields: 4 cups
Serving Size: ½ cup

Amount per serving

Calories: 162.69	Potassium: 141.74 mg
19.10% from Fat,	Magnesium: 6.98 mg
3.29% from Protein	Zinc: .19 mg
77.60% from Carb	Copper: .02 mg
Protein: 1.39 g	Manganese: .02 mg
Total Fat: 3.58 g	Vitamin A: 328.96 IU
Saturated Fat: 2.18 g	Vitamin E: 28.74 mg
Monosaturated Fat: 1.04 g	Thiamin: .02 mg
Polyunsaturated: .418 g	Riboflavin: .08 mg
Cholesterol: 11.19 mg	Niacin: .54 mg
Carbohydrates: 32.68 g	Pantothenic Acid: .19 mg
Fiber: 1.41 g	Vitamin B6: .03 mg
Calcium: 34.28 mg	Folate: 3.25 ug
Phosphorous: 37.36 mg	Vitamin B12: 0.10 ug
Iron: .31 mg	Vitamin C: 73.87 mg
Sodium: 17.13 mg	Selenium: .93 ug
Sugar: 30.02 mg	

Nutritional Information

Yields: 3 ½ cups
Serving Size: ½ cup

Amount per serving

Calories: 80.99	Potassium: 173.17 mg
1.02% from Fat	Magnesium: 13.39 mg
12.00% from Protein	Zinc: .33 mg
87.00% from Carb	Copper: .05 mg
Protein: 2.50 g	Manganese: .26 mg
Total Fat: .10 g	Vitamin A: 24.37 IU
Saturated Fat: .04 g	Vitamin E: .26 mg
Monosaturated Fat: .02 g	Thiamin: .05 mg
Polyunsaturated: .02 g	Riboflavin: .14 mg
Cholesterol: 1.17 mg	Niacin: .20 mg
Carbohydrates: 18.20 g	Pantothenic Acid: .28 mg
Fiber: .54 g	Vitamin B6: .08 mg
Calcium: 83.82 mg	Folate: 7.84 ug
Phosphorous: 67.56 mg	Vitamin B12: 0.26 ug
Iron: .16 mg	Vitamin C: 46.56 mg
Sodium: 37.89 mg	Selenium: 1.89 ug
Sugar: 5.72 mg	

Strawberry Cheesecake Soft Serve

8 oz. French Vanilla nondairy creamer

1 3-ounce packet instant cheesecake pudding

½ cup strawberry pie filling

2 ½ cups ice

Directions: Place ingredients in jar in order listed, and secure the lid. Press the **Ice Cream** button.

Nutritional Information

Yields: 4 cups
Serving Size: ½ cup

Amount per serving

Calories: 95.57	Potassium: 36.71 mg
51.30% from Fat	Magnes08mg
3.30% from Protein	Copper: 0.00mg
45.40% from Carb	Manganese: 0.00 mg
Protein: .80 g	Vitamin A: 185.98 IU
Total Fat: 5.52 g	Vitamin E: 50.46 mg
Saturated Fat: 3.42 g	Thiamin: .01 mg
Monosaturated Fat: 1.58 g	Riboflavin: .04 mg
Polyunsaturated: .22 g	Niacin: .02 mg
Cholesterol: 18.71 mg	Pantothenic Acid: .08 mg
Carbohydrates: 10.98 g	Vitamin B6: .01 mg
Fiber: .06 g	Folate: .57 ug
Calcium: 27.75 mg	Vitamin B12: .06 ug
Phosphorous: 22.89 mg	Vitamin C: .23 mg
Iron: .102 mg	Selenium: .27 ug
Sodium: 91.50 mg	
Sugar: 7.77 mg	

Astronaut Surprise

1 cup French Vanilla nondairy creamer

2 Tbsp orange drink Mix

1 Tbsp instant vanilla pudding

3 cups ice

Directions: Place ingredients in jar in order listed, and secure the lid. Press the **Ice Cream** button.

Nutritional Information

Yields: 3 cups
Serving Size: ½ cup

Amount per serving

Calories: 155.08	Potassium: 62.86 mg
45.90% from Fat	Magnesium: 3.86 mg
2.95% from Protein	Zinc: .11 mg
51.20% from Carb	Copper: .01 mg
Protein: 1.13 g	Manganese: .01 mg
Total Fat: 7.78 g	Vitamin A: 345.73 IU
Saturated Fat: 4.82 g	Vitamin E: 71.20 mg
Monosaturated Fat: 2.24 g	Thiamin: .01 mg
Polyunsaturated: .31 g	Riboflavin: .09 mg
Cholesterol: 26.40 mg	Niacin: .37 mg
Carbohydrates: 19.55 g	Pantothenic Acid: .11 mg
Fiber: .10 g	Vitamin B6: .05 mg
Calcium: 54.75 mg	Folate: .80 ug
Phosphorous: 39.47 mg	Vitamin B12: 0.09 ug
Iron: .03 mg	Vitamin C: 10.32 mg
Sodium: 127.12mg	Selenium: .37 ug
Sugar: 19.76 mg	

Chocolate Mint Truffle Ice Cream

3 Tbsp Stephen's Gourmet™ Mint Truffle Chocolate Mix

1 cup French vanilla nondairy creamer

3 cups ice

Directions: Place ingredients in jar in order listed, and secure the lid. Press the **Ice Cream** button.

Fresh Apricot Ice Cream

⅔ cup whole apricot juice

⅔ cup nonfat dry powdered milk

½ banana – peeled

½ cup peaches - do not peel

¼ cup sugar

3 cups ice

Directions: Place ingredients in jar in order listed and secure the lid. Press the **Ice Cream** button

Nutritional Information

Yields: 3 cups
Serving Size: ½ cup

Amount per serving

Calories: 78.06	Potassium: 62.86 mg
87.20% from Fat	Magnesium: 3.86 mg
5.43% from Protein	Zinc: .16 mg
7.41% from Carb	Copper: .02 mg
Protein: 1.08 g	Manganese: .02 mg
Total Fat: 7.72 g	Vitamin A: 266.18 IU
Saturated Fat: 4.81 g	Vitamin E: 71.20 mg
Monosaturated Fat: 2.23 g	Thiamin: .02 mg
Polyunsaturated: .29 g	Riboflavin: .09 mg
Cholesterol: 26.40 mg	Niacin: .05 mg
Carbohydrates: 1.48 g	Pantothenic Acid: .18 mg
Fiber: .01 g	Vitamin B6: .02 mg
Calcium: .23 mg	Folate: 1.19 ug
Phosphorous: 38.62 mg	Vitamin B12: 0.12 ug
Iron: .02 mg	Vitamin C: .35 mg
Sodium: 16.03 mg	Selenium: .24 ug
Sugar: .06 mg	

Nutritional Information

Yields: 4 cups
Serving Size: ½ cup

Amount per serving

Calories: 93.37	Potassium: 266.95 mg
1.27% from Fat,	Magnesium: 16.35 mg
16.30% from Protein	Zinc: .45 mg
82.40% from Carb	Copper: .03 mg
Protein: 3.94 g	Manganese: .04 mg
Total Fat: .14 g	Vitamin A: 396.41 IU
Saturated Fat: .06 g	Vitamin E: .60 mg
Monosaturated Fat: .03 g	Thiamin: .05 mg
Polyunsaturated: .02 g	Riboflavin: .17g
Cholesterol: 2.00 mg	Niacin: .33 mg
Carbohydrates: 19.89 g	Pantothenic Acid: .43 mg
Fiber: .85 g	Vitamin B6: .08 mg
Calcium: 129.14 mg	Folate: 7.75 ug
Phosphorous: 104.65mg	Vitamin B12: 0.40 ug
Iron: .18 mg	Vitamin C: 17.21 mg
Sodium: 55.34 mg	Selenium: 2.94 ug
Sugar: 18.29 mg	

Berry Ice Cream

⅔ cup berry juice concentrate - thawed

⅔ cup non-fat dry powdered milk

4 large strawberries - remove stems

½ banana - peeled

3 cups ice

Directions: Place ingredients in jar in order listed, and secure the lid. Press the **Ice Cream** button.

Strawberry Ice Cream

1 cup nondairy creamer

½ cup sugar

½ tsp vanilla

2 ½ cups frozen strawberries

Directions: Place ingredients in jar in order listed, and secure the lid. Press the **Ice Cream** button.

Nutritional Information

Yields: 4 cups
Serving Size: ½ cup

Amount per serving

Calories: 82.72	Potassium: 248.66 mg
2.22% from Fat,	Magnesium: 18.20 mg
18.60% from Protein	Zinc: .47 mg
79.20% from Carb	Copper: .03 mg
Protein: 3.94 g	Manganese: .20 mg
Total Fat: .21 g	Vitamin A: 14.98 IU
Saturated Fat: .08 g	Vitamin E: .60 mg
Monosaturated Fat: .03 g	Thiamin: .06 mg
Polyunsaturated: .05 g	Riboflavin: .18 mg
Cholesterol: 2.00 mg	Niacin: .29 mg
Carbohydrates: 16.77 g	Pantothenic Acid: .42 mg
Fiber: .59 g	Vitamin B6: .10 mg
Calcium: 130.89 mg	Folate: 11.05 ug
Phosphorous: 105.10 mg	Vitamin B12: 0.40 ug
Iron: .18 mg	Vitamin C: 25.48 mg
Sodium: 55.05 mg	Selenium: 2.96 ug
Sugar: 15.29 mg	

Nutritional Information

Yields: 3 cups
Serving Size: ½ cup

Amount per serving

Calories: 176.29	Potassium: 185.95 mg
38.40% from Fat,	Magnesium: 13.77 mg
3.22% from Protein	Zinc: .23 mg
58.30% from Carb	Copper: .05 mg
Protein: 1.48 g	Manganese: .27 mg
Total Fat: 7.83 g	Vitamin A: 303.84 IU
Saturated Fat: 4.81 g	Vitamin E: 71.20 mg
Monosaturated Fat: 2.24 g	Thiamin: .03 mg
Polyunsaturated: .34 g	Riboflavin: .10 mg
Cholesterol: 26.40 mg	Niacin: .45 mg
Carbohydrates: 26.71 g	Pantothenic Acid: .21 mg
Fiber: 1.93 g	Vitamin B6: .04 mg
Calcium: 53.34 mg	Folate: 16.45 ug
Phosphorous: 43.99 mg	Vitamin B12: 0.09 ug
Iron: .71 mg	Vitamin C: 38.26 mg
Sodium: 17.87 mg	Selenium: .99 ug
Sugar: 21.09 mg	

Chocolate Ice Cream

1 cup half & half

½ cup chocolate milk mix

½ cup sugar

½ cup non-fat dry powdered milk

Directions: Place ingredients in jar and press the Pulse button for approximately 5 to 10 seconds.

Add:

1 tsp vanilla

3 cups ice

Directions: Press **Ice Cream** button

Vanilla Ice Cream

⅔ cup milk

⅔ cup non-fat dry powdered milk

2 tsps milk

¼ cup sugar

2 ½ cups ice

Directions: Place ingredients in jar in order listed and secure the lid. Press the **Ice Cream** button.

Nutritional Information

Yields: 4 cups
Serving Size: ½ cup

Amount per serving

Calories: 154.20	Potassium: 222.46 mg
22.50% from Fat,	Magnesium: 16.78 mg
10.50% from Protein	Zinc: .53 mg
67.00% from Carb	Copper: .03 mg
Protein: 4.06 g	Manganese: .02 mg
Total Fat: 3.88 g	Vitamin A: 108.74 IU
Saturated Fat: 2.34 g	Vitamin E: 29.19 mg
Monosaturated Fat: 1.12 g	Thiamin: .05 mg
Polyunsaturated: .26 g	Riboflavin: .20 mg
Cholesterol: 13.26 mg	Niacin: .13 mg
Carbohydrates: 25.99 g	Pantothenic Acid: .45 mg
Fiber: .17 g	Vitamin B6: .05 mg
Calcium: 140.00 mg	Folate: 5.03 ug
Phosphorous: 120.78 mg	Vitamin B12: 0.44 ug
Iron: .13 mg	Vitamin C: .78 mg
Sodium: 84.73 mg	Selenium: 2.67 ug
Sugar: 23.62 mg	

Nutritional Information

Yields: 3 ½ cups
Serving Size: ½ cup

Amount per serving

Calories: 84.05	Potassium: 249.18 mg
3.99% from Fat	Magnesium: 16.47 mg
24.70% from Protein	Zinc: .57 mg
71.30% from Carb	Copper: .01 mg
Protein: 5.05 g	Manganese: .01 mg
Total Fat: .36 g	Vitamin A: 50.07 IU
Saturated Fat: .23 g	Vitamin E: 14.98 mg
Monosaturated Fat: .10 g	Thiamin: .06 mg
Polyunsaturated: .01 g	Riboflavin: .22 mg
Cholesterol: 3.22 mg	Niacin: .14 mg
Carbohydrates: 14.59 g	Pantothenic Acid: .50 mg
Fiber: 0.00 g	Vitamin B6: .05 mg
Calcium: 177.13 mg	Folate: 7.12 ug
Phosphorous: 136.71 mg	Vitamin B12: 0.56 ug
Iron: .05 mg	Vitamin C: 1.06 mg
Sodium: 74.84 mg	Selenium: 3.75 ug
Sugar: 13.20 mg	

Apple Pie Ice Cream

1 cup frozen apple juice concentrate

2 Tbsp low-fat vanilla yogurt

⅓ cup non-fat dry powdered milk

½ apple – quartered

1 Tbsp vanilla

¼ tsp cinnamon

1 banana - cut in half

2 ½ cups ice

Directions: Place ingredients in jar in order listed and secure the lid. Press the **Ice Cream** button.

Raspberry Delight

1 cup non dairy creamer

¾ cup sugar

½ tsp vanilla

2 ½ cups frozen raspberries

Directions: Place ingredients in jar in order listed and secure the lid. Press the **Ice Cream** button.

Nutritional Information

Yields: 4 cups
Serving Size: ½ cup

Amount per serving

Calories: 93.81	Potassium: 302.18 mg
2.58% from Fat,	Magnesium: 16.55 mg
10.20% from Protein	Zinc: .31mg
87.20% from Carb	Copper: .04 mg
Protein: 2.37 g	Manganese: .13 mg
Total Fat: .27 g	Vitamin A: 17.98 IU
Saturated Fat: .10 g	Vitamin E: .76 mg
Monosaturated Fat: .03 g	Thiamin: .03 mg
Polyunsaturated: .05 g	Riboflavin: .12 mg
Cholesterol: 1.19 mg	Niacin: .23 mg
Carbohydrates: 20.32 g	Pantothenic Acid: .33 mg
Fiber: 0.74 g	Vitamin B6: .13 mg
Calcium: 77.45 mg	Folate: 6.98 ug
Phosphorous: 65.80 mg	Vitamin B12: 0.22 ug
Iron: .36 mg	Vitamin C: 2.94 mg
Sodium: 36.72 mg	Selenium: 1.85 ug
Sugar: 17.44 mg	

Nutritional Information

Yields: 4 cups
Serving Size: ½ cup

Amount per serving

Calories: 237.46	Potassium: 134.10 mg
35.10% from Fat,	Magnesium: 15.20 mg
3.07% from Protein	Zinc: .34 mg
61.80% from Carb	Copper: .05 mg
Protein: 1.89 g	Manganese: .33 mg
Total Fat: 9.59 g	Vitamin A: 331.12 IU
Saturated Fat: 5.78 g	Vitamin E: 85.44 mg
Monosaturated Fat: 2.71 g	Thiamin: .03 mg
Polyunsaturated: .53 g	Riboflavin: .10 mg
Cholesterol: 31.68 mg	Niacin: .32 mg
Carbohydrates: 37.92 g	Pantothenic Acid: .29 mg
Fiber: 3.20 g	Vitamin B6: .04 mg
Calcium: 58.73 mg	Folate: 11.29 ug
Phosphorous: 52.69 mg	Vitamin B12: 0.11ug
Iron: .36 mg	Vitamin C: 13.27 mg
Sodium: 19.73 mg	Selenium: .57 ug
Sugar: 32.51 mg	

Healthy Peach

1½ cups soy milk*

2 ¼ cups frozen peach slices*

¼ cup sugar

½ Tbsp vanilla

Directions: Place ingredients in jar in order listed, and secure the lid. Press the **Ice Cream** button.

*May substitute vanilla soy milk
*May substitute with any frozen fruit

Citrus Tofu Ice Cream

6 oz. tofu

½ orange peeled

½ cup sugar

¾ cup cranberries

3 cups ice

Directions: Place ingredients in jar in order listed, and secure the lid. Press the **Ice Cream** button.

Nutritional Information

Yields: 3 cups
Serving Size: ½ cup

Amount per serving

Calories: 85.86	Potassium: 183.01 mg
12.60% from Fat	Magnesium: 15.06 mg
11.30% from Protein	Zinc: .22 mg
76.20% from Carb	Copper: .10 mg
Protein: 2.43 g	Manganese: .13 mg
Total Fat: 1.20 g	Vitamin A: 201.07 IU
Saturated Fat: .12 g	Vitamin E: 0.00 mg
Monosaturated Fat: .20 g	Thiamin: .10 mg
Polyunsaturated: .47 g	Riboflavin: .06 mg
Cholesterol: 0.00 mg	Niacin: .54 mg
Carbohydrates: 16.45 g	Pantothenic Acid: .11 mg
Fiber: 1.51 g	Vitamin B6: .04 mg
Calcium: 5.76 mg	Folate: 3.29 ug
Phosphorous: 36.47 mg	Vitamin B12: 0.00 ug
Iron: .44 mg	Vitamin C: 3.74 mg
Sodium: 6.32 mg	Selenium: .77 ug
Sugar: 13.68 mg	

Nutritional Information

Yields: 4 cups
Serving Size: ½ cup

Amount per serving

Calories: 72.19	Potassium: 37.50 mg
9.45% from Fat	Magnesium: 6.36 mg
7.54% from Protein	Zinc: .15 mg
83.00% from Carb	Copper: .04 mg
Protein: 1.43 g	Manganese: .12 mg
Total Fat: .80 g	Vitamin A: 38.93 IU
Saturated Fat: .11 g	Vitamin E: 0.00 mg
Monosaturated Fat: .17 g	Thiamin: .01 mg
Polyunsaturated: .45 g	Riboflavin: .02 mg
Cholesterol: 0.00 mg	Niacin: .25 mg
Carbohydrates: 15.78 g	Pantothenic Acid: .04 mg
Fiber: .52 g	Vitamin B6: .03 mg
Calcium: 30.32 mg	Folate: 9.46 ug
Phosphorous: 23.54 mg	Vitamin B12: 0.00 ug
Iron: .26 mg	Vitamin C: 5.16 mg
Sodium: 2.03 mg	Selenium: 1.98 ug
Sugar: 14.56 mg	

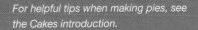
For helpful tips when making pies, see the Cakes introduction.

Soybean Oil Pie Crust

1 cup flour

Directions: Preheat oven to 425° F. Place flour in blender and press the Pulse button 3 to 5 times (Do not hold the button down for more than 2 seconds at a time).

¼ cup soybean oil

2 ½ Tbsp cold water

Directions: Pour ingredients in hole that has formed in the flour. Press the Pulse button 10 to 15 times. You may need to remove jar and use a rubber spatula to scrape ingredients off the sides of the jar, towards the center. When finished, roll dough into a piecrust and place in a round 9x9" tin/baking dish. Place filling crust and bake 15 minutes.

Nutritional Information

Yields: 1 9-inch pie shell.
Serving Size: 1 pie crust

Amount per serving

Calories: 936.78	Magnesium: 27.80 mg
53.70% from Fat	Zinc: .88 mg
5.53% from Protein	Copper: .18 mg
40.80% from Carb	Manganese: .85 mg
Protein: 12.91 g	Vitamin A: 0.00 IU
Total Fat: 55.72	Vitamin E: 0.00 mg
Saturated Fat: 12.81 g	Thiamin: .98 mg
Monosaturated Fat: 32.07 g	Riboflavin: .62 mg
Cholesterol: 0.00 mg	Niacin: 7.38 mg
Carbohydrates: 95.39 g	Pantothenic Acid: .55 mg
Fiber: 3.38 g	Vitamin B6: .05 mg
Calcium: 19.34 g	Folate: 228.75 ug
Phosphorous: 135.00 mg	Vitamin B12: 0.00 mg
Iron: 5.81 g	Vitamin C: 0.00 mg
Sodium: 3.09 mg	Selenium: 42.38 ug
Sugar: .34 mg	
Potassium: 133.75 mg	

Flaky Pie Crust

1 ¾ cups flour

1 tsp salt

¾ cup butter flavored shortening

Directions: Preheat oven to 350°F. Make sure blender jar is completely dry. Press the Pulse button approximately 15 to 20 times. When pulsing, the ingredients will fall towards the center of the jar. When the ingredients are no longer moving, remove the lid and with a rubber spatula, scrape the ingredients from the sides of the jar towards the center. Place the lid back on the jar and continue pulsing. Repeat this process until ingredients have turned into small granules.

¾ cup cold water

1 egg yolk

Directions: Beat together ingredients in separate bowl. Then add to jar and other ingredients. Repeat the pulsing process as described in the directions above. The dough should form into a ball on top of the blade. When this happens, stop pulsing. Add flour to your hands and separate the dough into two halves. Roll each half into a piecrust. You may use these as a double layer pie crust, or for two separate pies. Place in round 9" pie tin. Bake for 2530 minutes.

Nutritional Information

Yields: 1 double 9" pie crust
Serving Size: 1 slice

Amount per serving

Calories: 139.59	Potassium: 15.79 mg
65.20% from Fat,	Magnesium: 3.17 mg
4.56% from Protein	Zinc: 1.12 mg
30.30% from Carb	Copper: .02 mg
Protein: 1.58 g	Manganese: .09 mg
Total Fat: 10.02 g	Vitamin A: 14.96 IU
Saturated Fat: .3.99 g	Vitamin E: 3.85 mg
Monosaturated Fat: 4.40 g	Thiamin: .11 mg
Polyunsaturated: 1.15 g	Riboflavin: .07 mg
Cholesterol: 18.18 mg	Niacin: .81 mg
Carbohydrates: 10.47 g	Pantothenic Acid: .09 mg
Fiber: .37 g	Vitamin B6: .01 mg
Calcium: 3.70 mg	Folate: 26.53 ug
Phosphorous: 18.81 mg	Vitamin B12: 0.02 mg
Iron: .66 mg	Vitamin C: 0.00 mg
Sodium: 148.35 mg	Selenium: 5.22 ug
Sugar: .04 mg	

Pumpkin Pie

2 large eggs

1 ¾ cups canned pumpkin

¾ cup sugar

½ tsp salt

1 tsp cinnamon

½ tsp ground ginger

¼ tsp ground cloves

1 ½ cups evaporated low-fat milk

Directions: Preheat oven to 350° F. Place ingredients in blender jar and press **Batters** button.

1 unbaked 9-inch pie shell

Whipped Topping

Directions: Pour ingredients into pie shell. Bake for 60 minutes. After cooled, top with whipped topping.

Graham Cracker Pie Crust

13 to 14 whole graham crackers

Directions: Place crackers in jar and secure the lid. Press the Pulse button, and hold down until the graham crackers have blended into a fine consistency.

¼ cup melted butter

3 Tbsp sugar

1 tsp lemon juice

Directions: Preheat oven to 350°F. Add ingredients to jar. Use spatula to push ingredients towards the center of the jar. Hold down the Pulse button until the ingredients have blended into a pie crust. Press crust firmly into a round 8x8" baking pan.
Bake for 5 minutes. Allow crust to cool prior to filling.

Nutritional Information

Yields: 1 9inch pie/ 8 slices of pie
Serving Size: 1 slice

Amount per serving

Calories: 151.47	Potassium: 293.26 mg
9.89% from Fat,	Magnesium: 27.57 mg
15.50% from Protein	Zinc: .70 mg
74.60% from Carb	Copper: .08 mg
Protein: 6.06 g	Manganese: .19 mg
Total Fat: 1.72 g	Vitamin A: 8601.85 IU
Saturated Fat: .59 g	Vitamin E: 76.69 mg
Monosaturated Fat: .61 g	Thiamin: .04 mg
Polyunsaturated: .22 g	Riboflavin: .25 mg
Cholesterol: 63.25 mg	Niacin: .30 mg
Carbohydrates: 29.14 g	Pantothenic Acid: .78 mg
Fiber: 1.75g	Vitamin B6: .08 mg
Calcium: 165.06 mg	Folate: 17.76 ug
Phosphorous: 140.46 mg	Vitamin B12: 0.30 mg
Iron: 1.28 mg	Vitamin C: 2.97 mg
Sodium: 78.46 mg	Selenium: 6.17 ug
Sugar: 26.22 mg	

Nutritional Information

Yields: 1 pie crust
Serving Size: 1 slice

Amount per serving

Calories: 262.23	Potassium: 83.12 mg
35.20% from Fat,	Magnesium: 27.02 mg
4.92% from Protein	Zinc: .89 mg
59.90% from Carb	Copper: .01 mg
Protein: 3.24 g	Manganese: 0.00 mg
Total Fat: 10.30g	Vitamin A: 177.39 IU
Saturated Fat: 4.35 g	Vitamin E: 7647.60 mg
Monosaturated Fat: 3.13 g	Thiamin: .10 mg
Polyunsaturated: .43 g	Riboflavin: .11 mg
Cholesterol: 15.25 mg	Niacin: 1.72 mg
Carbohydrates: 39.45 g	Pantothenic Acid: .01 mg
Fiber: 1.55 g	Vitamin B6: .05 mg
Calcium: 37.74 mg	Folate: 21.23 ug
Phosphorous: 93.65 mg	Vitamin B12: 0.01 mg
Iron: 1.88 mg	Vitamin C: .29 mg
Sodium: 340.71 mg	Selenium: .10 ug
Sugar: 15.21 mg	

Non Dairy Low-fat Pumpkin Pie

2 cups canned pumpkin

2 cups lite tofu

⅔ cup honey

1 tsp vanilla

1 tsp cinnamon

½ tsp ground ginger

¼ tsp ground cloves

Directions: Preheat oven to 350° F. Place ingredients in blender. Press the **Speed Up** button until speed 7 is reached. Allow the blender to run a complete cycle. Pour into pie crust and bake for 60 minutes.

Nutritional Information

Yields: 1 9" pie
Serving Size: 1 slice

Amount per serving

Calories: 139.59	Potassium: 15.79 mg
52% from Fat,	Magnesium: 3.17 mg
2.62% from Protein	Zinc: 1.12 mg
95.90% from Carb	Copper: .02 mg
Protein: 1.58 g	Manganese: .09 mg
Total Fat: 10.02 g	Vitamin A: 14.96 IU
Saturated Fat: .3.99 g	Vitamin E: 3.85 mg
Monosaturated Fat: 4.40 g	Thiamin: .11 mg
Polyunsaturated: 1.15 g	Riboflavin: .07 mg
Cholesterol: 18.18 mg	Niacin: .81 mg
Carbohydrates: 10.47 g	Pantothenic Acid: .09 mg
Fiber: .37 g	Vitamin B6: .01 mg
Calcium: 3.70 mg	Folate: 26.53 ug
Phosphorous: 18.81 mg	Vitamin B12: 0.02 mg
Iron: .66 mg	Vitamin C: 0.00 mg
Sodium: 148.35 mg	Selenium: 5.22 ug
Sugar: .04 mg	

Yogurt Cream Cheese Pie

2 Tbsp cold water

1 (8 oz.) package cream cheese

8 oz. plain yogurt

2 tsp unflavored gelatin

¼ cup honey

1 tsp vanilla

Directions: Place ingredients into blender jar and secure the lid. Press the Pulse button and hold until well blended.

1 graham cracker crust

2 cups sliced fresh fruit

Directions: Pour mixture into baked graham cracker crust. Refrigerate 2 or more hours. Top with sliced fruit when ready to serve.

Nutritional Information

Yield: 2 cups filling/ 1 pie
Serving Size: 1 slice

Amount per serving

Calories: 136.79	Potassium: 97.97 mg
38.40% from Fat	Magnesium: 6.09 mg
12.80% from Protein	Zinc: .41 mg
48.80% from Carb	Copper: .02 mg
Protein: 4.44 g	Manganese: .01 mg
Total Fat: 5.91 g	Vitamin A: 220.56 IU
Saturated Fat: 3.74 g	Vitamin E: 58.97 mg
Monosaturated Fat: 1.66 g	Thiamin: .01 mg
Polyunsaturated: .21 g	Riboflavin: .13 mg
Cholesterol: 19.56 mg	Niacin: .08 mg
Carbohydrates: 16.91 g	Pantothenic Acid: .12 mg
Fiber: .02 g	Vitamin B6: .03 mg
Calcium: 66.98 mg	Folate: 7.46 ug
Phosphorous: 76.27 mg	Vitamin B12: .27 mg
Iron: .54 mg	Vitamin C: .19 mg
Sodium: 122.26 mg	Selenium: 2.20 ug
Sugar: 14.95 mg	

Chocolate Crumb Pie

Premade graham cracker pie crust

1 ½ cups milk

1 (8 oz.) package cream cheese - softened

2 Tbsp margarine, melted

1 (3 oz.) box instant vanilla pudding

8 oz. whipped cream

½ large package chocolate cookies

Directions: Make graham cracker pie crust. Place remaining ingredients into blender jar and secure the lid. Press the **Batters** button.

Nutritional Information

Yield: 4 cups/ 12 slices
Serving Size: 1 slice

Amount per serving

Calories: 208.50	Potassium: 126.61 mg
58.30% from Fat	Magnesium: 12.70 mg
7.90% from Protein	Zinc: .42 mg
33.80% from Carb	Copper: .05 mg
Protein: 4.17 g	Manganese: .06 mg
Total Fat: 13.68 g	Vitamin A: 466.49 IU
Saturated Fat: 6.73 g	Vitamin E: 122.80 mg
Monosaturated Fat: 4.56 g	Thiamin: .03 mg
Polyunsaturated: 1.69 g	Riboflavin: .16 mg
Cholesterol: 32.79 mg	Niacin: .29 mg
Carbohydrates: 17.84 g	Pantothenic Acid: .18 mg
Fiber: .39 g	Vitamin B6: .04 mg
Calcium: 81.75 mg	Folate: 11.55 ug
Phosphorous: 84.55 mg	Vitamin B12: .29 mg
Iron: .77 mg	Vitamin C: .49 mg
Sodium: 221.24 mg	Selenium: 2.22 ug
Sugar: 9.16 mg	

PUDDINGS

You can turn any pudding recipe into a mousse by pressing the **Smoothie** button instead of the **Batters** button.

Instant Pudding

2 cups cold milk

3.4 oz. package instant pudding, any flavor

Directions: Place ingredients into blender jar and secure the lid. Press the **Batters** button. Refrigerate immediately for at least 10 minutes.

Whipped Gelatin

1 cup boiling water

6 oz. package flavored gelatin any flavor

Directions: Place ingredients into blender jar and secure the lid. Press **Speed Up** button until speed 4 is reached. Allow it to run for 20 seconds, then press any lower row button to stop.

3 cups ice

Add ice to blender and press **Speed Up** button until blender reached speed 8.   Allow it to run for 20 seconds, then press any lower row button to stop.

1 cup whipped topping - frozen

Directions: Press **Speed Up** button until blender reaches speed 9. Let it run for 10 seconds and then refrigerate for 3 hours.

Nutritional Information

Yield: 2 ½ cups
Serving Size: ½ cup

Amount per serving

Calories: 111.70	Potassium: 180.52 mg
9.80% from Fat	Magnesium: 15.74 mg
14.00% from Protein	Zinc: 45 mg
76.20% from Carb	Copper: .01 mg
Protein: 3.92 g	Manganese: 0.00 mg
Total Fat: 1.22 g	Vitamin A: 199.75 mg
Saturated Fat: .73 g	Vitamin E: 60.02 mg
Monosaturated Fat: .34 g	Thiamin: .04 mg
Polyunsaturated Fat: .07 g	Riboflavin: .19 mg
Cholesterol: 3.94 mg	Niacin: .10 mg
Carbohydrates: 21.34 g	Pantothenic Acid: .37 mg
Fiber: .10 g	Vitamin B6: .05 mg
Calcium: 140.58 mg	Folate: 5.90 ug
Phosphorous: 109.56 mg	Vitamin B12: .42 mg
Iron: .07 g	Vitamin C: 1.18 mg
Sodium: 185.33 mg	Selenium: 2.61 ug
Sugar: 12.37 mg	

Nutritional Information

Yield: 4 cups
Serving Size: ½ cup

Amount per serving

Calories: 124.81	Potassium: 16.04 mg
32.50% from Fat	Magnesium: 1.77 mg
6.18% from Protein	Zinc: 04 mg
61.30% from Carb	Copper: .03 mg
Protein: 1.98 g	Manganese: 0.00 mg
Total Fat: 4.64 g	Vitamin A: 151.95 mg
Saturated Fat: .2.90 g	Vitamin E: 41.10 mg
Monosaturated Fat: 1.36 g	Thiamin: 0.00 mg
Polyunsaturated Fat: .13 g	Riboflavin: .03 mg
Cholesterol: 16.65 mg	Niacin: .01 mg
Carbohydrates: 19.69 g	Pantothenic Acid: .304 mg
Fiber: 0.00 g	Vitamin B6: 0.00 mg
Calcium: 11.58 mg	Folate: 1.24 ug
Phosphorous: 39.13 mg	Vitamin B12: .03 mg
Iron: .03 g	Vitamin C: .09 mg
Sodium: 104.78 mg	Selenium: 1.50 ug
Sugar: 19.26mg	

Cooked Pudding

3 cups steaming milk

1 package (3.4 oz.) instant pudding mix

3 Tbsp cornstarch

Directions: Place ingredients into blender jar and secure the lid. Press the Pulse button for approximately 3-6 seconds or until well blended. Stop and pour into serving bowls. Pudding will set within approximately 5 minutes.

Vanilla Soy Pudding

1 ½ cups soy milk

½ cup sugar

2 Tbsp cornstarch

Directions: Place ingredients into blender jar and secure the lid. Press the **Soups** button 3 times. Mixture should be steaming. Allow it to cool for 2 minutes.

1 tsp vanilla

Directions: Add vanilla to jar and press the Pulse button for approximately 10 seconds. Pour into container and refrigerate for at least 1 hour.

Nutritional Information

Yield: 3 cups
Serving Size: ½ cup

Amount per serving

Calories: 135.17	Potassium: 224.73 mg
10.00% from Fat	Magnesium: 19.80 mg
14.50% from Protein	Zinc: 56 mg
75.50% from Carb	Copper: .02 mg
Protein: 4.89 g	Manganese: .01 mg
Total Fat: 1.51 g	Vitamin A: 249.69 mg
Saturated Fat: .91 g	Vitamin E: 75.03 mg
Monosaturated Fat: .42 g	Thiamin: .06 mg
Polyunsaturated Fat: .08 g	Riboflavin: .24 mg
Cholesterol: 4.92 mg	Niacin: .12 mg
Carbohydrates: 25.46 g	Pantothenic Acid: .46 mg
Fiber: .13 g	Vitamin B6: .06 mg
Calcium: 175.54 mg	Folate: 7.38 ug
Phosphorous: 137.37 mg	Vitamin B12: .53 mg
Iron: .11 g	Vitamin C: 1.48 mg
Sodium: 192.83 mg	Selenium: 3.33 ug
Sugar: 11.68 mg	

Nutritional Information

Yield: 3 cups
Serving Size: ½ cup

Amount per serving

Calories: 107.27	Potassium: 87.85 mg
10.50% from Fat	Magnesium: 11.80 mg
8.43% from Protein	Zinc: 14 mg
81.10% from Carb	Copper: .08 mg
Protein: 2.30 g	Manganese: .11 mg
Total Fat: 1.28 g	Vitamin A: 19.60 mg
Saturated Fat: .13 g	Vitamin E: 0.00 mg
Monosaturated Fat: .20 g	Thiamin: .10 mg
Polyunsaturated Fat: .51 g	Riboflavin: .05 mg
Cholesterol: 40.00 mg	Niacin: .09 mg
Carbohydrates: 25.16 g	Pantothenic Acid: .03 mg
Fiber: .82 g	Vitamin B6: .03 mg
Calcium: 2.75 mg	Folate: 1.23 ug
Phosphorous: 30.40 mg	Vitamin B12: 0.00 mg
Iron: .37 g	Vitamin C: 0.00 mg
Sodium: 7.65 mg	Selenium: .97 ug
Sugar: 17.18 mg	

Chocolate Tofu Pudding

10.5 oz. soft tofu

¼ cup soy milk, plain or vanilla (may use evaporated milk)

5 Tbsp margarine, melted

2 (1 oz.) squares semisweet chocolate, each broken in half

½ cup sugar

Directions: Place ingredients into blender jar and secure the lid. Run soup cycle three times. Mixture should be steaming. Let pudding set for 2 minutes.

1 tsp vanilla

Add vanilla to jar and press Pulse button for approximately 6 seconds. Chill for at least 1 hour.

Nutritional Information

Yield: 3 cups
Serving Size: ¼ cup

Amount per serving

Calories: 107.86	Potassium: 57.10.86 mg
8.50% from Fat	Zinc: .27 mg
8.11% from Protein	Copper: .07 mg
33.40% from Carb	Manganese: .13 mg
Protein: 2.23 g	Vitamin A: 221.74 IU
Total Fat: 7.15 g	Vitamin E: 47.39 mg
Saturated Fat: 1.70 g	Thiamin: .03 mg
Monosaturated Fat: 3.01 g	Riboflavin: .03 mg
Polyunsaturated Fat: 2.07 g	Niacin: .16 mg
Cholesterol: 1.09 mg	Pantothenic Acid: .04 mg
Carbohydrates: 9.19 g	Vitamin B6: .02 mg
Fiber: .28 g	Folate: 11.64 ug
Calcium: 38.53 mg	Vitamin B12: .04 mg
Phosphorous: 36.52 mg	Vitamin C: .06 mg
Iron: .42 g	Selenium: 2.52 ug
Sodium: 61.76 mg	
Sugar: 178.27 mg	

Yogurt

3 ¾ cups warm water

1 cup instant nonfat dry milk

Directions: Place ingredients into blender jar and secure the lid. Hold down Pulse button for 5 seconds.

Add: 3 Tbsp plain yogurt

Hold down the Pulse button for 5 seconds. Pour into container, cover and keep at 115 ° (46 ° C) for 4 to 8 hours. Yogurt is done when it is thick and the consistency of heavy cream. If it is liquid, let it sit longer. Once it is ready, store in refrigerator.

Nutritional Information

Yield: 4 cups
Serving Size: ½ cup

Amount per serving

Calories: 116.82	Potassium: 457.40 mg
3.65% from Fat	Magnesium: 29.30 mg
39.60% from Protein	Zinc: 1.05 mg
56.80% from Carb	Copper: .02 mg
Protein: .94 g	Manganese: .01 mg
Total Fat: 9.24g	Vitamin A: 11.18 IU
Saturated Fat: .38 g	Vitamin E: 3.05 mg
Monosaturated Fat: .25 g	Thiamin: .11 mg
Polyunsaturated Fat: .01 g	Riboflavin: .40 mg
Cholesterol: 5.75 mg	Niacin: .24 mg
Carbohydrates: 13.26 g	Pantothenic Acid: .91 mg
Fiber: 0.00 g	Vitamin B6: .09 mg
Calcium: 323.42 mg	Folate: 12.90 ug
Phosphorous: 247.46 mg	Vitamin B12: 1.03 mg
Iron: .08 g	Vitamin C: 1.73 mg
Sodium: 138.61 mg	Selenium: 6.95 ug
Sugar: 13.26 mg	

Chocolate Cream Mousse

¾ cup steaming milk

¾ cup milk chocolate chips

2 Tbsp sugar

1 tsp vanilla

1 (3 oz.) package cream

Directions: Place ingredients into blender jar and secure the lid. Press the **Smoothie** button.

Nutritional Information

Yield: 2 cups
Serving Size: ¼ cup

Amount per serving

Calories: 163.30	Potassium: 279.03 mg
36.80% from Fat,	Magnesium: 23.21 mg
15.80% from Protein	Zinc: .86 mg
47.30% from Carb	Copper: .08 mg
Protein: 6.40 g	Manganese: .08 mg
Total Fat: 6.63 g	Vitamin A: 27.48 mg
Saturated Fat: 3.48 g	Thiamin: .07 mg
Monosaturated Fat: 2.63 g	Riboflavin: .25 mg
Polyunsaturated Fat: .20 g	Niacin: .18 mg
Cholesterol: 11.83 mg	Pantothenic Acid: .48 mg
Carbohydrates: 19.17 g	Vitamin B6: .05 mg
Fiber: .54 g	Folate: 9.43 ug
Calcium: 183.18 mg	Vitamin B12: .61 mg
Phosphorous: 157.21 mg	Vitamin C: .77 mg
Iron: .59 g	Selenium: 4.22 ug
Sodium: 104.15 mg	
Sugar: 17.20 mg	

For helpful tips while making desserts,
see the cakes introduction

DESSERTS

Cream Puffs

½ cup butter

1 cup water

3 large eggs

Directions: Preheat oven to 400° F. Place ingredients in blender jar and secure the lid. Press the **Batters** button.

1 cup flour

¼ tsp salt

1 Tbsp sugar

Add ingredients to the mixture in jar and secure the lid. Press **Soups** button twice. During the second cycle, the sound of the motor will change and the mixture will begin to harden. You may stop the blender mid cycle by pressing any lower row button, or you may allow the cycle to finish. Spray a cookie sheet. Form the cream puffs by spoonfuls and place them 2 inches apart on the cookie sheet. Bake for 35 minutes. Cream Puffs are done when the tops are golden brown and crisp. After having cooled for a few minutes, cut the top half off, place cream filling (See Cream Puff Filling Recipe) in the middle, and then replace the top.

Optional: Top with chocolate syrup or powdered sugar

Cream Puff Filling

1 ½ cups milk

3.4 oz. vanilla instant pudding*

3.4 oz. powdered whipped topping mix

Directions: Place ingredients in blender jar and secure lid. Press **Batters** button. Place filling cream puffs.

*For a chocolate cream filling, may use chocolate instant pudding

Nutritional Information

Yields: 12 cream puffs
Serving Size: 1 cream puff

Amount per serving

Calories 131.11	Potassium: 32.88 mg
63.20% from Fat	Magnesium: 4.42 mg
9.08% from Protein	Zinc: .24 mg
27.80% from Carb	Copper: .03 mg
Protein: 2.98 g	Manganese: .08 mg
Total Fat: 9.22 g	Vitamin A: 306.98 IU
Saturated Fat: 5.32 g	Vitamin E: 83.62 mg
Monosaturated Fat: .2.55 g	Thiamin: .09 mg
Polyunsaturated Fat: .53 g	Riboflavin: .12 mg
Cholesterol: 81.67 mg	Niacin: .63 mg
Carbohydrates: 9.12 g	Pantothenic Acid: .26 mg
Fiber: .28 g	Vitamin B6: .03 mg
Calcium: 11.95 g	Folate: 26.16 ug
Phosphorous: 41.22 mg	Vitamin B12: .20 mg
Iron: .75 mg	Vitamin C: 0.00 mg
Sodium: 124.50 mg	Selenium: 8.23 ug
Sugar: 1.19 mg	

Nutritional Information

Yields: 2 ½ cups
Serving Size: 1 cup

Amount per serving

Calories: 180.45	Potassium: 205.88 mg
9.92% from Fat	Magnesium: 13.80 mg
9.23% from Protein	Zinc: .52 mg
80.90% from Carb	Copper: .03 mg
Protein: 4.51 g	Manganese: .01 mg
Total Fat: 2.15 g	Vitamin A: 249.90 IU
Saturated Fat: 1.20 g	Vitamin E: 74.72 mg
Monosaturated Fat: .50 g	Thiamin: .06 mg
Polyunsaturated Fat: .44 g	Riboflavin: .23 mg
Cholesterol: 2.45 mg	Niacin: .12 mg
Carbohydrates: 39.52 g	Pantothenic Acid: .44 mg
Fiber: 155.70 g	Vitamin B6: .05 mg
Calcium: 134.01 mg	Folate: 6.13 ug
Phosphorous: 134.01 mg	Vitamin B12: 0.65 mg
Iron: .07 g	Vitamin C: 0.00 mg
Sodium: 327.77 mg	Selenium: 4.25 ug
Sugar: 33.01 mg	Selenium: .19

Snickerdoodles

½ cup flour
¼ tsp baking soda
½ tsp baking powder

Directions: Preheat oven to 375° F. Make sure jar is dry. Place ingredients in jar and secure the lid. Press the Pulse button approximately 5 times (make sure to not hold button for more than 2 seconds at a time). Place dry mixture in separate bowl.

½ cup margarine - softened
1 cup sugar
1 egg
½ tsp vanilla

Place ingredients in jar and secure the lid. Press the **Batters** button. After cycle is done, if necessary, press the **Batters** button again. Add mixture in jar to dry mixture set aside in bowl. Mix together well.

2 Tbsp sugar
2 tsps cinnamon

Form dough into ball and roll in cinnamon/sugar mix. Place on sprayed cookie sheet. Bake for 10 minutes.

Nutritional Information
Yields: 27 cookies
Serving Size: 1 cookie

Amount per serving

Calories: 92.27		Potassium: 12.82 mg
35.70% from Fat		Magnesium: 1.98 mg
4.27% from Protein		Zinc: .07 mg
60.00% from Carb		Copper: .01 mg
Protein: .99 g		Manganese: .08 mg
Total Fat: 3.70 g		Vitamin A: 162.33 IU
Saturated Fat: .71 g		Vitamin E: 35.37 mg
Monounsaturated Fat: 1.65 g		Thiamin: .06 mg
Polyunsaturated Fat: 1.12 g		Riboflavin: .05 mg
Cholesterol: 7.79 mg		Niacin: .41 mg
Carbohydrates: 13.98 g		Pantothenic Acid: .06 mg
Fiber: .28 g		Vitamin B6: .01 mg
Calcium: 5.53 mg		Folate: 13.67 ug
Iron: .42 g		Vitamin B12: 0.03 mg
Sodium: 54.75 mg		Vitamin C: 0.16 mg
Sugar: 8.53 mg		Selenium: 2.99 ug

Lemon Bars

Crust:
2 cups flour
½ cup powdered sugar
⅛ tsp salt
1 cup butter, melted

Directions: Preheat oven to 350° F. Press the Pulse button 4 to 5 times. Press the **Speed Up** button until speed 1 is reached. Allow the blender to run for 10 seconds. Use a rubber spatula to scrape flour off the sides of the jar towards the center. Press crust into a sprayed 9x13" baking pan. Bake for 15 minutes.

Filling:
4 eggs
6 Tbsp lemon juice
2 cups sugar
¼ cup flour

Directions: Place ingredients in blender jar and secure lid. Press the **Batters** button. Pour into slightly cooled crust. Bake for 35 minutes. After baked, sprinkle with powdered sugar.

Nutritional Information
Yields: 24 lemon bars
Serving Size: 1 bar

Amount per serving

Calories: 200		Potassium: 32.04 mg
38.80% from Fat		Magnesium: 4.23 mg
4.97% from Protein		Zinc: .20 mg
56.20% from Carb		Copper: .03 mg
Protein: 2.52 g		Manganese: .08 mg
Total Fat: 8.76 g		Vitamin A: 248.22 IU
Saturated Fat: 5.18 g		Vitamin E: 76.90 mg
Monounsaturated Fat: 2.37 g		Thiamin: .10 mg
Polyunsaturated Fat: .47 g		Riboflavin: .11 mg
Cholesterol: 61.23 mg		Niacin: .71 mg
Carbohydrates: 28.56 g		Pantothenic Acid: .20 mg
Fiber: .33 g		Vitamin B6: .02 mg
Calcium: 9.77 mg		Folate: 26.65 ug
Phosphorous: 33.73 mg		Vitamin B12: 0.14 mg
Iron: .73 g		Vitamin C: 0.95 mg
Sodium: 81.35 mg		Selenium: 7.25 ug
Sugar: 19.44 mg		

Marbled Brownies

1 package fudge brownie mix

Directions: Preheat oven to 350° F. Prepare brownies in blender, according to package directions. Blend by placing ingredients in blender, secure the lid, and press the Pulse button. Hold the button down for 15 to 20 seconds, or until blended. Pour ¾ of the brownie batter in a sprayed 9x13" pan. Optional, add 6 oz. chocolate chips cookies. Mix into brownie batter by pressing the Pulse button approximately 5 times.

1 (8 ounce) package cream cheese - softened

¼ cup sour cream

¼ cup sugar

1 egg

½ tsp vanilla

Directions: Make sure jar has been cleaned. Add ingredients and secure the lid. Press the **Batters** button. Pour on top of the brownie batter in the pan. Pour remaining brownie batter on top of the mixture.

Cream Cheese Frosting

1 (8 ounce) package cream cheese

¼ cup butter - softened

1 tsp vanilla

2 cups powdered sugar

Directions: Place ingredients in jar and secure lid. Press **Speed Up** button until speed 1 is reached. Allow the blender to run and complete one cycle (50 seconds), after which, it will stop on its own. Remove the lid and mix the ingredients in the jar with a rubber spatula. Place the lid back on and press the **Speed Up** button again until blender is at speed 1. This cycle will run for 50 seconds, but you may stop the blender midcycle if the frosting is blended to desired consistency, by pressing any lower row button to stop.

Nutritional Information

Yields: 16 Brownies
Serving Size: 1 brownie

Amount per serving

Calories: 180.53 (	Potassium: 50.84 mg
44.50% from Fat	Magnesium: 9.72 mg
5.52% from Protein	Zinc: .26 mg
50.00% from Carb	Copper: .07 mg
Protein: .2.526g	Manganese: .11 mg
Total Fat: 9.16 g	Vitamin A: 216.29 IU
Saturated Fat: 3.86 g	Vitamin E: 57.60 mg
Monosaturated Fat: 2.50 g	Thiamin: .07 mg
Polyunsaturated Fat: 2.30 g	Riboflavin: .09 mg
Cholesterol: 29.09 mg	Niacin: .51 mg
Carbohydrates: 23.17 g	Pantothenic Acid: .12 mg
Fiber: .66 g	Vitamin B6: .02 mg
Calcium: 16.69 mg	Folate: 18.08 ug
Phosphorous: 39.40 mg	Vitamin B12: 0.10 mg
Iron: .78 g	Vitamin C: 0.35 mg
Sodium: 49.44 mg	Selenium: 4.27 ug
Sugar: 16.15 mg	

Nutritional Information

Yields: 2 ½ cups
Serving Size: ½ cup

Amount per serving

Calories: 432.53	Potassium: 60.18 mg
52.00% from Fat	Magnesium: 3.12 mg
3.27% from Protein	Zinc: .26 mg
44.70% from Carb	Copper: .01 mg
Protein: .3.60 g	Manganese: 0.00mg
Total Fat: 25.43 g	Vitamin A: 908.18 IU
Saturated Fat: 16.03 g	Vitamin E: 242.73 mg
Monosaturated Fat: 6.97 g	Thiamin: .01 mg
Polyunsaturated Fat: .96 g	Riboflavin: .11 mg
Cholesterol: 75.44 mg	Niacin: .06 mg
Carbohydrates: 49.16 g	Pantothenic Acid: .14 mg
Fiber: 0.00 g	Vitamin B6: .02 mg
Calcium: 40.42 mg	Folate: 6.37 ug
Phosphorous: 51.03 mg	Vitamin B12: 0.21 mg
Iron: .57 g	Vitamin C: 0.00 mg
Sodium: 203.28 mg	Selenium: 1.52 ug
Sugar: 47.21 mg	

Cookie Bars

2 (18 ounce) packages cookie dough

Directions: Spread first package of cookie dough on sprayed 9x13" baking pan.

1 ½ cup silken tofu

2 eggs

1 cup sugar

1 tsp vanilla

Directions: Preheat oven to 350° F. Place ingredients in blender jar and secure the lid. Press the **Batters** button. Pour mixture onto cookie dough. Place contents of second package of cookie dough over filling. Bake 40 to 45 minutes. When done baking, allow to cool before cutting.

Whipped Cream

2 cups whipping cream

3 Tbsp sugar

1 tsp vanilla flavoring

Directions: Place ingredients in blender jar and secure the lid. Press the Pulse button seconds until blade spins freely. Remove the lid and with rubber spatula, stir cream. Place lid back on jar and press Pulse button approximately 3 to 5 seconds.

Nutritional Information

Yields: 36 bars
Serving Size: ½ cup

Amount per serving

Calories: 154.88	Potassium: 66.74 mg
35.40% from Fat	Magnesium: 9.81 mg
5.42% from Protein	Zinc: .21 mg
59.20% from Carb	Copper: .07 mg
Protein: .2.13 g	Manganese: 0.15 mg
Total Fat: 6.17 g	Vitamin A: 17.45 IU
Saturated Fat: 1.96 g	Vitamin E: 5.10 mg
Monosaturated Fat: 3.04 g	Thiamin: .06 mg
Polyunsaturated Fat: .83 g	Riboflavin: .07 mg
Cholesterol: 6.80 mg	Niacin: .62 mg
Carbohydrates: 23.22 g	Pantothenic Acid: .10 mg
Fiber: .45 g	Vitamin B: 20.78 ug
Calcium: 18.76 mg	Vitamin B12: .02 mg
Phosphorous: 29.35 mg	Vitamin C: .02 mg
Iron: .75 g	Selenium: 2.74 ug
Sodium: 63.17 mg	
Sugar: 5.70 mg	

Nutritional Information

Yield: 2 cups
Serving Size: 2 Tablespoons

Amount per serving

Calories: 61.46	Potassium: 11.65 mg
79.90% from Fat	Magnesium: 1.08mg
1.97% from Protein	Zinc: .03 mg
18.10% from Carb	Copper: 0.00 mg
Protein: .31 g	Manganese: 0.00 mg
Total Fat: 5.53 g	Vitamin A: 219.58 IU
Saturated Fat: 3.44 g	Vitamin E: 60.50 mg
Monosaturated Fat: 1.60 g	Thiamin: 0.00 mg
Polyunsaturated Fat: .21 g	Riboflavin: .02 mg
Cholesterol: 20.46 mg	Niacin: .01 mg
Carbohydrates: 2.81 g	Pantothenic Acid: .04 mg
Fiber: 0.00 g	Vitamin B6: 0.00 mg
Calcium: 9.76 mg	Folate: .60 ug
Phosphorous: 9.28 mg	Vitamin B12: .03 mg
Iron: .01 g	Vitamin C: .09 mg
Sodium: 5.70 mg	Selenium: .09 ug
Sugar: 2.41 mg	

Fruit Pizza

Crust: See recipe for Graham Cracker Pie Crust
Filling:

1 cup whipping cream

Directions: Place ingredients into blender jar and secure the lid. Press the Pulse button for approximately 10 seconds, or until thickened.

1 tsp vanilla
4 Tbsp powdered sugar

Directions: Add above ingredients and press the Pulse button 3 to 4 times until well blended. Spread on graham cracker pie crust and top with slices of fruit.

Nutritional Information

Yield: 1 ½ cups/ 8 slices
Serving: 1 slice

Amount per serving

Calories: 59.95	Potassium: 15.43 mg
69.50% from Fat	Magnesium: 1.12 mg
2.17% from Protein ·	Zinc: .04mg
28.30% from Carb	Copper: 0.00 mg
Protein: .33 g	Manganese: 0.00 mg
Total Fat: 4.64 g	Vitamin A: 15.195 IU
Saturated Fat: 2.90g	Vitamin E: 41.10 mg
Monosaturated Fat: 1.37 g	Thiamin: 0.00 mg
Polyunsaturated Fat: .13 g	Riboflavin: .02 mg
Cholesterol: 16.65 mg	Niacin: .01 mg
Carbohydrates: 4.25 g	Pantothenic Acid: .04 mg
Fiber: 0.00 g	Vitamin B6: 0.00 mg
Calcium: 10.45 mg	Folate: .60 ug
Phosphorous: 9.18 mg	Vitamin B12: .03 mg
Iron: .01 g	Vitamin C: .09 mg
Sodium: 5.19 mg	Selenium: .10 ug
Sugar: 3.76 mg	Protein: .13 g

NOTES: